DEATH, BURIAL AND REBIRTH IN THE RELIGIONS OF ANTIQUITY

Christianity came into existence in a world in which religion was of central importance. In any religious culture, the treatment of death is of central importance.

In *Death, Burial and Rebirth in the Religions of Antiquity*, Jon Davies charts the significance of death in the religions and cults of the pre-Christian and early Christian world. He analyses varied funerary rituals and examines different notions of the afterlife. Among the areas covered are:

- Isis and Osiris, Baal and Ahura Mazda: the thanatologies of Ancient Near East
- Burying the Jewish dead
- Roman religion and Roman funerals
- Christian burial
- The nature of martyrdom

Jon Davies also draws on the sociological theory of Max Weber to present a comprehensive introduction to and overview of death, burial and rebirth in the first Christian centuries which offers insights into the relationship between social change and attitudes to death and dying.

Jon Davies was until recently Head of Department of Religious Studies at the University of Newcastle, where he now teaches part-time.

RELIGION IN THE FIRST CHRISTIAN CENTURIES
Edited by Deborah Sawyer and John Sawyer,
Lancaster University

Too often the religious traditions of antiquity are studies in isolation, without any real consideration of how they interacted. What made someone with a free choice become an adherent of one faith rather than another? Why might a former pagan choose to become a 'godfearer' and attend synagogue services? Why might a Jew become a Christian? How did the mysteries of Mithras differ from the worship of the Unconquered Sun, or the status of the Virgin Mary from that of Isis, and how many gods could an ancient worshipper have? These questions are hard to answer without a synoptic view of what the different religions offered.

The aim of the books in this series is to survey particular themes in the history of religion across the different religions of antiquity and to set up comparisons and contrasts, resonances and discontinuities, and thus reach a profounder understanding of the religious experience in the ancient world. Topics to be covered will include: women, conversion, language, death, magic, sacrifice and purity.

Also available in this series:

WOMEN AND RELIGION IN THE FIRST CHRISTIAN CENTURIES
Deborah F. Sawyer

THE CRUCIBLE OF CHRISTIAN MORALITY
J. Ian H. McDonald

SACRED LANGUAGES AND SACRED TEXTS
John Sawyer

DEATH, BURIAL AND REBIRTH IN THE RELIGIONS OF ANTIQUITY

Jon Davies

London and New York

First published 1999
by Routledge
11 New Fetter Lane, London EC4P 4EE

Simultaneously published in the USA and Canada
by Routledge
29 West 35th Street, New York, NY 10001

Routledge is an imprint of the Taylor & Francis Group

© 1999 Jon Davies
The right of Jon Davies to be identified as the Author of this Work
has been asserted by him in accordance with the Copyright, Designs
and Patents Act 1988

Typeset in Garamond by Routledge
Printed and bound in Great Britain by Biddles Ltd,
Guildford and King's Lynn

British Library Cataloguing in Publication Data
A catalogue record for this book is available from the British Library

Library of Congress Cataloguing in Publication Data
Davies, Jon, 1939–
Death, burial, and rebirth in the religions of antiquity/Jon Davies.
p.   cm. – (Religion in the first Christian centuries)
Includes bibliographical references and index.
1. Death–Religious aspects–History of doctrines.
2. Funeral rites and ceremonies, Ancient.
3. Future life–History of doctrines.
4. Middle East–Religion.
5. Rome–Religion.
I. Title.   II. Series.
BL504.D295   1999
291.2'3'093–dc21   98-49845
                                                                   CIP

ISBN 0–415–12990–7 (hbk)
ISBN 0–415–12991–5 (pbk)

TO JEAN, MY WIFE, FOR THE
SOCIETY, HELP AND COMFORT
WHICH SHE HAS AFFORDED ME,
AND TO MY CHILDREN,
DANIEL, JACOB AND ESTHER,
MY DAUGHTER-IN-LAW ANNABEL,
AND MY GRANDDAUGHTER JESSIE,
FOR THE CHEERFULNESS THEY
BRING TO MY LIFE

CONTENTS

CONTENTS

LIST OF PLATES

PREFACE AND
ACKNOWLEDGEMENTS

This book is an exercise in historical sociology. It seeks to find patterns or regularities in the processes of social change, in this case in the relationship between social change and attitudes to death, dying and the afterlife. Social statisticians look for variables with the greatest explanatory power: what factor, or factors, explains or explain most of the variance in, or the stability of, a given set of outcomes?

At one level, this turned out to be fairly straightforward. It is clear, for example, that there is a hierarchy in funerary ornament and ostentation (including negative ornament and ostentation) which parallels a social hierarchy. At its simplest and most general, this is reflected in male power. Men dominate the cemetery just as they dominate society. Rich and powerful men dominate both. A similar gender-split characterises behaviour at funerals: men do one thing, women do another.

It proved much more difficult to establish patterns and processes of social change in, for example, the relationship between such matters as attitudes to the corpse and the method of corpse-disposal, including the quality and quantity of grave ornament or grave goods. Ornate sarcophagi can be found in association with rich grave goods, or not. Cremation is sometimes associated with a sense that the corpse is a pollutant, and sometimes not. A benign afterlife is sometimes seen as a 'reward' for this-worldly virtue, and sometimes not. The same society can demonstrate very different behaviour at different times, and for no apparent reason.

What, though, can be found in the data which 'explain' the core beliefs of a culture about death, burial and the afterlife, beliefs within which these other, lesser, matters can be located? After considerable tussle between the Marxist and the Weberian in my intellectual pedigree, I came to the view that Weber was right: *first* look for the basic values of a society, *then* for its material reality. I came to the view that we must start with the creation stories of each culture. Paradoxically, perhaps, it is in the stories of origins, the stories of life, that we can find explanations for the stories of endings, the stories of death. It is from the ideational or symbolic record, rather than from the material remains, that we can construct some sense of, some empathy with the death cultures of the Ancient Near East, the Hellenistic world and the early Roman Empire. *Their creation stories contain the prime explanation: their history, transacting with their creation stories, gives us a large part of the explanation of their attitudes to death.* This, then, is a Weberian rather than a Marxist approach: consciousness comes first, the material is derivative.

For me, this was a journey, with Max Weber as a guide, into worlds both new and fascinating. I would have been totally, rather than occasionally, lost in those worlds without the help and example of the two editors of this series, John and Deborah Sawyer. I hope that my efforts at reaching back into the pasts with which they have been so long familiar are a fair response to their support. Wilfred Watson gave sage advice – and gave me free run of his library. The University of Newcastle provided ample sabbatical and technical support. Staff at the libraries of the Universities of Newcastle and Durham have been generous with their time and have allowed me considerable latitude in use of the book stock. To the authors of innumerable books and articles I owe more than the simple listing in a bibliography can express. Students in the Department of Religious Studies at Newcastle University have been generous in their interest in what I was doing.

My friends and colleagues have long since grown accustomed to my preoccupation with death, and have ceased avoiding me (I think). Thank you Paul and Lesley Fallon, Joan and Gavin Aarvold, Brian Pearson, Gerard Loughlin, Isabel Wollaston, John Lazenby, Max Sussman, Norman Dennis, Patricia Tyson, Ros and David Place, Sam and Bobby Shuster. Editorial staff at Routledge have been supportive, helpful and patient – in particular Simon Coppock.

My children, now mature adults, occasionally, but cheerfully, mock this interest of mine, as does my daughter-in-law, Annabel. My wife Jean knows how much her love and support mean to me. My 'death' and her midwifery make a most balanced team, I think.

I am grateful to Greg Harsley for permission to reproduce the extract on pp. 168–9 which is taken from *New Documents Illustrating Early Christianity* (Horsley, 1987). I am also grateful to the following individuals and institutions for permission to use the photographs and drawings that feature in the text:

1   Prof. John Lazenby, Department of Classics, University of Newcastle upon Tyne, for plates 1–3.

2   R. Stoneman for plate 4.

3   Dr Graham Davies, editor of *Palestine Exploration Quarterly*, and Dr Rachel Hachlili, of the University of Haifa, Israel, for plates 5–7.

4   Dr Alan Bowman, Christ Church, Oxford, for plate 8.

5   The Egypt Exploration Society for plate 9.

6   The Museum of Antiquities (curator: Lindsay Allason-Jones), University of Newcastle upon Tyne, for plate 11.

7   The directors of l'Ecole Française de Rome, Groupe de Recherches sur l'Afrique Antique, for plates 12 and 13, and for permission to translate the poem which appears as the appendix to this volume.

8   Plate 14, courtesy of the Shefton Museum of Greek Art and Archaeology, University of Newcastle upon Tyne, cinerarium on permanent loan from the Wellcome Institute.

INTRODUCTION

The most profound boundary in the Late Antique world was the one drawn after death. The invisible chasm between the 'saved' and the 'damned' stood like a deep moat between the little groups, pagan and Christian alike, that came to chisel out a position for themselves at the expense of the time-honoured consensus of traditional public worship.

(Brown 1971: 57)

It is the central thesis of this book that it was on matters to do with death that 'Christianity' successfully defined an identity for itself that was both distinctive and, at the same time, sufficiently eclectic as to enable it to relate to aspects of some of the other religious cultures within which it found itself. 'Death' was a debated issue at the time – as it has been at most times other than the present. So was 'religion'. As Robin Lane Fox puts it, 'in the early Christian period, *atheism* ... was not an option' (Fox 1988: 30; my emphasis). Christianity came into existence in a world in which religion was of central importance; and in any religious culture, the treatment of death is itself of central importance. However one tracks Christianity, from its ancient antecedents to the story of its precarious early existence to its political triumph under Constantine, one has to consider a variety of religious views of death and burial – death and burial in scripture and in art, in theology, ritual, architecture, pilgrimage and martyrology, in cosmogony – which represent the summation of the moral meaning of both collective and individual life. This is true of any religion worthy of the name, and certainly of the religions and cults of the Ancient Near East and the Roman Empire that constitute the major part of this book. While, clearly, there is more to religion (Christian or otherwise) than death, a religion which ignored it or down-played it would be no religion at all.

1

Since the last Ice Age approximately one hundred billion (100, 000, 000,000) people have died. We know little now and will never know much about how they died, how their deaths were received, where they now lie, where their souls went, or even if, in their own minds, they had souls. We have perhaps, in our own experience of death and in our own common humanity, some human empathy, some sense of the pain of death and its association with the joy of life. Donovan Ochs asserts that:

> The phases of personal bereavement are universals indepen-dent of culture. There is no reason to doubt that the shock, sense of loss, grief, and pain experienced by the parents who lost a son or daughter in Vietnam or Iraq is different in degree or kind from those experienced by parents who lost a son in the Persian or Peloponnesian or Punic wars.
>
> (Ochs 1993: 16)

In *Grief and Mourning in Cross-Cultural Perspective*, Rosenblatt and his co-authors put forward the view that there are universal practices around death and burial which are to be found in all societies:

> For people in all human societies, the death of familiar people is a constant. ... Grief feelings are not unique to people in Western civilization. The experience of grief seems to be one of the costs of being human. The gains from long term contact and interdependence are often followed by the agony, anger and feelings of emptiness and sorrow that result from the death of someone who has been important to one. ... Two areas of emotionality [are] funda-mentally human: the universality of emotional expression in bereavement and the universality of sex differences in the expression of emotion during bereavement.
>
> (Rosenblatt *et al.* 1976: 1–11)

Rosenblatt's data are essentially those of anthropology rather than of archaeology, of Greco-Roman history or of theology, but both Rosenblatt and Ochs are making the same basic point, namely that human response to death tends to be conservative, to refer back to old or existing or even universal practices for meaning and conso-lation. The Ancient Near East was covered with death memories and death memorials, and with graves, sepulchres and cemeteries, the repositories of cultural comment on death.

Aubrey Cannon, in trying to construct a general theory for mortuary behaviour, insists that it has to be seen as a cyclical process, involving an initial period of ostentation, followed by a levelling-out period and then by one of societal regulation. It is, he says, not simply a matter of high status leading to high mortuary expenditure, but of ostentation in such matters being a function of *uncertainty* in social status: 'it is the historical process of social challenge and adjustments that is played out in the material expression of status and not the static structure of social relations that is being materially recreated' (Cannon 1989: 456). This is a valuable observation. The major changes in funerary liturgy and mortuary practice which take place in the centuries which are the concern of this book took place in cultures experiencing radical forms of social change, including war and conquest. Cannon's article is mainly concerned with the archaeological record – with the material remains. Such remains are, as he says, understandable only within some understanding of the symbolic language and theological thinking of the societies which produced them.

We can with benefit retain Cannon's emphasis on social change, and radicalise it to include social turmoil and social collapse, as these appear in the historical and scriptural–theological record. We can then define our subject as a concern for the most general of human speculations about the meaning of *life as seen through the lens of death*, that is 'thanatology'. Thanatologies vary, but they all involve, as part of their central moral drama, a cosmology, a Creation story and an account of the relationship within that story of the Creator-God(s) with his creation, including human beings. Since this relationship is mediated or revealed within history, in events in the Creation, we can say that thanatology is cosmology sculpted by history. When history is force, conflict and violence, then thanatology becomes cosmology sculpted by force, conflict and violence. For example, in Mesopotamian cosmology (see Part I) human beings are created by the gods to serve them and then to die. They had to die as a condition of being allowed to exist. This bleak religion offered, as far as we can see, no consolatory notion of salvation: even the 'heroes' fail (Dalley 1991). Even the most exemplary human beings are unable to reverse the original hostile attitude of the Creator. By contrast, in Egyptian Heliopolitan cosmology humans come into being as the *tears of joy* of Atum, and humanity will one day return, *as joy*, to Atum or one of his equivalents at Memphis or Hermopolis (Ions 1968; Lamy 1997). The canonical Creation story of the ancient Israelites (a story adopted by Christianity as its own) sees God creating humanity in His own image, seeing that it was 'good' and blessing it: the Creation-purpose achieves perfection in the creation of human beings. The ensuing thanatology develops, however painfully, within this initial understanding of the loving relationship between the Creator and the created. The promise, in ancient Egypt and in the Bible, is of the eventual 'return' of the created to the Creator, that is to a beatific afterlife, to 'salvation', a notion absent from ancient Mesopotamia.

When expressed as memorial, the transactions between cosmology and history are most visible as communal or dynastic monuments to societal leaders and exemplars. These may take the form of great mausolea, obelisks, megaliths and funerary mounds, all proclaiming the importance in history of political, military or religious leaders, the 'heroes' of that particular society. Theologically, such exemplars and heroes become the 'gatecrashers of heaven' as they seek, as recognition of their terrestrial virtue, some release from the general sameness of human death in a special relationship with the deity and with posterity. In every one of the cultures we will be looking at, the role of these heroes is to break, or to try to break, the barrier set between mortals and immortals, between humanity and the gods. They operate as thanatological pioneers, pushing into forbidden territory.

The focus on the Creation stories is the most general perspective from which we can try to understand the boundaries of possible 'options' for and of the various thanatologies which are the subject of this book: thanatology is cosmology sculpted by history. Throughout this book I will use this perspective to try to give some 'order' to the complexity of data which I will have to use. This is a 'Weberian' standpoint, in that it accords explanatory primacy to ideas or values rather than to material circumstances. Having said that, we have also to recognise that it is not possible to attach one particular thanatology to, say, one particular style of corpse-disposal. As Caroline Bynum puts it, 'cross-cultural work in both anthropology and history suggests that we can never find a causal relationship between doctrine and burial practices' (Bynum 1995: 51). A thanatology provides a sense of the overall 'death culture', a discursive picture of the transactions between cosmology and ontology, between the living god and the dying human. It permeates the ecology and liturgy of death, and makes sense of the events and emotions of dying, death and burial: it provides the 'atmosphere' around the deathbed and the funeral.

Thanatologies, however, do not 'predict' a specific form of corpse-disposal or of commemorative monument. I will conclude this intro-duction with a more extended discussion of the implications of having such an imprecision at the heart of my methodology. The problem might, though, be better understood if at this stage we could consider some of the data, the physical artefacts which we are trying to 'explain'.

The actual built forms which symbolise thanatologies are many and varied. There were in the Ancient Near East the huge and highly visible mausolea of the great and powerful, such as the pyra-mids or the burial places of the kings of Persia and other Eastern lands, as well as the humbler (and long-vanished) burial pits, *necropoli*, rock-cut tombs, *arcosolia* and *loculi* of lesser and ordinary people. As an example of the concern of Egypt for its dead, we could refer to the body-shaped coffins of the Egyptian Middle Kingdom, in which even ordinary Egyptians were buried well into the Roman period. Such coffins found in Canaan (at Deir el-balah) have been interpreted as the graves of Egyptian soldiers, dying far from home, unable to be returned to Egypt (the preferred option) but at least interred in the appropriate manner in a coffin shaped to the human form (Levy 1995: 341).

Concern for the proper burial and commemoration of the mili-tary and of the war dead is a constant theme in human history. The burial of the war dead is one of the few occasions when burial is seen as the responsibility more of the community than of the family. In general the burials of the war dead are surrounded with ornate public ritual and ornament, signifying the permanence of the community for which the soldiers died, and the death-transcending permanence of their connection with it. Egyptians, Greeks and Romans expressed much of their funerary and commemorative ritual and art in their memorials to their heroic dead.

The 'war dead' of the early Christians were, of course, their early martyrs – and, centrally, their martyred leader. A very large part of the views on death of the early Christians is associated with their experience and symbolic evaluation of martyrdom. Indeed, in the minds of the majority populations of the Hellenic world, and often to their astonishment, it was the zeal with which Christians sought and welcomed death and martyrdom which most radically identi-fied them. Christianity very early on began to confer upon the deaths, burial places and burial remains ('relics') of their martyr-heroes and -heroines the ostentatious funerary architecture which characterised both earlier and later cultures. Death, while always democratic in nature, is seldom democratic in expression.

Tombs, together with their grave-goods, location, epitaphs and internal design, constitute the major part of the archaeological record. The graves of Egyptian soldiers mentioned above can be used to trace the ebb and flow of war between Egypt and its various enemies on its north-eastern frontier. Cultural interpenetrations and modifications can also be traced through graves and epitaphs. In Beth Shearim, an extensive Jewish necropolis consisted of catacombs dug into the hills, with sarcophagi being placed in the spaces so provided. The town at Beth Shearim, which functioned as a kind of Jewish capital after the Roman destruction of Jerusalem, was the home and workplace of Rabbi Judah ha-Nasi, 'editor' of the Mishnah. Given its roles as a kind of Jerusalem-substitute and as a major rabbinical centre, Beth Shearim was the place to which many Diaspora Jews returned to be buried. Of the several hundred legible inscriptions found in the necropolis, the majority were in Greek (including Greek inscriptions relating to wives of rabbis), and only a fifth in Semitic and/or Hebrew. Greek names were common. Greek ornament included a depiction of the god Eros and representations of Amazons, along with Jewish representations of the Menorah. Older Hebrew words such as *hapsis*, *krepis*, *osta*, *nepes* became neologisms, so *nepes*, for example, functioned as a synonym for tomb. There are Greek references to eternal life and to Hades. More specifically, Jewish words and phrases reflect the Jewish beliefs of this period in the resurrection of the dead after the general Judgement, as well as the view that the wicked would not enjoy the future life of the just. Inscriptions warned that Jews (or others) who disturbed the resting place of the dead would suffer in the next life. References to 'soul' and 'immortality' are transposed onto more particularly Jewish views of the resurrection of the body (Freedman 1992: vol. 5, 133–4; Goodenough 1953).

In this necropolis we see one of the fundamental facts about the period with which we are concerned, which is the pervasive influence of 'Hellenism', ubiquitous and subtly influential, affecting in this case the burial practices of what is generally regarded as one of the most insistently self-defining of the cultures of the Ancient Near East. Religious tolerance and syncretism seem to have been features of both Persian and Greek (or Hellenistic) systems, and the result was a world of cultural variety and of cultural borrowing and lending – nowhere more so than in the sphere of death and burial. The cultural 'mix' typified by Beth Shearim finds another expression in the early fourth century CE Via Latina Catacomb, Rome, in which one cubiculum is decorated with Christian catacomb and sarcophagus imagery, while another is just as exclusively pagan, employing images of the hero Hercules, his protectress Athena and associated figures from Greek mythology (Elsner 1995: 274; Goodenough 1953).

It is not as if there were, in these separated centuries, a small number of well-defined religions fully in place, from which more numerous and marginal religious groups would pick bits and pieces *en route* to their own orthodoxy. Except at a rather abstract level, the 'major religions' were but tentatively in existence; the religious world was in essence a pluralism, an about-to-be-worked-out set of competitive and complementary ideas, operating under the (to us) surprisingly permissive culture of Hellenism, with its extraordinary competence in the import and export of religious, philosophical and aesthetic ideas.

Pluralistic? Yes, but as far as death and burial were concerned the heir of some potent traditions. Death asks many questions: Why do we die? Why do the good die just as certainly as the wicked? Are the wicked and the good, equal at death, equal also in the life after death? Is death an expression of God's anger or of his love? Behind the burial practices and beliefs of first century CE Greeks and Romans (and of Jews and Christians) were the long shadows of ancient Egypt and Persia, each of them with complex and detailed thanatologies and burial practices. Behind *them*, and part of them, are the endless complicated and relatively unattested religions of Ugarit, Akkad and Mesopotamia, the religions of El, Baal, Marduk, the worlds of Gilgamesh and Enkidu. In a variety of ways, by being 'brought to an end' by the Greek conqueror Alexander the Great, these cultures were 'brought into' the Hellenistic world. Thus, for example, the idea of a Day of Judgement, of being weighed on the moral scales of God, is a feature of both Egyptian and Persian religion. Related to the idea of judgement is a serious concern with (though not necessarily for) the body, a concern which is as much to provide the living with a definite focus for post-mortem ritual as for maintaining the identity of the deceased. I say *with*, rather than *for* the body, because it has proved very difficult indeed to relate actual burial practices to death beliefs. We may quote Bynum again:

> We can never find a causal relationship between doctrine and burial practice. Scholars have not, to my knowledge, been able to adduce a single case where a change in eschatology dictates precise changes in death rituals or where

changing practice immediately entails a new theory of the afterlife.

(Bynum 1995: 51)

Zoroastrians of the Seleucid and Arsacid periods (358–250 BCE, 250 BCE–230 CE) maintained a clear belief in the immortality of the soul and individualised post-mortem judgement and existence, yet combined this with disincarnation practices quite alien and incomprehensible to (for example) early Christians, to whom a whole-cadaver interment was important precisely because the body was so essential to post-mortem identity, judgement and resurrection.

Cremation, for many centuries the standard Roman mortuary practice, may again seem to indicate a lack of concern for post-mortem survival and identity: yet most cremations did (and do) produce physical remains which can be, and often were, venerated as much as the full-body cadaver. Jews have always practised full-body interment, and have also (perhaps paradoxically) regarded corpse-handling as polluting and unclean. Yet Jews, certainly from the end of the first century BCE to about 70 CE and probably for a lot longer, created and maintained large ossuaries in which individual identity is lost and for which repeated corpse- and bone-handling is required. This may (as some suggest) reflect a period of Sadducean dominance, or it may reflect not so much a diminished respect for the long-dead as a powerful and prioritising respect for the *newly*-dead, as tombs and *loculi* were used over and over again, with the space vacated by the former now available to facilitate the proper treatment of the latter.

What do we then make of the insistence in three of the Christian Gospels (Mark excepted) that Jesus is interred in a 'new sepulchre, wherein was never man yet laid' (John 19: 41)? This phrasing clearly implies that not all interments were similarly conducted. Where, as in Jesus' case, the tomb is new, does this indicate the presence of a cadaver of particular importance or the burial of an individual destined to mark a radical break with kin and cultural antecedents? We will see below how important it was to Abraham to purchase and occupy his own tomb at Machpelah so as to establish beyond doubt the distinctive nature of his people the Jews. The tomb marks territory, dynasty and tribe. Jesus' new and empty tomb marks the real beginning of a new religion.

While there are clearly some important aspects of death and burial which seem to be fairly constant cross-culturally, it is also the case that death and its relationship with life (both in this world and the next) resonates and changes with historical experience. Certain attitudes and practices are historically new and specific. Burial and memorial practices which encapsulate historical experience differentiate and divide both one *individual* from another and differentiate and divide one *society* or *community* from another. This is what such practices are meant to do. Death in this sense is neither democratic nor irenic. Burial practices will on occasion be required to distinguish between the dead, seeing in some of them an exemplary, emblematic or heroic moral quality, and in others merely a set of negative virtues or positive failings. This mechanism is most pronounced with death in war, but such a moral categorising of the dead goes on at every level of society, and in stable and peaceful societies. At such times of peace this moral differentiation can apply to citizens of superordinate civic worth, those leading citizens of Greek cities, for example, commemorated for constructing temples or sanctuaries, or for providing bequests for annual religious processions. Greek cities, in the centuries which are our concern, *seem* to have led a relatively quiet life, secure within a well-run Roman Empire, and their religious and death practices reflect this. In a complicated book, Christiane Sourvinou-Inwood provides a general summary of the Homeric understanding of life and death. 'All men must die' and go to Hades was the central 'tenet of mainstream Homeric eschatology in all its strands', and this was true for the children of the gods and even Hercules, the greatest of the heroes:

> But there is also a very thin layer of belief, not integrated within the remaining funeral ideology, according to which a few select people connected with the gods escape death and gain some sort of immortality. Menelaos, who is Zeus's son-in-law, will go to a paradise with ideal weather, the Elysian fields at the ends of the earth. The Dioscuri were given a kind of eternal life on alternating days. These are the first signs of a divergence from the inescapable fate of death; in the archaic period this divergent trend will grow and develop into an important new eschatological strand that will provide the common man with a model of hope for a better life after death.
>
> (Sourvinou-Inwood 1995: 17–8)

Sourvinou-Inwood concludes this paragraph by noting that it is the Homeric heroes who went to the Islands of the Blessed, and it is clear (whether with Greeks or with other cultures) that such a moral differentiation of the dead, which is in effect a formulation of a moral covenant between the living and the dead, is likely to become more urgent and more sharp-edged in a society characterised by serious communal emergency or crisis. The obvious instance is war, when (whether victorious or defeated) the remaining populace will have the task of incorporating or reincorporating into their moral framework the memory and meaning of their own 'sacrificial dead', and of the enemy dead who their soldiers (dead or alive) have killed on behalf of the general populace. Greek and Roman wars made soldiers out of all men. Between 490 and 338 BCE Athens was at war for two years out of every three and saw no period of peace longer than ten years. Between the seventh century BCE and the end of the first century BCE the Roman temple to Janus was 'closed' (which signified peace) only twice (Garlan 1975: 15).

Jews, under the same Roman Empire as the Greeks, had their political life and capital city destroyed, and their temple obliterated for a second time. Such an experience reinforced Jewish collective memory of danger, war, persecution and political disaster; and Jewish views on life and death, be it of their community or of individuals, reveal a very deep concern indeed for the moral calculus of death as a complement to a differentiation of the living in this world. Clear evidence for the effect of war on attitudes to death and to the relationship of these attitudes to the living is to be found in 2 and 4 Maccabees, and in the Dead Sea Scrolls, which will be discussed later. At a collective level, the mechanism operated to differentiate a moral community, the people of Israel (of which both the living and the dead are members), which stands, superior either in this world or in the future, over and against those other communities or societies which beset it. Jewish millenarianism, expressing both the moral reversal of actual military defeat and the spiritual triumph of the morally superior (if militarily defeated) Jews, represented this response.

A morally impregnated historical experience is difficult to accommodate to a morally neutral afterlife or post-apocalypse new world. Eschatology (individual or collective) makes sense of history. It makes it bearable. To a large extent the early Jesus Movement shared in this tradition, and soon added to it that form of death in which so much of early Christian thanatology found its origin and rationale: the death of martyrs. In Roman history and in Greek history, *heroes* have greater salience than martyrs. Part III will deal with this in greater detail. At this point all I wish to do is to repeat the point that death practices will have built into them a sense of history, of a differentiated moral evaluation of individuals and collectivities. In the centuries with which we are concerned this has to be borne in mind when we consider the variety of death practices under study.

In recounting the Christian story – a story which is but part of this book – many authors distinguish between 'early Christianity' (in which a *collective* moral language of salvation was deployed – the millenarian expectations of the Second Coming and consequent wholesale salvation and damnation) and a Pauline accommodationist Mission Theology (in which millenarianism is played down and a more respectable *individualised* soteriology deployed). The change, the move away from radical social transformation, is generally held to have taken place in order to make the Jesus Movement acceptable to the more laconic religious lifestyles of the Greek cities into which the Pauline missionaries were moving.

I discuss the 'Greek religion problem' below, but would here like to suggest that to see millenarianism (Christian or otherwise) as separate from or the antithesis of individualised or personal salvation is mistaken. While there may well be differences in emphasis, or indeed differences in audience reception or 'hearing' of a particular theology, it is best to see both forms of other-worldly visions and constructions as part and parcel of each other. This is certainly how Origen saw things – in his *Exhortation to Martyrdom* he urged martyrs to see themselves as part of the great cosmic struggle:

> A great assembly is gathered to watch you as you do combat and are called to bear witness. ... The whole universe and all the angels on the right and on the left, all human beings, those on God's side and those on the others – all will hear us doing battle for Christianity.
>
> (Ramsey 1986: 134)

Origen, who sought (and eventually found) martyrdom, is saying that the blood of the individual martyr ransoms others; and all this in the context of the great earth-shattering story of the cosmic struggle between good and evil. It is this Salvation Christianity which flows into the Greco-Roman cities of Late Antiquity. The cosmic drama of Christianity centres on death from its very beginnings, the salvific death-refuting death of the human-god from whom the new religion derived its name. Christ's religion was and is a death-obsessed religion, centred on the figure of the martyr-hero. The death-world of early Christianity was collective/millenarian and individual/soteriological at one and the same time. This millenarian or apocalyptic message of Jesus presented the Hellenic world with a particular set of opportunities and problems, which will be discussed below.

Christianity is also (as story, narrative and drama) the story of a highly individualised, lonely dying and death. The journey to Calvary is marked by the progressive isolation and betrayal of Jesus. On his own, and by voluntarily dying alone, Jesus saves the entire world and all who could and would follow him. Even those who abandoned and betrayed him are themselves 'saved', precisely by (and from) their betrayal. Judas, the first serious Christian sinner, is the first Christian martyr or (perhaps more accurately) the first martyr to Christ. He is a lonely, muddled man, moving via sin, error and treachery towards a highly moralised, self-salvific, voluntary death. He is, that is to say, an ordinary man (see Klassen 1996). The deaths of the early Christians are the deaths of ordinary men and women, dying for reasons of individual conscience rather than being apotheosised as military heroes or as exemplary and emblematic figures of particular nations or societies. The martyrs of Christianity are ordinary individuals; it is in its foundational martyrology that Christianity locates its death-message, its newness, its power both to persuade and to repel (see Perkins 1995).

Some methodological comments

Throughout the period with which we are concerned, Christianity was a ragged-edged religion, feeling for its boundaries. System (be it systematic theology or systematic liturgy) is usually *post facto* and reflects the optimism and myth-making competence of intellectuals. This is as much true of the Christian view of death as it is of other aspects of that religion. At no time did anyone sit down to provide 'comprehensive answers' to the matter of death, although Paul is ceaselessly moving in that direction, consciously seeking to both respect and add to the Pharisaic traditions of which he was so proud.

Like most religious undertakings (and most of the other things that humans do) the Christian project stumbled into existence, reacting to accident and to happenstance and opportunity neither anticipated nor welcome, as well as devising deliberate constructions and reconstructions of its own history, meaning and purpose. Paul, the most prominent early Christian, was by his own account born 'out of due time' (1 Cor. 15: 8), meaning that direct personal experience of Christ was already a diminishing reality and that he, and the vast bulk of Christians, would henceforward have to live in a secondhand world of things remembered and reported at two or more removes. Paul, his contemporaries and their successors were engaged in the construction of what Peter Berger and Thomas Luckmann (Berger and Luckmann 1966; Berger 1980) call 'plausibility structures', endeavouring to create 'a direct relation between the cohesion of institutions and the subjective cohesiveness of beliefs, values and worldviews' (Berger 1980: 18). In this the early Christians were seeking to explain and to legitimise (both to themselves and to indifferent or hostile others) the origin, nature and narrative of their movement, and to do so in the face of the existence, power and persuasive competence of rival religions. Early Christianity could neither claim to be nor was a monopoly: we can perhaps see it, anachronistically, as a religion operating in what (following Berger) can be seen as a prototypically *modern* frame of reference. It was a matter of *choosing* a religious preference, for 'tradition' was neither guide nor practicality. *The novelty* – a novelty which Berger sees as a modern innovation – *lay in the very fact of being able to or having to choose*: Jews and Gentiles, men and women, slaves and free, were being offered the choice of creating new traditions, a process which could perhaps only in retrospect be seen as abandoning old traditions.

For cultists and missionaries of endless variety, there seems to have been no problem in establishing the validity of a generally *religious* view of life, a choice, that is, to be or remain religious. This is, of course, the contemporary problem. In the world of the Romans and Greeks, *secularism* was not a problem – see Robin Lane Fox's comment at the start of this introduction. *Pluralism*, however, was: the early Christian records depict a movement of people who had taken 'the leap of faith' (often enough, in several different directions) confronted by an almost desperate need for both subjective and institutional coherence in a world in which the truth they had to offer – to them, the one and only truth – was just one of many. The only thing more problematic than persuading Greeks and Romans to take them seriously, was the need to find the institutional and ideational grounds that would enable them to believe in the possibility of success, to create, that is, the subjectively validating plausibilities which would enable them to take themselves seriously.

In such a social environment, it is difficult to sort out the causes and effects of the Christian story: there is no clear history which makes evident sociological sense. Did, for example, Christianity attain a significant degree of presence in at least some of the cities of the

Hellenistic world because it was 'new', or was its 'newness' a disadvantage? Eusebius addressed this problem when he commented that, while Christians were 'a youthful people [with an] undeniably new name',

> Nevertheless our life and mode of conduct, together with our religious principles, have not been recently invented by us ... the religion proclaimed in recent years to all nations through Christ's teachings [is] none other than the first, most ancient, and most primitive, of all religions, discovered by Abraham and his followers, God's beloved.
>
> (Eusebius 1986: 46)

Eusebius clearly recognised that while a degree of innovation was clearly necessary for a 'New Religious Movement' to be perceived as new, so also was an ancient tradition necessary to persuade people that it wasn't!

Eusebius and other early Christian authors clearly understood that 'new traditions' are much more persuasively presented as *biographies, events* and *stories* than as complex theologies – which usually come later and are less readily propagated. In telling stories about a martyred and self-resurrecting God, in detaching the death of men and women from an association with their *natal* ethnic or civic group membership, in individualising both death and its salvific consequence, and *in making martyrdom ordinary*, early Christianity began, in its unfolding story, to set itself apart from the death-traditions of the cultures and religions in which its origins lay. However martyrdom, expressed as martyria, had the almost opposite advantage of being 'localisable', the 'property' of a particular city or town. In this way, a universal religion could become a civic cult, very familiar *in that sense* to the religions of the Greeks and Romans. In these various ways, the new religion seems to have been able to 'make sense' to a surprisingly wide range of the inhabitants of the Empire. By the year 300 CE there were Christian churches in northern England, Upper Egypt, western Spain and eastern Syria – the frontiers of the Roman Empire – and sizeable Christian congregations at many points in between.

This 'success' is probably because of the fact, noted above, that (in addition to the task of being 'new') the business of death and burial, of funerals and post-mortem practices tends also to be an area of social concern heavily grounded in conservatism and tenacious tradition. This is partly due to the nature of death and of local topographies and practicalities – the 'neutral technology' of life and death as Robin Lane Fox puts it, pointing out the difficulty of envisaging such things as a Christianised design for an automobile or a Marxist-designed wrist-watch (Fox 1988: 22). A Christian body would share with all other bodies a propensity to decay and smell: burying went on all the time, and to an extent Christian funerary practice was conservative. Jesus is, after all, interred in the pre-Christian tomb of a member of the Sanhedrin. He is wrapped in a shroud, a burial practice evidenced in the ancient Epic of Gilgamesh and a standard part of Persian, Greek and Hellenistic prothesis. The usual colour of Greek shrouds was white. The spices which St John describes as being wound in with Jesus' shroud 'as the manner of the Jews is' (John 19: 40) were also used in Greek cadaver care, and were indeed part of the burial customs of Dynastic and Ptolemaic Egypt (Goody 1993: 43). The differential roles of men and women which accompany the death of Jesus would have made sense in the world of Late Antiquity, as would other Greek burial customs. These included a period of time and a set of ceremonies (which took place both at the tombside and away from it) in which the dead were held to be not yet properly dead and were therefore, in a variety of ways, problematic to the living: 'Touch me not', said Jesus to Mary Magdalene, 'for I am not yet ascended to my Father' (John 20: 17). Greek funeral ceremonies for the period immediately following the death included a three-day fasting period, followed by a banquet at which the deceased person was held to be present as the host – that is, they were held to be properly dead, and therefore no longer dangerous to the living. During that three-day period the deceased was not properly dead and was dangerous to know or to touch. The parallels with the three-day period immediately after the Crucifixion seem clear.

The sepulchre in which Jesus was placed was clearly a 'chamber tomb' of some kind, as Simon Peter is described as going *into* it (John 20: 6). Such rock-cut tombs have a very long pedigree indeed, as does the reuse of such tombs implied in the Gospel statements that Joseph of Arimathea's tomb had not yet been used. In interring Jesus as they did, and no matter how idiosyncratic were the pre- and post-death events surrounding his death, the early Christians were living and dying within very ancient funeral traditions derived from the endless interplay of the cultures of the Ancient Near East, and determined to some extent by the geology and geography of the lands in which the deaths occurred. To try to do justice to this complexity, this book will mobilise a wide range of data, archaeological and historical as well as theological. While the immediate world of the early Christians was the violent world of Israel-Palestine (set paradoxically within the broader and well-policed 'peace' of the Roman Empire), the setting also included a much older inheritance of funeral architecture, art, emblem and archaeology, together with associated thanatologies. Such an inheritance was not 'coherent' – any more than is ours – and any 'theology of death', be it Christian, Jewish or Gentile, will almost inevitably be both syncretistic and untidy. This would be particularly true of a religion lacking both internal definitive creeds and external validating authorities.

What we see, in the slow elaboration of the Christian story, and indeed of the other cults of the Empire, is a process of reciprocally adaptive theologies and liturgies. The extent and nature of the reciprocity would be a function of the relative power and status of, say, a Jewish and a Christian community in an Hellenic city. The outcome would be partly a question of mind or intellectual conversion, partly a question of circumstance, the two combining to produce Peter Berger's 'plausibility structures' in which early Christians found some semblance of coherence.

Precise 'cause' and exact 'consequence' are not to be found in such a world, now so far from us. More usefully, perhaps, the term 'elective affinity' might serve to explicate the methodological style of this book. Within broad (and often unexplained) theories of social causation, this concept enables us to cope with the fact that while some factor – such as, for example, the Platonic notion of the soul – may explain some part of the attractiveness of Platonism to early Christians (and vice versa), it does not always do so; it may indeed be associated with a quite different outcome. A Greek member of the Isiac cult may after all have found a Christian 'soul theory' *less* rather than more acceptable precisely because it was rather like his own – *too* close, that is. The *circumstances* under which two ideas, on the surface compatible, are in real life actually conjoined may also vary. A relatively powerless religion such as early Christianity may well have been willing, if not eager, to go along with a degree of mutual tolerance which would not be acceptable or even advisable in other circumstances: the prime task of early Christians was, above all, to get themselves tolerated. Such a process may well underly the (still continuing) controversy about the early third century BCE 'Christian' funerary inscriptions discovered by W.M. Ramsay at Kelendres and Eumeneia (in Asia Minor), which seemed to show early Christians accommodating themselves in 'heretical' ways to their pagan host-communities (Frend 1996: 91–104). Eumeneia had possessed a bishop since *c.*160 CE, and seems to have been a strongly Christian city where the conversion process had been led by the leading citizens. Gravestones carried a mixture of Greek, Jewish and Christian attitudes, with Christians (for example) seemingly happy to follow Greek custom in writing upon the actual tombstone a curse upon anyone trying to insert into a tomb a body not part of the family of the owner, and requiring that anyone found guilty of so doing pay a fine *to the local public treasury* – the offence, that is, being seen *as to the entire polis* and not solely to the particular religious community involved. Additional inscriptions indicate a Christian presence: 'he who will judge in the future the living and the dead' added to the more pecuniary sanctions of the rather conventionally minatory Greek epitaphs. All of this seems to indicate a practical and diplomatic relationship between Greek and Christian citizens of Eumeneia, rather than one of principled or dogmatic agreement. In such circumstances, of course, either one or both parties to the original compromise may come to discover that the temporary arrangement has a persuasive intellectual and communal competence exceeding the originally more grudging accommodation; a new morality can emerge, which may or may not be proclaimed as what was initially intended anyway. To complicate things even further, the historical record may or may not be 'honest' about such reflexive transactions!

In such an area of study as this, and at so many centuries remove, one has to adopt both the flexibilities of 'elective affinity' and to make use of other Weberian tactics of understanding such as the framework of 'social action', in which a disciplined effort has to be made to see social reality from the various points of view of the various 'actors', free from any obligation to determine which is 'correct'. The world of early Christianity was a cosmopolitan world, with a multiplicity of cultures and polities, some ancient and decayed, some ancient and prosperous, some relatively new and inchoate, some relatively new and adamant. From such a world what would have seemed least likely at the time of the death of Christ must surely have been the conversion of the Roman Emperor and Empire to something called 'Christianity' and the transformation of a small intra-Jewish argument into a major orthodoxy and dominant religious system of the Empire.

In seeking to make sense of and confer order upon the great welter of data which are invoked in a study of death, we could perhaps carry in our minds the major variables of a 'death culture'. One (and by far the most important as I have said above) is the foundational cosmology, the view the culture takes of the purpose of the creation of the world and of the relationships of God or the gods with their human creation and its cosmic purpose within that Creation. This cosmology attends to the problems raised by the very evident fact of physical decay and human ephemerality (individual and communal), and seeks to examine it to see whether it is a tragedy or a glory. Second, there is the material culture – that is, the actual locations, topographies, architecture and design of corpse-disposal, whether this is interment or cremation (or some blend of both), primary or secondary burial, straight into the ground or into a tomb or mausoleum, and whether the grave is an actual grave or a death-memorial and locator. Third, there is the nature of the actual funeral – that is, the presence, performance, ritual movements and gestures of people who have been mobilised by a death to enter into ritual behaviour which both prepares for and attends to the disposal of the physical remains of the deceased and the concomitant restructuring of their social relationships. In many cultures the funeral is aimed at neutralising the dead, to render them indifferent to the new social arrangements from which they are excluded. Fourth, and tied in with the first, there will be some view of the meaning of the historical experience and trajectory of the collectivity. This may be most explicit at the occasion of the death of the mighty kings and rulers, or of large numbers of deaths in war, when the death-memorial elicits a sense not simply of the movements of the universe and of 'humanity' but of *these* humans, *this particular piece* of the universe of which we, the dead, the dying and the living are the cultural and moral representatives. This set of concerns may be simply those of 'dynasty', when title to land-possession or to social status are safeguarded by proclamatory ritual. When however such sentiments lead to repeated post-mortem rituals at the burial site or monument, and to tendencies to ascribe intercessory competence to the dead, then we can speak of a 'cult of the dead'. As we shall see, it is this aspect of death which gives rise to repeated controversy in, for example, Judaism, where temptations to accord to the dead a capacity to help or advise the living, or even to intercede with God, are regarded by 'the authorities' as a most dangerous heresy. It is difficult, however, to find any religious culture which is able to suppress such 'cults of the dead' completely, while many of them make it a major part of their thanatological practices. As Berger might say: there must be some plausible interconnection between these four variables for them to constitute a viable death culture.

In the chapters that follow, I will endeavour to show how the people living in the three or four centuries before Christ, and the three or four hundred centuries after him (centuries in which Christians were merely one of many religious groups), tried to construct a sense of meaning for their deaths. The general format will be a presentation of the particular thanatology, followed by an account of actual funeral practice, with a short summary which will be amplified in the epilogue.

A concluding point

This book will, unavoidably, use terms imputing cultural reality to social entities such as 'the Jews' or 'the Romans' or 'the Christians'. Yet, in death as in life, the historical record is neither comprehensive nor statistically unbiased in its data-selection processes. Of the approximately 100,000,000,000 people who have died since the last Ice Age only a tiny fraction are 'remembered'. Ian Morris, for example, discusses the relationship between burial practice and social structure. 'Burials', he writes, 'are the material remains of self-representations of social structure through the agency of ceremony' (Morris 1987: 8). In demonstrating very clearly that burial within Greek cemeteries (in particular the Athenian Kerameikos) was neither available to everyone nor statistically representative of the population as a whole, he shows that a major portion of the population would have been disposed of 'informally' or 'invisibly'.

In the Greece about which Morris is writing (about 1100–500 BCE) rank or social status was the main criterion for burial within the Kerameikos, as well as for the particular location within it of the actual interment. The more democratic the *polis*, the more 'collective' the funerary architecture and the greater the disinclination to encourage or condone individual or status distinctions in access to or use of cemetery space and elaborate sepulchral ornamentation. However, whether elitist or democratic, status, whether emphasised or muted, was determined by the rank of the *male* citizen. Athenian cemeteries were statistically 'short' of women, children and non-citizens, slaves in particular. Sarah Pomeroy writes that:

> the skewed sex ratios of Greek cemeteries testify to the devaluation of women. ... To the twenty per cent of female infanticide postulated by Golden, we may add the lack of burial with a marker of another ten per cent of women resulting from disrespect and neglect.
>
> (Pomeroy 1997: 104–5)

Exclusion by age, whether by infanticide followed by informal 'disposal' or by simply inserting a dead baby in an adult coffin or burial place, is something marking nearly all societies, including our own where aborted remains generally have no known grave. Over and above infanticide (usually of female babies rather than male) children died in enormous numbers. Scheidel provides figures for Roman Egypt: of every 100,000 girls born, 49,000 would be dead within five years; of 100,000 boys born, 45,000 would be dead within five years (for most of our period, female death-rates exceed male death-rates). For late antique Rome, and from Christian tomb inscriptions, Scheidel shows that whereas only 3 per cent of Christian funerary inscriptions refer to children under one year old at death, a proper statistical representation would produce a number ten times that amount (Scheidel 1996: 152).

In Roman Carthage, conversely, the Tophet (itself a word and location associated with Jerusalem and Gehenna) seems to have been the location for the burial of children sacrificed by their parents to Kronos-Baal Hamon. Far from children being absent from the mortuary record, they are only too present. Lawrence Stager gives a figure of 20,000 children sacrificed between 400–200 BCE (Stager 1980: 3). Stager comments that the rate of child sacrifice seems to have been associated with the degree of military danger for Carthage: the children, willingly or not, were in death pressed into the service of the community.

Money also determined how one died – then as now. Bowman, writing about the continuation into the Ptolemaic and Roman periods of ancient Egyptian burial customs, comments that they show:

> the care and expense that was lavished upon those who could afford the embalming, the elaborate bandaging, the highly decorated woven mummy cloths, the very life-like portraits painted in encaustic on wooden boards set into the headpiece of the mummy or the gilt masks which served as headpieces, the painted boxes which contained ritual texts to accompany the deceased on his journey. The rich might be laid in massive stone sarcophagi, set in lavishly decorated tombs; the more modest might afford a ceramic coffin; the poor would end up simply as plainly bandaged mummies, soaked in pitch and consigned, with a label bearing the name of the deceased, to a communal pit or graveyard.
>
> (Bowman 1986: 186)

For the very poor, other places existed. The Romans had places for collective, anonymous corpse disposal – the *puticuli*. The Jews had Gehenna, a valley to the west of Jerusalem with long-standing associations with human sacrifice, later becoming the place where dead animals, the city's garbage and the bodies of criminals were burnt, and as such full of fire and associated fears and anxieties – a warning to all of the fate of those in essence treated as 'unburied'. To be unburied seems to have been the ultimate degradation for the people of the Ancient Near East, it being proof of abandonment by both humanity and the gods. Huge and consistent efforts went into the management and government of the dead, even though within that the inequalities and injustices of human society are replicated in grave, sepulchre and cemetery.

For whatever reason, whether of cost, or for reasons of status and rank, or because of the appetites of the gods, the burial places of humanity reflect the power and control systems of the societies out of whose life they come. In the centuries of interest to us, these societies are dominated by upper-class men, 'citizens' when such a status was a relatively rare thing, men who would, in their respective elites, monopolise the military, political, economic and intellectual resources of the worlds they governed under the gods. However, death and burial practices are *often enough* successful attempts by less powerful and prestigious people to create their own monuments for their lives and deaths, and *often enough* ruling elites step aside and let them get on with it. Indeed, the 'sumptuary laws' through which both Greeks and Romans sought to limit the funeral expenditure and ostentatious ornamental extravagances of the rich are clear evidence of the fact that, at death, the transient hierarchies of humanity are radically subverted by the commonality of life. The deaths of the poor and lowly must be respected. Graves and monuments always reflect society, but they do so within the radically egalitarian empire of death. To be totally 'ignored' at death, to be left without an 'address' (in the various senses of that word) is rare indeed. True, time has eroded most of these addresses and no amount of archaeology or textual exegesis can ever bring them to life as fully and graphically as the monuments of the powerful, but the addresses are there, and can in varying degree and in various ways, be noted and examined and set within the context of the historical record. Slaves, the poor, children, women, ordinary people – not quite invisible in history, because not quite invisible in death.

Part I

DEATH IN THE
ANCIENT NEAR EAST

There is continuity in our funeral rituals and traditions extending back to the ancient Near East.

(Kennedy 1987: 227)

The Greeks burn their dead, the Persians bury them; the Indian glazes the body, the Scythian eats it, the Egyptian embalms it.

(Lucian of Samosata 1905: vol. 3, 217)

Van der Meer and Mohrmann's *Atlas of the Early Christian World* records the existence of approximately forty-two churches or Christian congregations of the first century of the Common Era. Of these, all but two were in the Eastern or Greek-speaking end of the Roman Empire, including ten in 'Palestine'. The two main concentrations were in 'Palestine' and in what is now Turkey. By the year 300 CE concentrations of Christian churches are to be found in Africa (around Carthage), Spain (in the south-east in 'Baetica'), and in Italy and Syria, as well as in Mesopotamia, Armenia and Egypt. In these areas Van der Meer and Mohrmann classify the population almost exclusively as 'majority or large number of the people Christian' (Van Der Meer and Mohrmann 1959: Maps 1, 2 and 3).

The cities and lands in which Christian churches and congregations are nearly all to be found are often enough identical with the cities and lands of the Jewish diaspora or galut, as well as of the Jewish 'homelands'. The earliest Christians were of course Jews. At one time or another, and in one way or another, Jews had travelled to and lived in (voluntarily or otherwise) most of the major cultures and religions of the Ancient, Classical, Hellenic and Roman Near East.

The story of Abraham and his descendants, of the sojourn in Egypt and of the wandering Israelite tribes who became the 'Kingdom of Israel' as well as 'The Jews' of the Exile and the 'Judaism' of the Septuagint, the Dead Sea Scrolls and the Mishnah, takes us on a journey through the lands and homes of the most ancient of their (and our) religious ancestors. If travel, trade and propinquity result in an ingestion and exchange of religious ideas, then the people of the Jewish scriptures must have been among the most influenced, if not necessarily the most influential of cross-cultural receivers, transmitters and messengers. Given the religious importance of the people and the lands through which they moved or on which they settled, it is not surprising that they (both land and people!) have been extensively 'dug over' by archaeologists and other antiquarians. As a consequence, we know a great deal about the Prehistoric and Ancient Near East, as well as about the succeeding periods of history.

This part of the book will concern itself first with the more prominent of the religious death cultures of the lands over which the Jews wandered or to which they were exiled, that is the death cultures of Egypt to the south and of Mesopotamia and 'Persia' to the east. Egypt had a relatively self-contained death culture. To the east, however, 'Persia' and 'Mesopotamia' have to represent the various religions of 'Babylon' ('Assyria' or 'Syrio-Mesopotamia'), as well as an Iranian-Zoroastrian manifestation. While all of these religions are 'old' by most standards, there are to be found in the Ancient Near Eastern archaeological and other records evidence for even earlier 'tribal' religious cults and associated burial practices. We see these practices, carried out in the names of their gods and goddesses: El, Marduk, Atargatis, Astarte, Anat, Asherah, Dagan, Baal and Melkart, and a host of others, gradually becoming involved in the larger empires of the area. In the 'Christian centuries' all these and others are encountered in most of the cities of the Ancient Near East in bewildering and endlessly reconfigured variety, what Ramsey MacMullen calls the 'pullulation of beliefs' of the lands of what became the Roman Empire (MacMullen 1981: 1).

The 'standard' Greco-Roman city referred to by MacMullen would contain temples to Jupiter, Juno and Minerva, Mercury, Isis and Serapis, Apollo, Liber Pater, Hercules, Mars, Venus, Vulcan, Ceres, and these in turn would be manifestations of other gods or aspects of gods, under different names. As an example we could perhaps take the Syrian city of Edessa, a city associated in Christian tradition with Jesus himself. In one version of the Edessa story, Jesus wrote a letter to Abgar, King of Edessa, in response to a request for help with a royal illness. This is clearly apocryphal. By the second century CE the city of Edessa, the home of the religious teacher and philosopher Bardesanes, had strong Parthian-Iranian (Zoroastrian) religious influence co-existing with a Judaism connected with the large Jewish colonies of Babylonia. Edessa's Christianity, initially Jewish-Christian, would have probably also entered from the east, producing a variety of Judeo-Christian texts such as the Odes of Solomon. In addition there were Gnostics, such as the Quqites, who mixed a Samaritan tradition with Iranian elements. All of this, in the second century CE, 'existed beside and on the basis of' (as Hendrik Drijvers puts it) 'an authochthonous Semitic religion, in which Baal and Nebo were worshipped and an important place was reserved for Atargartis to whom the sacred fish in the lake of Kallirhoe were dedicated'. Astrology flourished in Edessa, with a seven-planet Empire under one Ruler-God, and separate worship of the Sun and Moon. Sanctuaries to these cults were being built in the second century CE. Eastern philosophy made an appearance, in the form of the thoughts of Diogenes of Babylon and others, and from the west came knowledge of Greek Stoicism. In addition, over the early Christian centuries the city became the location of persistent intra-Christian disputes, 'an amorphous mass of Christians', with heresies in various forms (such as the teachings of Marcion and Tatian), as well as Bardesanes' own version, all adding to the available menu of theologies and philosophies (Drijvers 1965: 215–6; Klijn 1962: 33). It is perhaps small wonder that when Christianity came to Edessa it became itself riven by argument and heresy: the local 'mix' was simply too rich!

I will discuss the thanatologies of these cults, as well as those of Egypt, Canaan, Mesopotamia and Persia, in the following chapters of Part I. In Part II, I will try to relate all of this to the specifically Jewish variants of this Ancient Near Eastern culture, as this Jewish tradition developed in the course of Jewish history from the Iron Age into the Hellenistic and Roman periods. There is, of course, no implication in this that the movement of history in the Ancient Near East was aimed at 'producing' Judaism. Jews and Judaism were always, and remain, a minority presence in the Ancient Near East. However, it was there that Judaism developed, and I will use Part II to present an analysis of Jewish death culture, archaeology and attitudes, which evolved as we approach the centuries which are the focus of this book.

In the chapters of Part III, I will address the other obvious fact arising out of a perusal of the map presented by Van der Meer and Mohrmann – that is, that the early Jewish-Christian congregations are to be found primarily in the *Greek*-dominated part of the *Roman*

Empire. We will therefore be interested in Greek and Roman attitudes to death and burial – which are themselves, of course, part of the general death culture of the Ancient Near East, although with their own very distinctive imprint. Indeed, it was Hellenism very much more than Judaism which 'imported' Egypt, in the form of cults (including the cult of Isis), into the Roman Empire. Egypt is therefore more relevant to these later chapters than to the discussion of Judaism. Again in these cities of the Greco-Roman world we find the 'pullulation of beliefs' referred to by MacMullen.

The 'pantheon' of each city was not simply a list of gods; it was a list of the dangers and disasters against which the gods, properly worshipped, would offer protection. In the multiplicity and ubiquity of the gods lies the evidence for the multiplicity and ubiquity of the dangers the people of the Ancient Near East and the Roman Empire sensed in the world around them. The gods were protectors of animals, crops and human beings. They were the guarantors (when properly worshipped) of 'fertility' in its widest sense, the basis of communal life. In the city of Mantineia, which was thirteen by (at most) seven kilometres, there were (in the actual city) six temples with six or more statues, eight sanctuaries, three grave-shrines and various public monuments (Zaidman and Pantel 1992: 207–13). At five separate sanctuaries Zeus was worshipped for five different functions: Zeus Thunderbolt, Zeus Saviour (i.e. guarantor of the city after it had to be rebuilt following a Spartan sacking in 385 BCE), Zeus as War Lover, Zeus as Counsellor, Zeus as Bountiful. In the country zone of Mantineia, there was a sacred wood to Demeter and a sanctuary to Poseidon Hippios, itself a modern version built by Hadrian (died 138 CE) around the earlier sanctuary. There were sanctuaries to Artemis, Penelope, the mysteries of Dionysus, Black Aphrodite, Pelias' daughters, Areithos, Ankhises and, again, Aphrodite. No citizen of Mantineia could have avoided one or more of these shrines, statues, sanctuaries and temples on a short evening walk: if they followed the Athenian example, then 120 days in each year would have been devoted in whole or in part to religious festivals of one kind or another, including especially processions – the public celebration of the protective cults. To be irreligious in such contexts was practically impossible, as well as dangerous. The citizens of such cities were heirs to an extraordinary religious inheritance to which I will now turn.

1

OSIRIS AND ISIS

The life-theology of Ancient Egypt

The Egyptians alone believe in the resurrection, as they
carefully preserved their dead bodies. They have a custom
of drying up their bodies and making them as durable as
brass.

(St Augustine, in Pettigrew 1834: 15)

Of any Egyptian doctrine of a final catastrophe there is no
record.

(Hastings 1912: vol. 5, 374)

[For over four thousand years] of eventful history ... the
care of the Egyptians for their dead remained the striking
and constant feature of their religion. ... Several of the
old-world customs survive in almost their ancient form.
Among these are the periodical visitation to the tombs, the
feastings and observances on these occasions, the prayers
and invocations made almost directly to the dead, the
belief of the presence either in or near the tomb of the 'good
spirit' or double of the deceased, and the provisioning of
the tomb with food.

(Garstang 1907: 1–2)

Amongst the oldest thanatologies of the Ancient Near East were those
of Egypt and Persia. In both cases the religious systems were both
formalised and 'official', although the sacred texts of Persia are much
more elusive than those of Egypt. The Egyptian texts are more
extensive. Both sets of texts present problems for interpretation,
translation and comprehension; and in both cases there are additional
problems of establishing the degree, if any, of their cultural influence.

In the case of Egypt, there is very considerable debate about
the precise nature of Egyptian (or 'African') influence on the

Greco-Roman world. This controversy enlivens the pages of *Black Athena* (1987), by Martin Bernal, and *Not Out of Africa* (1997), by Mary Lefkowitz. The controversy was reviewed by John Ray in 1997. Whether with Herodotus in the fifth century BCE, with Diodorus Siculus in the first century BCE, with Plutarch in the first century CE, or with contemporary writers, 'Egypt' seems to be a culture reported and exported as much by creative misrepresentation as by accurate understanding.

Egypt was ancient when Abraham was merely old. The Egyptian dynasties date from about 4400 BCE. Egypt accounts for seven-tenths of the period from the invention of writing to now (see Ray 1978–9). The average Egyptian of the Dynastic periods had a life expectancy at birth of 30–36 years. Half of the population died by the age of 30 and few excavated burials contain people over the age of 60. Few of these deaths would have been attended by any medical personnel, as the court and its high officials had a virtual monopoly of such care, sharing it only on occasion with the army. Ordinary Egyptians died young and ill (Nunn 1996: 22, 118).

Yet they had been created lovingly. The 'Monologue of the Creator God' describes the acts of Creation:

> I did four good deeds
> within the portal of the horizon.
> I made the four winds
> so that every man might breathe in his surroundings.
> I made the great flood
> so that the poor and the rich might have power.
> I made every man like his fellow.
> I did not ordain that they do wrong;
> their hearts disobeyed what I had said.
> I caused that their hearts did not forget the west,
> so that the offerings be presented to the gods of the locality.
> (Hornung 1983: 198)

A humanity created so lovingly lived in the same way: in a real sense Egyptians did not 'die'. Augustine was probably wrong in using the term 'resurrection', since the Egyptian fourfold concept of the person in effect sees it as immortal, with 'death' providing more of an opportunity for fulfilment, rather than experienced as a negation requiring a rebirth, a resurrection. The whole point of Egyptian funerary ritual was to prevent a *second* death (feared as oblivion) from taking place by transcending any gulf there might be between the two worlds. The central religious preoccupation of Egyptian religion was with life, a sanguine philosophy perhaps engendered by the annual gift of water from the Nile and of the benign cosmology which saw 'nature' attached to the life-giving inundation and the seemingly uninterruptible miracle of crops and food. Egyptian cosmology was without an End Time, an Apocalypse, and it is in this that the Egyptians are perhaps most distinctive, even unique. Zandee (1960) has taught us not to downplay the dark or 'hellish' side of Egyptian religion, but both Spencer (1982) and Henk Milde (1994: 15–35) would agree with the editors of the *Encyclopedia of Religion and Ethics* (Hastings 1912) and with Cohn, who argues that the idea that 'time was moving towards a universal consummation ... had no place at all in Egyptian thinking' (Cohn 1995: 30). To put this point in another way, there is no radical dualism in Egyptian theology which would invoke, for either individual or humanity, some crisis-ridden eschatological drama.

The Egyptians feared *chaos* in this world and the next: the whole purpose of their spells and rituals was to deny the chaos implicit in death and to preserve continuity at the time of death so that its divisive and dis-membering consequences could be pre-empted. Death was an opportunity to reassemble life, with all of the threatening elements removed, in unity with Osiris and the eternal journey of Ra in the skies and in the underworld.

In their pyramids and their associated mastabas and cemeteries, in their mummification practices (of both humans and animals) and in the associated construction of a sense of 'person', the Egyptians elaborated a theology in which individual life was so important and valuable that every effort had to be made to ensure that death and burial provided cause and occasion for the affirmation of that life rather than for fatalistic acceptance or sufferance. The spells and incantations of the various *Books of the Dead* were aimed at bringing the dead 'out into the day', which as a title would be a much more accurate translation of the purpose and spirit of the *Books* than the translation we tend to use. The Egyptians themselves called the papyri 'Books of Going out into the Day':

> Beginning of the spells of the Offering Field,
> spells of Going out into the Day, of coming and going in the realms of the dead,
> of entering the Field of Rushes, of staying in the Offering Field, the great abode 'Mistress of Winds'.
> Having power there, being glorious there,

ploughing there and reaping,
eating there, drinking there,
making love there;
doing everything that used to be done on earth
by the copyist of the temple of Ptah, Nebseny, lord of reverence,
engendered by the draughtsman Thenna, justified,
born to the housewife Mutresti, justified.

(Milde 1994: 15)

The person with whom these incantations would have been concerned was held to be made up of four elements or aspects: a *ka* (a kind of vital force, an ability to act and do), a *ba* (an entity actually invigorated by death, with the all-important task of binding together the *ka* and the mummy/body), the *xu* (a shiningness or evidence of location around the polestar and evidence also of heart-conscience, weighed at judgement against the balance of a feather) and the *body*. While there are various versions of this fourfold division, the essential point is the emphatic denial of death in complex rituals designed to maintain the unity and integrity of the person: hence the importance of the mummy, the body to which – on death – the other aspects of the person would have to be re-attached, at various times, if that person were to live, to become Osiris. There is, then, neither resurrection nor metempsychosis in Egyptian thanatology: the full, embodied person retains their life, 'justified' and revitalised.

To support this extraordinary view of life/death, there existed the central triad of Osiris, Isis and Horus, the tripartite centre of a pantheon and post-mortem system which, while considerably mutated by later Greek and Roman syncretism, constituted the benign life-culture (rather than death-culture) of Egypt. In texts issued and reissued and changing over many centuries, Osiris, once a mythical human king, is transformed into the immortal god of the dead. In this, his sister–wife Isis plays the central role.

The cult of Isis goes back as far as the fourth millennium BCE, dated by a document which associates her with insisting on a respectful attitude to the dead. She is herself immortal, and the life-giver to and sexual partner of her brother Osiris; Isis saves and restores Osiris. Furthermore, it was by becoming Osiris, and through the salvific intercession of and reflexive identification with Osiris, that Egyptians of all status would experience a 'going out into the day', something which made their funerals an experience of hope and rebirth. Osiris had been killed and dismembered by his brother Set, a figure who remains to threaten the introduction of a rather alien dualism into the predominantly benign system. The sister–wife of Osiris, Isis (goddess of resurrection, of fertility, of the moon), was the deity whose activities made the whole cult of Osiris possible. When, with the aid of Horus and of the dog-headed god Anubis, Isis reassembled the body of her murdered and dismembered brother Osiris, she laid the basis of a major cult of death and rebirth. Osiris presided over the Day of Judgement, with each incoming person being weighed against a feather. Failure would result in being eaten by the Eater of the Dead, the crocodile-headed Ammit, and thus sent to the 'second death', to the total oblivion and chaos beyond the grave which was the greatest dread of the Egyptians. Death is followed by a journey; this journey after death, through a series of tests and trials, was aimed at passing the Judgement, at 'becoming Osiris', at salvation. In the Judgement Hall of Osiris lay eternal life. Forty-two netherworld judges assessed the deceased, who then passed into the abode of Osiris, in a chamber or place whose roof was of fire, whose walls were of gigantic living cobras and whose floor was primeval water from which sprang the blue lotus, symbol of the external womb.

Evolving over many centuries, the necessary spells and incantations (originally in Pyramid Texts, then in the Coffin Texts and lastly in the papyrus 'Books of Going out into the Day') provided a guide, a map to salvation: 'there was never really any doubt concerning the success of the soul in making the journey', writes Alan Spencer, 'because the papyri always record that the individuals for whom they were written overcame all difficulties and eventually reached the domain of Osiris' (Spencer 1982: 144). Death, the Journey and the Judgement before Osiris gave individuals an opportunity to articulate the exculpatory spells and prayer-offerings which would guarantee them Justification, the Coming out into the Day.

Various Egyptian texts, spread over many centuries, show the evolution of this thanatology, with a clear sense of death being an occasion for judgement with, of course, the implicit danger of punishment for those who were unfamiliar with the words of the 'Books of Going out into the Day'. In general, though, the entry into the abode of Osiris, indeed the entry into and becoming Osiris, was entry into the abode of the dead, into paradise, though the deceased must be pure. Various roads ran through the Egyptian netherworld. In the netherworld, the deceased might spend a very long time, in netherworlds both paradisical and gloomy. The crocodile-headed Ammit instantly devoured those who failed the Judgement, and other demonic beings provided a series of tortures and attacks. The emphasis though was always on the hope of arrival at the resurrection point on the eastern horizon, where the deceased will enter a cosmic permanency, sharing in the daily rebirth of the sun god Re or Ra. In this journey, Re travelled in the night-time in a boat to the land of the dead, the Tuat, to feed and advise or admonish the dead. The end-concern of all Egyptian thanatology was to enable the deceased to participate in the daily resurrection of the sun god or (there being some variation in this) to join the equally immortal stars.

The Egyptian afterlife was seen as 'more life', not death, and life with the negativities removed. Egyptian cadaver-preparation, funerary arrangements and architecture were designed to ensure this. At death, the dissolution of the person was a threatening possibility. *Ba* and *xu* might wander off, perhaps for thousands of years, but on return must find the *ka* and an identifiable body – the *ka* in particular must have a proper place to live, a mummy, a real body. Logically enough, erotic power was held to have a competence to ensure existence after death, although the main concern seems to have been with the other-worldly sexual appetites of the male rather than the female: 'the sexual power of the mummy had to be maintained and stimulated. This is always visualised as pertaining to the mummy of a man, never that of a woman' (Manniche 1987: 10). To provide sexual stimulation for the male, Egyptian post-mortem provision included phallus worship, temple prostitution and concubine figures painted on the tomb walls (ibid.: 10–17).

Sex in the afterlife was not without problems. The hieroglyph for phallus includes an association of meanings of ' semen' and 'poison'. This is a reference to the poisonous semen of the god Seth, in his homosexual attack on Horus, and to the ability of a dead person to have sex with a sleeping person, a danger avoided by the use of the spell 'let your seed be ineffective' (Nunn 1996: 53). It is interesting to note that semen is indeed carcinogenic.

Egyptian tombs were an extension of life, indeed its affirmation: their grave goods and equipment, and the care lavished on funerals, prayers and spells, all emphasise the central importance of maintaining the integrity of the person as a vital, recognisable, busy, sexual human being. The Necropolis at Giza illustrates the way in which the 'social system' of the afterlife mirrored the social system of this world – or perhaps vice versa – as well as expressing the Egyptians' theological understanding of the nature of death.

The king [Cheops] lay in his pyramid provided with all the splendid equipment of his palace and person: the daily supply of food and drink was guaranteed by the endowments of the servants of the ka, who were engaged to make offerings and recite the necessary formulae in the temples attached to the pyramid. The king's ka was free to pass unhindered from the grave to the temple and to the outer world. His queens, his children, his officials and his attendants lay in the small pyramids and the mastabas east and west of the pyramid, and these were provided with similar equipment and similar daily offerings, each in proportion to his rank and means. Their kas, also, were free to pass unhindered to and fro from the grave to the outer world. ... Thus in the ghostly world of life after death, the court of the great king, with the queen-mother, the queens, the children, and the great officials, were assembled round the ka of the king and in daily association with him.

(Reisner 1942: 27–8)

Giza was laid out like a town, with the smaller mastabas running in straight lines to the east and west of the large Khufu pyramid. Other mastabas were built as houses, complete with lavatories and gardens (Spencer 1982: 72). In essence, Egyptian tombs, in all their varieties of size and ornateness, were homes, designed to provide all material support for the anticipated continuation of convivial and sociable life (it was partly for this reason that these lavishly equipped 'houses' were so attractive to robbers). Human beings were accompanied not only by food and furniture, but also by animals. Cats, imbued as were many animals with a religious significance, were mummified and placed within the tombs. Indeed, 'tombs' is perhaps too limiting a word, because in their zeal to recreate the world, to impose a humanly devised order upon the always threatening chaos, Egyptian architects and builders created structures – temples, sanctuaries, necropoli, pyramids – of a death-defying monumentality which has indeed outlasted mere history. The sanctuary at North Saqqara for example had, by 1976 when excavations ceased, been found to contain 'four million mummified ibises, half a million hawks, five hundred baboons (or at least their burial places), a score of sacred cows', as well as temples and thousands of statues (Ray 1978–9: 151). This ancient burial ground became, from the sixth century BCE, a pilgrimage centre for over a thousand years, neutralised only by the imposition on the old temple site of a Christian church.

In all of the complex death theology of Egypt, of particular interest is the concept of *ma'at* or Maat, the goddess of truth and divine order. Maat (see Proverbs for a parallel) has a very long pedigree, being a female deity, both mother and daughter of Amon, an 'assimilation' of Ra/Re, the Sun God. Maat's purpose or function is to look after and defend the orderly progress of creation and the human place within it. At some point, Maat's role is transferred to Isis, and linked by her to Demeter, although taking supreme power (with his agreement) from Osiris. At the moment of Judgement Maat would provide the feather against which the heart (symbol of the personality) of the deceased would be weighed in the scales before being allowed to enter the house of Osiris. The feather indicates the fineness of the judgement, i.e. the necessity at all times, pre-death and after, of being meticulous in form and substance. Maat is the embodiment of justice, the right ordering of all creation at the personal and collective levels. For the deceased individual, approaching the house of Osiris, the balancing of the heart of the deceased against *ma'at*, represented hieroglyphically by the feather, ensures that 'the balance is void of his guilt' (Milde 1994: 22). The heart, representing the *ka* of the deceased, is itself capable of being critical, i.e. it can behave like a conscience, separate from but part of the 'persona' of the deceased, and giving that part of the persona a chance to take part in the discussion of its own fate!

Ma'at, the feather, is not a marginal standard, facilitating a 'just-about' decision ('just-about passed' or 'just-about failed'), but is an absolute measure, the Egyptian principle of good order or justice, and is part of a prolonged funerary rite in which the deceased has to pass a series of tests before entering paradise, which is the presence
– of Osiris, in which the deceased must be pure, not just satisfactory: the balance must be void of all guilt. The principle or the Goddess Maat insists that human beings, in order to become one with Osiris, must live their lives in the expectation of having to be pure. Life must be lived in the expectation of a massively moralised but benign death. (The feather, as representative also of the fragility of 'truth', reappears many, many centuries later in Isaac Bashevis Singer's short story *A Crown of Feathers*.

The Egyptians were essentially ritual optimists, believing fervently in the 'resurrection' of the dead as an individualised, embodied self, with the whole purpose and point of the funeral rite being to rejoin the *ba* (soul) with the body. Cremation was abhorrent, reserved for evil-doers who would thereby be rendered totally non-existent. The point of the funeral was to accomplish the 'going out into the day', the new life with Osiris and as Osiris, in the delights of eternity. Henk Milde quotes from a 1450 BCE stela:

> A fair burial comes in peace, when your seventy days are completed in your embalmment place. You are placed on a bier ... and drawn by young cattle. May the ways be opened by milk, until you reach the entrance to your chapel. May the children of your children be collected all together, weeping with affection. May your mouth be opened by the lector priest, may you be purified by the sem-priest. Horus adjusts for you your mouth, he opens for you your eyes, your ears, your body, your bones, so that all of you is complete. Spells of glorification will be read for you, an offering will be made for you, while your heart is really with you, your heart of your earthly existence. You will come in your former appearance as on the day you were born.
>
> (Milde 1994: 17)

The actual funeral operated within this basic concern. The Greek writer and traveller Diodorus Siculus provided a first century BCE account of an Egyptian funeral (Diodorus Siculus 1933: 209 ff.). It should be noted that Wallis Budge (1995: 181–3) and Mary Lefkowitz (1996: 72–5) have some doubts as to the accuracy of Diodorus Siculus' reporting, though Budge says that he is basically correct on mummification practices. Budge's own, long account of an Egyptian funeral (Budge 1995: 153–73) is similar to Diodorus' account.

In his *Account of Egypt*, published between 30 and 20 BCE, following a visit there in 56 BCE, Diodorus Siculus describes how the Egyptian 'Judgement' was egalitarian, with even the kings, at death, being subject to a pre-burial, public evaluation of their reputations. In the event of an unfavourable evaluation, the deceased are denied a proper burial, either for ever *or until such time as their family is able to make some kind of restitution*. Diodorus tells us that on the death of an Egyptian, kinsman and friends daub their heads with mud and wander through the town lamenting. He gives the costs for 'three manners of burial': one 'very costly, one of medium cost, one very mean' (Diodorus Siculus 1933: 209), and goes on to say that:

> Those who attend to the bodies are craftsmen who have inherited their skill from their forefathers. They set before the relatives of the deceased an estimate of the expenses of

2

ZOROASTER, AHURA MAZDA AND AHRIMAN

> They [the Persians] have no images of the gods, no temples nor altars, and consider the use of them a sign of folly. This comes, I think, from their not believing the gods to have the same nature with men, as the Greeks imagine.
>
> (Herodotus 1996: 72)

> The complexity, lack of coherence, and apparent contradictions in the eschatological schemes, both in Iran and in Judaism, are quite considerable. Many of the events which the individual experiences after death, such as confronting a bridge, a weighing of his deeds, a judgement, are repeated in the accounts of universal eschatology. While it may be natural for such ideas to evolve in a somewhat inconsistent manner by transposing certain motifs from one area to another and by repeating them in both places, it is nevertheless striking that the similarities between the eschatology of Judaism and that of Iran are apparent not only in the use of such schemes but also in their seeming incoherence.
>
> (Davies and Finkelstein 1984: 321–2)

With this rather wry comment Davies and Finkelstein endeavour to make as much sense as it is possible to make of the undoubted, but complex, interplay of the religions of Syria, Mesopotamia, Iran – and the Jews.

In the sixth and fifth centuries BCE, the armies of Cyrus, Cambyses, Darius and Xerxes expanded and consolidated a 'Persian' empire stretching from Central Asia to the Mediterranean. This empire, inheriting the cities and cultures of several earlier empires of the Sumerians, Amorites, Hittites, Assyrians and Chaldeans, lasted until the invasion of Alexander the Great in the fourth century BCE. Much of the western area of the Persian Empire then became the centre of the Seleucid state, while the eastern part (Babylonia and modern Iran), although nominally part of the Seleucid regime, steadily achieved autonomy under the Parthians and then (224–636 CE) the Sassanians. In the seventh century CE Islam became the dominant regional power. In the middle of all of these military and political cataclysms were the Jews of the 'Babylonian Captivity'. Many, if not most of the exilic Jews stayed in 'Babylon', where the Jewish community, after the second destruction of the Temple, became the dominant Jewish culture, producing in the sixth century CE the great Babylonian Talmud.

Zoroastrianism became the official religion of the Persian Empire, whose first king, Cyrus, 'ended' the Jewish captivity in 539 BCE. If the Book of Ezra is an accurate history, then Cyrus was instrumental in rebuilding the Temple at Jerusalem (doing so, he insisted, in the name of Yahweh: Ezra 1: 1–5). An 'official' religion, therefore, does not mean uniformity throughout the Persian Empire, in which religious pluralism appeared to have been the norm, a feature continuing under the succeeding Hellenic empire and culture.

Zoroastrianism is a lot older than the texts through which we know it, the contents of which were in the main orally transmitted until the fourth or even fifth century CE. The religion pre-dates the Persian Empire and, as is usually the case, the 'new' faith had to struggle and compromise with antecedent, popular and plausible religions. Such a process generally involves as much compromise as conversion. Indeed, in their occupation of Mesopotamia the Persians inherited a complex cosmology, cultic religion and apocalyptic which can perhaps be symbolised by reference to the stories and cults of Baal-Shamin, of Marduk and of the half-god/half-man Gilgamesh, whose stories and cults flourished well before, well into and beyond the first Christian centuries, as the earlier reference to the multiplicity of faiths at Edessa indicates. The same pluralism is to be found in other cities, such as Palmyra, Dura-Europos and Babylon itself. This religious culture will be the subject of Chapter 3.

Alexander's conquest of the Persian Empire had the same effect on Zoroastrianism as on Egyptian religion: it pulled it into the generally tolerant and inquisitive world of Hellenism. Descendants of Iranian colonists lived in and maintained their religious practices and places in Asia Minor. At Sardis, for example, Jewish and Zoroastrian worshippers were a feature of the pluralist religious culture of that typically Hellenic city. Both religio-ethnic groups spoke and wrote in Greek, and shared a common Sibyllist tradition (Freedman 1992: vi, 1171). Zoroastrianism flourished under the Seleucids and under the (Arsacid) rulers of the Parthian Empire, and became a persecuted and eroded religion only later under increasingly hostile Christian and then Moslem hegemony.

While monotheistic (a rare feature in the religious world of its origins and early history) Zoroastrianism was very explicitly dualist, with the wholly good, eternal, uncreated being Ahura Mazda being perpetually opposed by the equally uncreated but wholly evil and malign Angra Mainyu, later known as Ahriman. A complicated assembly of greater and lesser immortals aid Ahura Mazda in his endless struggles against the evil Ahriman. In turn Ahriman mobilises a counterforce of evil, which among other things brings about human death. Death is the creature of evil. People and gods must perpetually struggle to restore themselves and the universe to its original state of goodness. While eternal life is part of this original, god-given goodness, it must also be earned through just beliefs and virtuous actions.

Human beings are part of Ahura Mazda's creation, part of the goodness of the material and spiritual which he created. As such, the welfare of human beings is of deep concern to Ahura Mazda, knowing as he does that they will be beset by Ahriman, the Adversary. In Ahura Mazda's creation, even the wicked who have been led astray by Ahriman will ultimately return to goodness. Ontologically, therefore, human beings are made with the potential to be saved: they exist in their own right, and not as appendages of gods or the playthings of fates or Fate. They possess souls and, following earlier Iranian belief, the soul on death ascends on the third day after death to the peak of Mount Hara, the centre of the earth, where its words and deeds are weighed. From Mount Hara, the souls of the dead depart on their journey to heaven – or its opposite. Zoroastrian dualism extends to a conception of the human being as composed of two states, that of the body ('with bones') and that of spirituality (or the soul). The 'soul' itself is at times seen as of two types, one a permanent pre-existing spirit, the Fravashi, a kind of immortal 'Platonic' higher perfection or celestial origin of each terrestrial existent, the other a more individualised existence, with the former generally regarded as spirit, the latter as near-corporeal (Nigosian 1993: 83; Boyce 1979: 14–5).

In Zoroastrianism, the spiritual is not seen as superior to the physical: rather, the two conjoined become the highest form of existence. This conjoining usually takes place after death – indeed, in a general, apocalyptic conjoining or resurrection, a physical resurrection. A particularly holy Zoroastrian initiate can achieve in this life the state which is available to most people only in the next life, i.e. after death and resurrection.

Heaven (a place of infinite light) is attainable after death by those deemed worthy by Mithra, Sraosha and Rashnu, Ahura Mazda's allies. Only with their help will the souls of the dead (the souls having been painfully separated from the body) be able to cross the Chinvat Bridge. The journey to judgement and to the bridge begins on the morning of the fourth day after death, after a three-day period in which the soul lingers near the body. The immediate post-mortem journey of the person is to judgement at the Chinvat Bridge. The dead person has already, in the days before appearing at the bridge, been the subject of dispute between the hovering spirits and angels of, respectively, good and evil. At the bridge, the dead are met by the soul's double. This, for the righteous, is a beautiful young girl under whose guidance the dead person is taken safely over the widening bridge to paradise. The wicked are met by *their* soul's double, a horrible old hag, who chases them over an ever-narrowing and sharpening bridge from which they fall into hell. Individuals whose good deeds exactly balance with their bad deeds are kept in *Hamestan*, an in-between place where the souls remain in a version of the ancient kingdom of the underworld, shadows in shadow, with neither joy nor terror, a limbo.

Mary Boyce (1979: 14) makes the point that in its earliest Indo-Iranian formulation, paradise, the presence of the gods, was probably only for princes, warriors and priests, and that 'all lowly persons, herdsmen, and women and children' would find themselves in that eternally dismal and joyless place that was hell. Zoroaster overturned this doctrine, insisting that for men and for women as well as for rich and poor, salvation was possible on the basis of the judgement made by Mithra and his attendant deities about the overall worth of each soul's thoughts, words and deeds. All people however await the final transfiguration.

The bodies of the righteous dead were the source of the greatest pollution, for evil had to concentrate its forces around them in particular. In the Videvdat, a set of rules dealing with demons, can be found the following:

> Let no man alone by himself carry a corpse. If a man alone
> by himself carry a corpse, the *Nasu* [corpse-demon] rushes
> upon him, to defile him, from the nose of the dead, from

the eye, from the tongue, from the jaws, from the sexual organ, from the hinder parts. This *Drug* [falsehood or disorder], this *Nasu*, falls upon him, stains him even to the end of the nails, and he is unclean, thenceforth, for ever and ever.

(Nigosian 1993: 55)

The body was regarded as highly infectious, to be handled only by professional undertakers and body handlers. Rules as complicated as those later to be found in the Mishnah governed the cleansing and disposal of household objects or clothing which came into contact with the corpse. The Towers of Silence, in which bodies were exposed for disincarnation, are in some accounts a later development, although Herzfeld (1988: 212–20) is clear that the buildings were *early* forms of corpse handling. Whichever is the case, from very early on the body was exposed on rocky or otherwise impervious ground, to prevent it polluting the sacred earth and its equally sacred plants and animals. In Videvdat 111.4, Ahura Mazda assures an interlocutor that:

If a man shall bury in the earth either the corpse of a dog or the corpse of a man, and if he shall [does] not disinter it within the second year...there is nothing that can pay, nothing that can cleanse from it...there is no atonement, for ever and ever.

(ibid.: 55)

Bleached or disincarnated bones were eventually gathered together and buried, to await the full body reassembly at the last days. Mary Boyce notes that the tombs of wealthy or important Zoroastrians of the Seleucid or Parthian period were buried in lavish, Hellenistically decorated tombs, but then comments:

Only the rich could have afforded such elaborate ossuaries at any epoch: and Pompeios Trogus, writing of the Parthians in the first century AC [CE] recorded that 'their general mode of sepulture is rending to pieces by birds or dogs; the bare bones they at last bury in the ground'. Evidence from Central Asia in the Sassanian period suggests, however, that this 'burial in the ground' often took place in a casket or urn.

(Boyce 1979: 91)

In the chief liturgy of the Zoroastrians, the Yasna and the Visparad, the living maintain a relationship with the Fravashis of the immortal saints and, through 'words of blessings' known as *Afringan*, maintain contact with the dead. The dead were remembered with honour, in particular on the last five days of the year when the souls of the dead revisit the earth (Nigosian 1993: 57). At the final transforming apocalypse, every human being, transfigured, will come to be a new body, formed by Ahura Mazda from all the old body's scattered parts, which have been stored in the now equally transfigured parts of the earth.

The fate of the individual is caught up in the overall eschatology of the faith. The dualism which is such a potent feature of Zoroastrianism (although it is qualified through the sense of the ultimate and indeed original sense of goodness) invites these notions of post-mortem judgement, creating as it does a sense of human beings as invariably embarked on a journey upon which they have to find their way between good and evil, truth and untruth, suffering and salvation. On both individual and collective/cosmic level, the same two forces of good and evil create the terms and conditions of salvation and damnation, of death or life. Fire, a son of Ahura Mazda, will come to separate good men from the evil ones by a river of fire. This will be associated with the Last Judgement, when the world and life will be transfigured. All the dead will come back to life, clad in glorious indestructible bodies. The body, as being not becoming, will exist in an individualised form, recognised and recognising, capable of friendship and pleasure – including sexual pleasure. Over a 12,000 year period, the world itself will in the last era take on a new form of material existence, transcending the dualism of good/evil and of ideal/material. Time will cease to be, all will be fully realised or made wonderful. This is summed up in Bundahishn 1, a section of the Book of Primal Creation:

> Then Ohrmazd [Ahura Mazda], in his omniscience, knew that the Destructive Spirit existed, that he would attack and ... knew that if he did not fix a time for battle against him, then Ahriman would do unto his creation even as he had threatened, and the struggle and the mixture would be everlasting. ... Then Ohrmazd chanted the Ahunvar [prayer], that is he recited the twenty one words of the Yatha ahu vairyo: and he showed to the Destructive Spirit his own final victory, the powerlessness of the Destructive

Spirit, the destruction of the demons, the resurrection, the Final Body, and the freedom of creation from all aggression for ever and ever.

(Nigosian 1993: 62–3).

It is within this triumphal eschatology that Zoroastrian teaching was able to ask its adherents to locate their lives in a this-worldly practical faith of minute-to-minute, day-to-day struggle and dangers, beset by demons and rules and prescriptions, a dense thicket of peril and evil, but helped by angels and by the hope and promise, tied into a sense of obligations and rewards, of salvation. This was a conscience-creating religion, not content with outer conformity. Salvation lay within. Death, be it the death of living sin or actual death in sin, was all around, rendered tolerable only by the promise of the Final Body. We can turn to the Denkard, a ninth century CE compilation of earlier traditions, for a summary of Zoroastrian thanatology:

A man who performs the worship of the gods with certainty as to the gods and with faith in the reality of the thing, is a son of the gods and his place is in highest heaven. ... A man who performs the worship of the gods with the thought that the gods do not exist and that the thing does not exist, is an enemy of the gods and his place is in Hell.

Every person ought to know: 'Where have I come from? For what purpose am I here? Where do I return?' I for my part [the author is speaking] know that I come from Ohrmazd the Lord, that I am here so as to make the demons powerless, and that I shall return to Ohrmazd.

(Nigosian 1993: 69)

3

CANAANITES AND MESOPOTAMIANS

I have a word to tell you,
a story to recount to you:
the word of the tree and the charm of the stone,
the whisper of the heavens to the earth,
of the seas to the stars.
I understand the lightning which the heavens do not know,
the word which men do not know,
and earth's masses cannot understand.
Come, and I will reveal it.
(The Ugarit god Baal to another god, in Coogan 1978: 9)

This 3,400-year-old text is from Ugarit, a city on the Mediterranean opposite Cyprus, which was destroyed in about 1200 BCE by the 'Sea Peoples'. Extensive archives, in one of the earliest surviving alphabets, provide texts for an understanding of ancient beliefs about the relationships between the gods, the immortals, and humans, the mortals. From further west, in Babylon, come other extensive records of antiquity, which also tell us much about gods and people, about life and death. Both these cities and their zones of influence had extensive panthea involving gods and goddesses whose shrines and cults are to be found in many cities in the lands which lay around and between them – in Ebla, Palmyra, Sardis, Pella, Dura-Europos, Antioch, Edessa and so on – the cities which rose and fell or rose and prospered in response to the ebb and flow of a series of states and empires. When, 1,200 years or so after the destruction of Ugarit, the first Jewish Christians moved into what had become the Hellenised cities of the same geographical area, they found in those cities flourishing cults and potent symbols descended from the ancient panthea, endlessly restructured, of Ugarit and Babylon. At Babylon itself, Herodotus had found the

Another they groan like professional mourners.
My god has not come to the rescue in taking me by the hand,
Nor has my goddess shown pity on me by going at my side.
My grave was waiting, and my funerary paraphernalia ready,
Before I had died lamentation for me was finished.
All my country said: 'How he is crushed!'.
(Babylonian 'Poem of the Righteous Sufferer', c.1500 BCE, in
Lambert 1975: 41–6)

Rather surprisingly for cultures which were in contact with Egypt – the Ugarit necropolis yielded among other objects a hawk statuette wearing the crown of Egypt – these stories reveal a great and unbridgeable gulf between humans and their gods. Egyptians, on dying, actually became Osiris and could live their life in that understanding. A Zoroastrian can look forward to individual and eventually eschatological salvation. In Ugarit and in Babylon, things were different. In all three cultures, as in all religions, the same questions were being asked about death: Why were human beings created? Why do humans die? Do the gods care? If all human beings must die, whether they have lived good or wicked lives, is there some afterlife in which these differences will be recognised? If so, can or should men seek to influence their post-mortem fates, or would the attempt to do so (in effect to claim immortality) further antagonise the gods?

Generally, the religions of ancient Canaan and of the various cultures of Mesopotamia provided bleak answers to most of these questions. In the Aquat story, Baal had initially responded to the pleas of Danel, Aquat's father, for a son: Aquat. But Aquat is killed by Anat, goddess of both love and war, and (on the Osiris–Isis model) both wife and sister of Baal. Baal does nothing to stop the murder of Aquat by his wife–sister and fellow god. From this story must come the message that even supportive gods are not to be relied upon. Aquat's comment about the inevitability of his death is a realistic if bitter refusal of Anat's earlier offer of immortality: Aquat knows that the goddess will either be unable to deliver what she is offering, or she will cheat.

Aquat's story has parallels also with the Gilgamesh story from Babylon, in that the hero of that epic also falls out with a senior female goddess, though in this case she is more interested in sex than in the hero's bow and arrows. The weapons/penis, war/women, heroism/domesticity pairings are major opposites or tensions in nearly all epics, which are mostly concerned with the appropriate way for men to die, given that they cannot attain immortality. In the

Epic of Gilgamesh, for example, Enkidu (the beloved companion of Gilgamesh) dies bemoaning the fact that he could not die 'like one who falls in battle' and goes on to say that 'he who falls in battle is blessed, but I shall die in disgrace' (Heidel 1975: 62). The Epic of Gilgamesh centres on the pursuit, by men, of immortality, ignoring, as does Gilgamesh, the 'lesser' if more realistic life-career of a this-worldly domesticity as they pursue their quests. Glorious death or fame, rather than immortality, is what they seek or attain, whether in the case of Gilgamesh or Aquat (or Achilles or 'heroes' in general). 'Heroism' is almost synonymous with death in battle, and is the closest *men* get to breaching the mortal/immortal divide. The death of men in nearly all ancient 'epics' is properly male when properly heroic. Men then achieve 'a name': they become memorable, monumental – and therefore, as their name lives forever, in a sense immortal. This is denied women, who in Gilgamesh for example are never named, and who are indeed, in another 'epic', explicitly told that their glory lay in not being talked about, not having a name (Thucydides 1972: 151).

These epics, then, were major configurers of the relationship between men and women, as well as between gods and humans, immortals and mortals (see Lyons 1997, and later in this book). In all their variety, they were the basis of the Ancient Near East's understanding of the fate of men and the role of the gods. Matthews and Benjamin, in lumping together the stories of Aquat, the Egyptian Diary of Wen-Amon and the Gezer Almanac, describe this thematic as 'very popular in the ancient Near East and in ancient Israel' (Matthews and Benjamin 1991: 85), and go on to compare Aquat with Gilgamesh, Danel's barren wife with Abraham's Sarah, and Aquat the 'mighty hunter' threatened by a woman with Ishmael threatened by Sarah (ibid.: 85–6). There can be little doubt about the general 'circulation' of such stories. They were the 'wisdom' which told human beings what they had been created for, and a rather bleak purpose it was.

The Epic of Creation of the Babylonians is primarily about war and conflict between the gods, and the eventual, if precarious, resolution of the conflicts by the elevation of Marduk as the supreme god (Dalley 1991: 228–77). In whatever version of the Creation story, humans appear as created *only* for the purpose of working for and servicing the gods.

In Atrahasis, the story is told of the origin of human beings (Atrahasis was a kind of Noah-figure, in origin Sumerian but much used by Babylonians and Assyrians). The gods created human beings as an alternative to an earlier form of workforce in which a class of lower-order gods, the Igigu, had done all the necessary manual labour. The Igigu went on strike on the grounds that they, like all gods, were immortal, and they resented the implication that, by being given all the work (which they did for 3,600 years!), they were something less than god-like. A plenary session of the gods, thoroughly alarmed at the withdrawal of labour, decided to create a substitute for the Igigu in the form of humans, a species intelligent and motivated enough to want to and to know how to work for the gods, but kept in their place by having death designed into them. This was accomplished by mixing the blood of a minor deity with clay, the blood providing the intelligence and motivation, the clay being that to which the creature would return on death. There was a period of 'settling in' of about 600 years (Dalley 1991: 18) as the new species, the humans, got on with their work and with reproducing themselves so as to be able to work all the more. Unfortunately, the noise they made by virtue of their numbers and zealous activity annoyed Enlil, Lord of the Earth:

> The country became too wide, the people too numerous ...
> Enlil had to listen to their noise ...
> The noise of mankind has become too much,
> I am losing sleep over their racket,
> Give the order that the suruppu-disease shall break out ...
> (Dalley 1991: 18)

In one version Enlil deals with 'the human problem' by inducing famine and drought to destroy humanity. In another he eventually destroyed most of humanity in a great flood, having earlier tried epidemics, droughts and famines. However, the god Ea had forewarned his human protégé, Atrahasis, also known as the 'Supersage', telling him how to build an ark. Atrahasis and the occupants and animals of the ark survived the flood, but this survival and that of his family annoyed Enlil even more, although several of the other gods were upset at what had happened. To avoid further trouble, Ea redesigned the human by building in population-reducing measures such as sterility and infant mortality, and by building death into human nature.

Humans, therefore, exist primarily to serve the gods, to provide them with food, drink, clothes and places to live – the temples and sanctuaries, the 'homes' of the gods. This is the predominant human function; anything else, including their own needs, is secondary. By existential definition, and because it suits the gods, humans are mortal: they die. They die in order to avoid provoking (merely by being alive) the gods, rather than because they have sinned, collectively or individually. They cannot achieve immortality, because their death is a necessary part of the ontology *of the gods*. This is as true for the hero Gilgamesh, even though he was two-thirds divine, as for anyone else. There is no such thing as 'salvation' and the only 'alternative' to humdrum death is a heroic death, in war. So Gilgamesh, after the death in conflict of his friend Enkidu, feels that he has been denied a similar opportunity for military prowess and turns therefore to a fruitless search for immortality (Dalley 1991: 92). The realistic Ut-napishtim tells him:

> Why do you prolong grief, Gilgamesh?
> Since the gods made you like your mother and father,
> Death is inevitable, at some time, both for Gilgamesh and for a fool ...
> Nobody sees Death,
> Nobody hears the voice of Death ...
> Savage Death just cuts mankind down ...
> The gods appointed life and death.
> They did not mark out days for death, but they did so for life.
> When the gods created mankind
> They appointed death for mankind
> Kept eternal life in their own hands.
>
> (Dalley 1991: 107–8, 150)

In the Enuma Elish story, officially 'published' in Babylon by Hammurabi (1792–1750 BCE) and 'reissued' by Ashurbanipal (668–626 BCE), the tale is again told of the creation of humans as the servants of the gods. The god Marduk battled his way to pantheonic supremacy, and proceeded to create the Universe, the Sky, the Earth, with the Waters of Apsu (the sea) kept out by the Horizons – he created, that is, the 'standard' cosmology of the Ancient Near East. From the blood of a defeated rival he made The Savage, The Aborigine:

> I will knead blood and bone into a Savage,
> Aborigine will be its name.
> The Aborigines will do the Gods' work
> The Savages will set the Gods free.
>
> (Mathews and Benjamin 1991: 13)

To 'police' this universe, Marduk positioned 300 of the Anunnaki (ancient chthonic deities of fertility) in the heavens, and another 300 on the earth. Every year, at Babylon (which was built by the gods to celebrate his victory) the story of Marduk's creation and activities was re-enacted.

For the human Aborigine-Savage, life in such cultures was highly ritualised, both in a day-to-day sense and at the time of death. The significance of the presence of the ubiquitous Anunnaki and associated 'demons' was expressed in hemerological texts and in standard incantatory or supplicatory texts, which were both a help to worried humans and a perpetual reminder of their precarious hold on life. The 'official' Babylonian hemerology ('written' or promulgated in the eleventh century BCE) promised, for example, a death in the family if garlic was eaten on the wrong day, and death by an irruption of the wind-demon if you went up on the roof on the wrong day (Hulin 1959–60: 45, 49). An 'incantatory tablet' from Nimrud describes the troubles of a man whose cattle are being eaten by demons and who has himself no fewer than seven demons attached to various parts of his body. He has to be 'purified', after which a bird will then carry his 'fate' up to heaven and his devil down to the deep waters under the earth. Then,

> The man, the son of his god
> Like the heaven he shall be pure
> Like the earth he shall be clean
> Like the sky he shall be bright.
> (Knudsen 1959–60: 60)

This seems like a large promise, but it is very clear that only the most rigorous observance of 'procedure' will attain the desired result – the implication being that 'lapses' could well make things much worse. In such a world, 'religion' would consist of meticulous attention to and attendance at the series of holy places, altars, places of sacrifice and meetings of like-minded 'brotherhoods' which made life possible: among such quotidian obligations would clearly be the matter of burial and its associated rituals, the 'cults of the dead'.

The 'cult of the dead' which many observers find in the Ancient Near East is associated both with the precariousness of the relationships between the 'savages' and the gods, and with the precariousness of the political position of the good, or pro-human, gods *within the pantheon*.

The cult of the dead was a family cult. The *etemmu* or spirits of the dead both required the services of family members and were in a position to assist them, the latter capacity because in some sense death conferred upon the deceased a degree of deification. In Atrahasis there seems to be an indication that the blood of the murdered (sacrificed?) god, which was mixed with clay to make man, separates from the clay (flesh) at death to become a 'ghost': 'let the ghost exist so as not to forget the slain god' (Dalley 1991: 15). This 'ghost' is the 'sign' of the individual, activated after death.

In Mesopotamian cosmology, the Below was both a space and a location for the ghosts of the dead. Bodies, always shrouded, were placed in the earth, directly, or in a tomb, or in a cave, and never cremated or sited above ground or left unburied. In the Underground – various terms were used for this place – were to be found the Anunnaki (referred to in the preceding paragraphs) and other deities such as Nergal and his wife Ereskigal, and Samas the Sun God, who (like Ra) moved between the Underworld and the Above, or Heaven. The family tombs were points of access to the Underworld, a reason why nonburial was so abhorrent to the Mesopotamians; the tomb was the first stage of the journey to the Underworld, *away from the rule of the gods in the Upper World*. In Ishtar's Descent to the Netherworld is to be found a description of 'the land of no return'. Ishtar is the goddess of fertility, and:

> To Kurnugi, land of no return,
> Ishtar daughter of Sin was determined to go;
> The daughter of Sin was determined to go
> To the dark house, dwelling of Erkala's god,
> To the house which those who enter cannot leave,
> On the road where travelling is one-way only,
> To the house where those who enter are deprived of light,
> Where dust is their food, clay their bread.
> They see no light, they dwell in darkness,
> They are clothed like birds, with feathers.
> Over the door and the bolt, dust has settled.
>
> (Dalley 1991: 155)

This story is comparable to the story of the descent of Persephone to Hades, and her periodic release, i.e. they may both be seen as seasonal-cyclical, involving the Underworld in the Upper World cycles of summer and winter, of the growing and the fallow seasons, the climatic bases of life. Ishtar returns to the Upper World after a series of ritual re-robings and re-ornamenting, together with appropriate mourning ceremonies, but she has clearly had a dangerous time: fertility is not to be taken for granted. Another fertility god, Telepinu, has also to be reconciled with humanity by a series of appropriate rituals and food offerings, and Telepinu can (as with Ishtar) be associated with the seasonal myths of the series of departing and (hopefully) returning gods – Tammuz, Osiris, Baal, Adonis, Attis, Persephone, etc. (Pritchard 1971: vol. 1, 87–91).

The dead, the departing, semi-deified, have also to be kept sympathetic – they were feared rather than venerated – and for this purpose Mesopotamian society had an elaborate 'cult of the dead', which of course included both burial and appropriate burial ceremonies. Baruch Margalit (1980: 251) suggests, on the basis of a comparison with finds at the Jericho cemetery (see below), that these included incising or 'grooving' the top of the head, and plastering or glazing it and removing the lower jaw. The care of the deceased person's *etemmu* was the task of the kin, delegated to a particular relative (the *paquidu*) whose task it was to feed and water the dead, to erect a memorial stele or pillar, to call out the name of the dead, often associating such naming with the arrival (actual or hoped for) of new family members: progeny were of central concern in these rites. The *etemmu* was believed to have powers both to assist and to harm the living, and had therefore to be propitiated and honoured by the appropriate family member, again within the context of rituals involving food and water. Family participation in and provision of these rituals was important in order to avoid bringing into being a 'strange ghost', that is one without a fixed abode. Sharing a meal with the ghost was one way of emphasising its family connections and of proving proper care. Bayliss offers data indicating that care of the *etemmu* was seen as an extension of care for one's parents, a particular duty of the eldest son. At Ugarit, the family basis of the rite was emphasised by the existence of domed tombs underneath the houses, a staircase going down into them and an entrance chamber under a high, corbelled roof (Curtis 1985: 56). Frankfort thinks that this style of burial-building indicates the presence of an 'Aegean element' in the Ugarit population (Frankfort 1996: 276), although evidence from 'Natufian' Eynan indicates that under-house burial was a common practice, it being the strongest possible way of proclaiming 'title' over a piece of land (Boyd, in Campbell and Green 1995: 17–23). Jean-François Salles (in Campbell and Green 1995: 171–84) notes, however, that the graves in an actual 'above-ground' cemetery near the Temple of Baal at Ugarit had been so disturbed as to permit few conclusions other than that not everyone was buried under-house at Ugarit and that cemetery burial seems to have been the norm.

Corpses would be shrouded, and perhaps placed in a reed coffin. Grave goods were common, and in some cases a cup for water was provided in the tomb. In Ugarit, as in the Ancient Near East in general, tomb violation was both a great fear and the occasion for most serious warnings and threats.

Salles (1995: 171–84) sees parallels between Ugarit funerary customs and those of biblical Israel. In Amos 8: 10, there is reference to the mourning practices of covering one's head with dust, shaving hair and the use of sackcloth – 'sackcloth and ashes' – and Salles sees evidence for this in the response of Aquat's father to the news of his son's death. The 'breath' which leaves the dying Aquat 'like the wind, his spirit like a breeze' occurs in many Jewish descriptions of the actual moment of death. The Ugarit and Babylonian stories contain references to the tearing of clothes, to prolonged (but time-limited) periods of mourning, to funeral meals, to female mourners, to the building of family shrines, to the importance of progeny and the particular tragedy of the early death of sons – Aquat's death threatens the future, it proclaims the triumph of the desert, and must therefore be denied. Danel, Aquat's father, received the news of his son's murder when he was in the fields kissing and talking to the crops, and telling them about his son. In response to the news of his death, he states that he will weep, then bury him: 'I will put him in the hole of the gods of the earth'. Baal then destroys some vultures, which Danel has called upon Baal to first kill, then recreate. Only when the body of the bird shows evidence of fat and bone, of vitality [*sic*], does Danel bury his son, now 'reconstituted' from the fat and bone of the vultures. In his palace, Danel is joined by keeners and mourners, who gash their skin, and weep and mourn. The mourning lasts for seven years, and is then formally ended by Danel with a sacrifice to the gods (Coogan 1978: 43–6). In Ugarit the tomb was essentially the dynastic title, the proof of the existence of a set of relationships conferring ownership of land and chattels.

Bayliss suggests that for ordinary people, the cultic responsibilities seem to have been restricted to the grandparental generation, and should not therefore be seen as a multigenerational tribal descent-line ritual (Bayliss 1973: 121–2). This perhaps reflects the sense that ordinary humans had that their arrangements lacked the support of the gods, a sense in which Mesopotamian thanatology is very unlike the Egyptian. Rites *for the monarch*, however, involved lengthy genealogies and lengthy pedigrees, real and mythical, and included as being associated with the royal dead all those without their own cult and those soldiers who had fallen in war – 'the Babylonian equivalent of the Unknown Soldier' (ibid.: 122). The royal cult at Ugarit, which would of course have involved military elements, monarchs being warriors as well as priests and rulers, seems to have called a monthly gathering, involving the reigning monarch and (in the case described by Bayliss) very lavish funeral offerings of food, wine and beer, as well as incense, all 'as a regular due' (ibid.: 124). The 'attendance' *by the departed monarch* at these meals was a central purpose of the rite (Healey 1995: 189). While this seems to be ill at ease with the general Mesopotamian belief that 'all men die', it would appear that in Mesopotamia as elsewhere special thanatologies apply to kings. In Bronze Age Syria, at Ebla and elsewhere, as well as at Ugarit, king-lists associate dead monarchs with the gods, although they do not equate them. These dead monarchs, as *Rephaim*, are invoked to proclaim the merit of the *reigning* monarch. The concern is with the continuity of the community through the continuity of the monarch.

In that sense, such cultic activity represents a beneficial and indeed 'rational' rite, in which the living and the dead remained related to each other through a complex cult 'of the dead', but also of 'the living and the dead', played out within a spiritual world of many gods and many demons, an endless invitation to regular anxiety-eliciting and anxiety-soothing rites, processions and ceremonies, expressed in formal hemerological and incantatory texts and formulae. This ritual activity took place under the shadow of a sombre thanatology. In ending with another version of the Gilgamesh Epic, it is perhaps not necessary to point out just how different it is to the good cheer and optimism of 'Going out into the Day' with which I concluded the chapter on Egyptian attitudes to death and dying.

> You have toiled without cease, what have you got?
> Through toil you are wearing yourself out,
> You are filling your body with grief,
> You are bringing forward the end of your days.
> Mankind, which is like a reed in the cane-break, is snapped off.
> Man and woman in full flower of youth
> Death
> No one can see death.
> But savage death snaps off mankind.

Suddenly there is nothing.
The prisoner and the dead are alike,
Death itself cannot be depicted,
Mammitum, creatress of destiny,
Decreed destinies with them.
They established life and death ...
Death they fixed to have no ending.
        (Lambert, in Alster 1980: 55)

It was, and remains, a problem to assess the relationship of the religions of the Ancient Near East to the progressive elaboration of Israelite-Jewish, and Israelite-Jewish-Christian religious identity. In Part II, I will address the story of the elaboration of a specifically 'Jewish' thanatology, as this developed from Iron Age tribal Israel through the Biblical period and towards some form of 'canonicity' in the Hellenic and Rabbinic periods. I will conclude *this* part with some general comments on the 'religious world' to which the interaction of the thanatologies outlined above seem to me to have given rise.

4

MERE TEXTS OR LIVING REALITIES?

The possible influence of the older thanatologies on Judaism and Christianity

There is risk here of anachronism, as Christianity was very much a late arrival on the Near Eastern scene. It makes some sense, however, to try to see what, if anything, of Egypt, Iran and Mesopotamia 'entered' Judaism and, later, Christianity.

Influence can be both positive and negative, providing opportunities for emulation and occasion for opposition. The Hebrew Bible is full of Israelite opposition to the various 'Baals' and the idolatries with which the Jewish leaders and prophets associated them. The Jews in their Exodus were only too aware of the altogether 'other' nature of their single God to be able to adapt, never mind adopt, the Osiris–Isis solution to death, with its radical indifference to the mortal/immortal dualism. Neither was the grim pessimism of the Babylonian Epics an object of interest, as the Bible insisted that God deemed his Creation to be 'good', and humans were in no sense to be seen as nothing more than discardable slaves of the gods. Whatever the temptations, and occasional backsliding, the Israelites were officially monotheistic, and their thanatology reflects this. Judaism, perhaps because of its monotheism, remained merely one of the innumerable sects of the Greek and Roman world.

We might consider here the city of Ephesus, scene of so much of the identity-forming Christian experience. Ephesus was visited, along with many other cities, in the second century CE by Publius Aelius Aristides, a somewhat hypochondriacal Greco-Roman citizen in search of, among other things, healing and 'salvation'. At no point in this search does he mention the healing or salvific attractions of either Judaism or Christianity, despite the oft-repeated view that the ancient cultic gods were in some sort of decay and disarray and that Christianity, with its promise of salvation and resurrection, simply occupied some pre-existing 'spiritual vacuum'. As Rick Strelan demonstrates, this was in no sense the case at Ephesus, where the cult of Artemis (Persian Anaitis) was not only of very ancient establishment, but was also flourishing and continued to do so long after the arrival of Christianity (Strelan 1996: 81). The Artemis cult (in part of Persian origin) was a religious cult – and more. Strelan quotes Oster's description of it as a 'social institution par excellence; it participated in the financial, legal, educational, family, civic and athletic activities of Ephesian society' (ibid.: 25). Strelan discusses the various scholarly opinions on the cult of Artemis, in which she is (often in error) cast as the 'demonic' goddess of the underworld, associated with death and magic, and with other underworld deities such as Hecate, Selene and Ereschigal. To a large extent, this depiction of Artemis is advanced to 'explain' the 'triumph' of Pauline Christianity, a notion of triumph made problematic by Strelan's most convincing demonstration of the great popularity of the cult of Artemis. Much more likely, writes Strelan, is the idea that the association of Artemis with death was (however difficult this association may be for us) seen by the Ephesians as part and parcel of her association with childbirth: they are both part of life, this life on earth, the life cycle, and honoured precisely for that reason:

> For people who lived constantly on the narrow line between life and death, and who did not hide disease or sickness away in institutions, death and burial was a *planting*. As Slater says: 'Tombs were ... not only final resting places but also sources of a kind of life, and were provided with attributes reminiscent of impregnation, pregnancy, and birth'.
>
> (Strelan 1996: 83)

It is possible that a polytheistic religion, in which the life–death drama does not have to be bifocalised, but in which gods and goddesses can be associated with 'attributes' that can themselves vary and migrate, is a religion which can just as readily see the human condition in a similar light, neither irrevocably alive nor irrevocably dead. It is true that tensions persist, because the gods and goddesses are often enough capricious and hostile – but that is the way they are; through cultic sacrifice, regular processions and formal routine rites, all that humans can do is precisely that: get on with it. Certainly, Javier Teixidor is of the view that 'to discuss the immortality of the soul or how to acquire true *gnosis* were not popular concerns ... the common man never rose above his daily prayers ... popular religion must have remained practically unchanged in Greco-Roman times' (1977: 4–6). Polytheism made *living* both more demanding and more immediate, and perhaps in so doing made ontological pessimism 'manageable'. Monotheism – as and when it appears – may well make death more promising, but also more remote and more frightening, given the omnipotence of the one all-demanding god. When the gods and goddesses are, as statues and processions, here (as well as there), when they have faces, gestures and expressions, they can be known, loved or feared perhaps, but they are amenable to conversation in *this* life, our life. The 'cults of the dead' which feature so largely in this book should, as Strelan is perhaps indicating, more properly be known as 'cults of the living'. They are in effect attempts to retain the presence and sociability of the dead in this world – just as the associated cultic processions and sacrifices of the pagan world were aimed at keeping the gods and goddesses present and sociable in this world, for at least some of their time. Monotheism tends to exile God to another world, and his presence and purpose *here* is inscrutable. Polytheistic cults, such as those at Edessa or Ephesus, or the dozens of other cities visited by the busy Aristides, were this-worldly, life-linked, death-caring religions, accepting death rather than disputing it. These polytheistic cults can be seen as a flow of prophylactic hemerologies, rather like Hellenistic medicine, concerned with life and distancing itself from dealing with death because it too evidently and finally demonstrated the end of human competence. What Amundsen writes of ancient medicine can also be applied to ancient cultic practices: 'the medical art's two functions were preserving and restoring health, not prolonging life *per se*' (1996: 33).

What can be said in more detail about the possible impact of 'Egypt' and 'Babylon' on the Jewish attitude to dying, death and the disposal of the dead? It is quite permissible to regard the extraordinary religion of Egypt as an ornate 'cult of the dead'. We will find below a more extended treatment of Elizabeth Bloch-Smith's discussion of the prevalence of an Iron Age (*c.*1200–580 BCE) 'Judahite' cult of the dead. It is sufficient here to note her summation, as well as the high degree of congruency her depiction has with the practices of Israel's neighbours.

> In Judahite culture the dead were an integral part of the social organisation. Individuals believed that their descendants would nourish and care for them following death, just as they had provided for their predecessors. Moreover,

the legitimacy of land holdings was validated by the ancestral tomb, and the prosperity of the land may have been
thought to have been insured or blessed by benevolent
ancestors. ... Neither the existence of powerful dead nor
the efficacy of necromancy could be negated.

(Bloch-Smith 1992a: 132)

Inevitably, 'the authorities' sought, in Judah as throughout Jewish
history, to moderate and hopefully to suppress this quintessentially
Ancient Near Eastern practice: the dialectic of the struggle
continued in both Jewish and Jewish-Christian religion and history.
Nicholas Tromp (1969) and Alexander Heidel (1975) have made
detailed analyses of the interpenetration of Israelite and other
Ancient Near Eastern thanatologies. As we have seen in the verse
from the Babylonian Descent of Ishtar to the Underworld, 'existence' in the Mesopotamian Underworld was essentially dark, dusty
and permanent, and the biblical Sheol carries the same connotation
of dimness and darkness. Heidel notes that the Babylonian
Pantheon, replete with its politics and turbulence, continues to
exist in the Underworld, while in the Israelite underworld the
tendency is towards a single god who is, of course, elsewhere, a god
of the heavens rather than of underneath. The Mesopotamian afterlife is, says Heidel, undifferentiated – all the dead go there, never to
reappear. In contrast, Old Testament Israel was already (see below
and Rosenberg 1981) moving towards the concept of a differentiated afterlife as well as towards the concept of resurrection. Both
these points are matters of considerable dispute. Elizabeth Bloch-
Smith has already been quoted to provide grounds for qualifying
Heidel's emphatic assertion that in Hebrew scriptures there is no
'traffic' between the living and the dead, a feature Heidel asserts to
be of Babylonian but not of Hebrew religion – the Witch of Endor
notwithstanding, might be a rejoinder. These clarities of 'either/or'
are both the strength and weakness of Heidel's approach, in that he
sees as 'resolved' matters on which an unresolved tension continues
in thanatology in general and certainly in the society of Iron Age
Israel and Biblical and Rabbinic Judaism. At all times and in
varying degree, ancient, perhaps demotic, perhaps pagan, perhaps
'heretical' ideas co-existed alongside the very orthodoxies to which
they were anathema, and in response to which the orthodoxies were
so resolutely articulated in the first place. As Shalom Spiegel puts
it, in commenting on the persistence of pagan legitimisation of
human sacrifice practices in Judaism:

Age-old beliefs continued to nest in the thickets of the soul. It is very hard to drive out pagan spirits, and each generation must renew the battle against them. What is more, the very measures adopted to expel them are frequently themselves a partial admission of the vitality of pagan ways.

(1979: 77)

In his quiet way, Spiegel at various points indicates a degree of agreement with the notion that, in Christianity, Judaism gave rise to a pagan cult of the dead, in particular a cult of sacrifice, a return (he implies) to an ancient legacy predating both Judaism and Christianity.

Less controversially, Theodore Lewis comments on how difficult the Yahwist leaders found it to 'lay pagan ghosts':

The Deuteronomistic legal material ... reflects clear restrictions against consulting the dead, giving offerings to the dead, and engaging in self-lacerating rituals which ... were typical of Canaanite death cult practice. The fact that we have similar laws against black magic in the Covenant Code (e.g. Exodus 22: 17) argues that such ideology may go back quite early. We may safely infer from these laws that cults of the dead existed and flourished in ancient Israel to the extent that they were considered a threat to what becomes normative Yahwism.

(1989: 172)

Israel-Judaism, whether in antagonism against or in imitation of the various ideas about death of the Ancient Near East, developed within that context, sometimes imitating, sometimes rejecting its inheritance. The 'cult of the dead' remained a point of serious tension for many, many centuries, precisely because it formed such a large part of the (repressed) inheritance.

At more detailed levels, also, there are parallels. Nearly all cults and religions agreed on, for example, the paramount importance of *formally* disposing of the dead, of providing special burial clothes, a shroud at least; associated (perhaps rather problematically) with this there was a sense of the 'uncleanness' of the corpse, where Jewish views would indeed appear to be paralleled in, for example, Zoroastrianism, and where later developments in both Judaism and Zoroastrianism seem to perpetuate a genuine and common tradition. In both religions the very 'uncleanness' would seem to prohibit or keep to the absolute minimum post-mortem handling of the dead.

Whoever in the open field touches one who is slain with a sword, or a dead body, or a bone of a man, or a grave, shall be unclean seven days.

(Numbers 19: 16)

A corpse, and whatsoever is severed from it, can convey uncleanness, through seven removes: viz., by touching (1) vessels which touch (2) a man who touches (3) vessels (all three becoming Fathers of Uncleanness).

(The Mishnah 1967: The Rules of Uncleaness, 17, 802)

If a man shall bury in the earth either the corpse of a dog or the corpse of a man, and if he shall not disinter it within the second year, what is the penalty. ... Can the eating vessels be made clean that have been touched by the carcass of a dog or by the corpse of a man?

(Videvat 3: 4, 7:10 in Nigosian 1993: 55–6)

There appears here, then, a widespread Near Eastern attitude to the dead, in agreement on the prime need for burial and on the contaminatory capacity of the corpse. Jewish–Persian contacts were prolonged and, after the advent of the Achaemenids, fairly friendly and constructive. The Jews who remained in Persian Babylon became the major diaspora community, producing in the Babylonian Talmud one of the great set pieces of Judaism. Cyrus, first Achaemenid king, is recorded (however problematically) in Ezra 1 and in 2 Chronicles 36: 22 as the man who fulfilled the word of Yahweh in destroying the Neo-Babylonian dynasty and in facilitating the rebuilding of the Temple. In Isaiah, Cyrus becomes the Lord's anointed (Isaiah 45: 1), and in the more obviously apocryphal Bel and the Dragon, an addition to the Book of Daniel, Cyrus is actually converted to Judaism (Nickelsburg 1981: 27).

The *Cambridge History of Judaism* (Davies and Finkelstein 1984: 314) suggests that there is a level of congruency between Persian Zoroastrianism and Jewish Apocrypha, Pseudepigrapha and the Qumran scrolls in such matters as dualism and on the idea of individual as well as of collective post-mortem judgement, with death involving a series of steps towards such judgement, with related ordeals, resurrection and eventual salvation. Both religions share a complex demonology and angelology. There are quite serious problems to do with the texts and dates of the Iranian material, but they do indicate mutual influence on matters to do with death. Lenore

Erickson (1994) sees the exiled Jews in Babylon moving away from polytheistic–cultic ideas towards the Zoroastrian position on such matters as the nature of the inherent Goodness of Creation, including Man, the Afterlife, Judgement, the role of Satan, angelology, the expectation of an apocalypse and 'ages of time' – all of these are matters that relate to ideas about death and the fate of humanity. This is *not* to say that the Jews who were exiled to Babylon went there as polytheistic–cultists, and came back monotheists, but that in exile the developing Yahwist orthodoxy could have found in Zoroastrianism some theological support for their purposes; and that, carried back to Jerusalem, such ideas, borrowed or otherwise, became part of the ideational resource of the restored Temple.

Zoroastrian teaching, of course, opposed the burial or entombing of a corpse. Herodotus (1996: 77) had reported on the practice of corpse-exposure by the Persians. He states that 'the body of a male Persian is never buried, until it has been torn by a dog or a bird of prey', although he is careful to say that this is a matter about which he is not certain, as it was something which 'is spoken of with reserve and not openly'. This practice of exposure and of secondary inhumation remained peculiarly Zoroastrian. Even here, though, there are ambiguities. Cyrus himself, having escaped being killed as a baby, died in battle and was embalmed, that was actually handled after death and not exposed. Then, though, he was placed in a stone chamber located well above the earth, in keeping indeed with the Zoroastrian concern to prevent the corpse polluting the earth. It seems to be the case that here, as so often in so many other cultures, the death of a powerful male, a king, permitted a funerary response quite incompatible with formal religious requirements. Nearly all Persian and successor dynasties followed Cyrus in adopting burial styles and funerary architecture out of keeping with basic Zoroastrian teaching against tombs for the dead. Cyrus' tomb, which is still in existence, was raised on a plinth well above the earth. An almost entirely aperture-free stone chamber, it was for two hundred years the location and occasion for daily and monthly animal sacrifices, arranged by Cyrus' son Cambyses (Boyce 1979: 53). Darius the Great, third Achaemenid king, had his own tomb cut into the cliffs above Persepolis, and in general the monarchs of the Achaemenid, Arsacid and Sassanian dynasties followed this pattern, expressing in their own funerary styles a concern for political or dynastic ambition rather than proper religious form. This pressure to endow political or military leadership figures with cultic forms of death remembrances becomes a major tension in Jewish history, with (as we shall discuss in Part II) such pressures proving particularly difficult to reconcile with an adamant monotheism.

At a less exalted level, Mary Boyce finds evidence for a more demotic and closer following of the Zoroastrian practice of exposure, disincarnation and secondary or ossuary-style bone-interment in a fifth century BCE rock-cut sepulchre in Lycia in western Asia Minor. She describes two chambers, with lidded floor cavities, containing the bones of several persons, 'gathered up', asserts Boyce, 'after the rite of exposure' (1979: 59). This may well have been the case, although it is not demonstrated, and in the context of discussing the possible connections between Judaism and Zoroastrianism her claim runs into the insistence from other scholars that such ossuary-type burials were normative in the Ancient Middle East long before either Judaism or Zoroastrianism could be said to have exercised much influence.

Eric Meyers states that at Catal Huyuk in the seventh century BCE 'secondary burials are entirely normative' (1983: 92). Meyers, in this article and in an earlier book (Meyers 1971), shows that this practice (of enormous antiquity) was common in Neolithic, Bronze and Iron (or Biblical) Ages, and simply continued into Hellenistic and Roman times, a burial practice, therefore, of extraordinary longevity. Against this we have to set Bloch-Smith's insistence that in the Judahite Iron Age 'the vast majority of individuals initially received primary inhumation' (Bloch-Smith 1992a: 70).

Meyers pursues his thesis by insisting that at the late (second century CE) and very important Necropolis of Beth Shearim 'secondary burial was the dominant mode of inhumation' (1983: 108). If Meyers is right, then whatever similarities there are between Jewish and Persian practices are a reflection perhaps of mutual influence, but more likely of the influence of earlier practices on both. If Meyers is wrong, then Jewish burial practices (which in the anti-Meyers school consisted of whole-body primary once-only inhumations) were unaffected by Zoroastrianism. The issue is important well beyond the question of various methods of 'bone disposal'. The implication is that a society in which the disarticulated bones of a number of people were regularly reordered and the tomb therefore regularly revisited, would or could be a society given to a this-worldly cult of the ancestral dead. Conversely, individualised primary inhumation, undisturbed, would or could indicate a society either indifferent to such concerns or sufficiently persuaded of the importance of individual other-worldly salvation as to require an undisturbed whole-body presence in the tomb.

As we will see in Part II below, the archaeological record is as problematic as the textual one when it comes to establishing either patterns of influence or of definite changes in burial practice which can be related to specific 'theories' about death and its purpose. Indeed, the archaeological record reveals, in burial practices, a homogeneity of considerable longevity, making it intriguingly difficult to equate one particular style of burial with a particular thanatology.

Before concluding this part and chapter, we should revisit the primary variable which affects attitudes to death and dying, i.e. the moral status of the created human being in the particular creation story of the particular religions under consideration. Generally, attitudes to what happens to an individual human at death is a function of how humans, as a species, are regarded at the moment of creation. We have seen that in Mesopotamian creation stories men and women are created, in some versions as an afterthought, in order to serve the prior interests of the gods. They die in order to prove or to reinforce this negative status. Their death can then in no way be glorious, merely dim. In Egyptian cosmogony The Shaper, one of many gods involved in creation, participates in the creation of human beings as part of the benign creation of the gods, the world, the animals, the plants. Humanity is a natural part of the creativity of the gods. In Zoroastrianism, man is created by god in his own image. In the Hebrew creation story, in Genesis, creation is presented as *completed and perfected* by the creation of humanity. As Rabbi Nehemiah put it, and he was only one of many sages who saw it this way, 'one man is equal to the entire work of creation' (Bialik and Ravnitzky 1992: 575.3): humanity is created in the image of God, a view quite alien to the Mesopotamian story, where gods do not die, but where dying and being dead is what humans do and are. In one strong Israelite tradition, death was unnatural, with life being seen as never ending, a matter for and of moral decision. There has never been, in Israelite-Jewish tradition, the notion that man is created inferior or evil – however much and however often he may have disappointed and offended his creator! To this story, the story of life and death in Judaism as expressed in their actual tombs, I will now turn.

The archaeological record of 'Judaism', the simple caves, rock-cut tombs, *tumuli* and *arcosolia* of the Ancient Near East, the forms of burial followed by Abraham when he bought the cave at Machpelah, and indeed by Joseph of Arimathea when he bought the tomb in which Christ was placed, may tell us as much about the Ancient Near East as the ancient texts with which we have been primarily concerned.

Part II

FROM CAVES AND ROCK-CUT TOMBS TO JUDAISM

5

THE GENERAL ARCHAEOLOGY OF THE ANCIENT NEAR EAST

Burial complexes with *kokhim* or *arcosolia* were apparently used by all the inhabitants of Palestine *without faith different-iation*. This tradition, which developed from the tombs of Iron Age Palestine, reached its peak in the Roman period. ... *There were no specific architectural traditions or burial customs in the cemeteries surrounding Roman-Byzantine Apollonia.*

(Tal 1995: 119; emphases added)

Archaeology reveals *no distinctively Israelite burial practices* during almost the whole of the biblical period. The Israelites continued to use modes of burial employed in Palestine long before the conquest.

(*Encyclopaedia Judaica* 1972: vol. 4, col. 1515; emphasis added)

[In Pella of the Decapolis the East Cemetery contains tombs and associated artefacts indicating] use totalling 2,400 years, from the middle Bronze Age to the late Byzantine period, and perhaps *from the 4th Millennium BCE to the 15th Century CE.*

(Smith 1973: vol. 1, 168; emphasis added)

From Apollonia and from Pella and from many other places comes evidence for the extraordinary persistence, over many hundreds of years, of common locations and styles of burial practice, and for what seems to be the relative weakness of correlation between particular religious attitudes and a particular manner of disposal of the dead. Grave-sites and cemeteries were used over and over again. Death was ecumenical, and topography probably as important as theology.

In the cities, towns and countryside of both east and west, and for the later Jews and Christians as well as for the much older and larger societies of which they were a small part, much of the historical record of and witness to the 'ancestors' in the Ancient Near East consisted of cave-tombs, *arcosolia*, cists, burial shafts, urn-burials, necropoli, catacombs, sarcophagi, mausolea, hypogea, ossuaries, *stelae* and related epitaphs, legends and proclamations of the dead, the 'death culture' of the Ancient Near Eastern world. Travellers through these lands must have been aware of this legacy, whether as detritus and rumour or as visible and visited holy places. As is obvious from the accounts of later travellers such as Pausanias, much of the 'built environment' of the Ancient Near East consisted of tombs and associated religious buildings, in ruins or in use; many of these sites and buildings were associated with notions of sacrifice, birth and rebirth, death and monuments to death, other worlds and other lives.

It is almost impossible, now, to know how these ancient death cultures presented themselves to travellers and nomads such as the early Jews. The main witness, the lapidary texts of great mausolea and small burial caves, of valleys of tombs, of necropoli and of funerary temples are relatively mute, although in many cases they were used and reused. In Babylon, Ctesiphon and Seleucia, at Palmyra (called Tamar or Tadmor in 1 Kings and 2 Chronicles) and at hundreds of other sites all over the Ancient Near East such as Pella, Neolithic and later settlements had become Parthian or Greek or Roman cities, well equipped with both ancient and 'modern' cemeteries, ossuaries, funerary temples and tower tombs. These cities stood in a landscape covered with evidence of earlier and more demotic funerary practices. Jewish travellers and traders, and Jewish armies and exiles, would, from both this evidence and from their own funerary practices, have been aware that the areas over which they moved and in which they settled were the homes of death cultures of considerable antiquity. When Abraham bought the cave at Machpelah he was working within a well-attested practice of burial style, for the land over which he travelled and over which his descendants also travelled, fought and which they occupied, was covered by the funerary and mortuary remains of many centuries of earlier occupation: Stone Age, Bronze Age and Iron Age societies, as well as those coming later, had all left behind their respective versions of grave pits, urns, cave-graves, loculi, *arcosolia*, ossuaria, catacombs, dolmens, temple-tombs, mortuary gardens and ceme-teries. In the Middle Paleolithic period (to which are dated the earliest burials found in Palestine) pit-burials took place in the Kebara cave on Mount Carmel, sometimes in pits which would be used many times over many hundreds of years. Mount Carmel was the site of Saul's memorial for the victory over the Amalekites, the home of Nabal, Uzziah and Hezro, and of Elijah's confrontation with the priests of Baal and of his own later translation (Negev 1986: 68 ff.; Levy 1995: 122–3; Cheyne and Black 1899: vol.2, 1270–4).

Natufian Late Mesolithic burials have been found in their hundreds, with either whole body or skull-only interments, as well as a mixture of single-body and collective styles of burial. Grave goods and cadaver-painting seem also to have been frequent. At the Mesolithic village of Eynan, in northern Palestine, one of the earliest known above-ground funerary monuments has a twenty-one-foot diameter stone circle surmounting a sixteen-foot diameter pit containing human bones covered by large stones. Fifty part-sunken huts seemed to have formed the actual village of Eynan (Negev 1986: 68–9). Dog burials have been discovered at Gilat (Wolf 1993: 140–1), and in-house under-floor human burial at Tuleilat Ghassul (op cit.). Such burials indicate a widespread propensity to make, as it were, permanent settlements with corpses, marking as they do a sense of community between the place, the dead and the living. It is by having the dead placed within it that the land truly becomes occupied by the living. This, as will be argued below, is the significance of the early Bronze Age cave-tomb of Abraham at Machpelah and of other Israelite burials, such as that of Joshua.

In the Chalcolithic period (taking us up to c.3500 BCE) Gilat, along with Ein Gedi and Tuleilat Ghassul, emerge as regional cult centres, associated with the provision of a variety of types of grave and mortuary structures, and with a series of formal cemeteries marking further stages of settlement and occupation of the land:

> The establishment of ceremonial sites such as Gilat, Ein Gedi and Tuleilat Ghassul, and formal cemeteries throughout the country, indicates access to territory was controlled by the symbolism of place.
>
> (Levy 1995: 239)

On coastal sites, such as Azor, clay ossuaries have been found, of about two feet in dimension, shaped like houses and with doors to permit the insertion of skulls (with the doors themselves sometimes carrying the representation of a human face). This practice of course requires a positive affirmation of corpse-disincarnation, disarticulation and the ensuing handling of remains.

A common form of tomb over this period was the natural cave, sometimes resculpted and ornamented to permit better access and use, and to facilitate reuse, often over many centuries. The Hebrew word *kokh*, in Aramaic *kokhah*, means cavity or cave, and fairly easily gives the meaning of a burial chamber cut into a rock (Van der Horst 1991: 154). Simple ledges might be cut out of the side of the cave, and the defleshed bones of earlier burials removed into a special ossuary-pit or stored, along with all the others, in a special bone cavern nearby, an early charnel house. Shallowly dug graves, developed into interlocking tunnels and separate chambers, could be covered over, forming the mounds which are a feature of so many landscapes, or later dug deeper to form underground burial chambers and catacombs. This gradual transformation of natural features would produce, logically enough, entirely man-made tombs and buildings, in particular the *arcosolia* and associated *kokhim* in which various forms of individual interment and primary burial could easily be associated with familial, quasi-dynastic tomb occupation, with or without secondary burial and ossuaria. Such structures would proclaim to all the fact of the occupancy of the land and of the death-transcending nature of familial, kin and tribal relations. The early (early to middle Bronze Age) occupants of Jericho, for example, devoted enormous effort to creating proper accommodation for their dead. John Bartlett notes that the 346 excavated tombs (containing 356 individuals) would have involved the digging out of an average of over fifty tons of rock per tomb; he comments that the people of this era seemed to have spent more energy on creating tombs than on building houses (Bartlett 1982: 78). As is nearly always the case, the tombs (of nearly every type) were 'family' tombs, occupied by a variety of numbers of corpses of mixed genders and ages, but with the primary criterion for being placed in the tomb being one of familial relationship.

Greenhut (1995: 3–46), in analysing the tombs of the broad area of Palestine, notes a complex interplay between tomb type, the matter of primary or secondary burial, and of various practices such as possible disincarnation and disarticulation of bodies before actual interment. Constant reuse of tombs (and the activities of grave robbers) so mixes up the actual remains as to make it difficult, later, to know whether clan, extended family or nuclear family burial was the norm. Bloch-Smith (1992a: 70–1; 1992b: 214) notes that very few people were buried alone, and concludes that:

> Both sexes and all ages were buried together in bench tombs, indicating that family relations (attested in biblical

references but not yet demonstrated archaeologically), rather than achieved status or affiliation in social units, determined one's place in burial.

(Bloch-Smith 1992a: 49)

'Family' is, of course, identified by reference to the male. John Abercrombie discusses the practice of couple or paired burial in Iron Age Siloam (Silwan, Shiloh). An inscription on one of them reads:

This is (the sepulchre of [Sheban?]) yahu, who is over the house. There is no silver and no gold here, but [his bones] and the bones of his slave-wife with him. Cursed be the man who will open this.

(Abercrombie 1984: 61)

Levy (1995: 422) states that it is this Sheban/Shebna who is admonished by Isaiah:

What have you to do here and whom have you here, that you have hewn a tomb for yourself, you who hew a tomb on the height, and carve a habitation for yourself on the rock?

(Isaiah 22: 15, 16)

Abercrombie's main concern is to point out the 'domestic' nature of this interment, i.e. of a paired burial, of husband and wife, even though other interments might surround this, the central feature. He notes other features, common in the Levant of that era (seventh to sixth century BCE), such as the paucity of precious metal grave goods or ornament, the use of the 'curse' formula and, of course, the masculine 'ownership'. The curse formula is a common feature of later Greek and Hellenic tomb inscriptions, and assumes the presence of 'strangers', i.e. it is a mark of a relatively cosmopolitan society, where the inscription-maker feels it necessary to give admonitory advice to passers-by who may be unfamiliar with the local funerary etiquette. Indeed, Isaiah's denunciation of the unfortunate Shebna is in part because he was a foreigner. The practice of burying man and wife in the same tomb emphasises the domestic nature of interment, no matter that another common practice, of reuse of tombs, might later 'scatter' the couple's bones inside the burial chamber. Abercrombie's data are, of course, from the Iron Age, not the Bronze Age, although he also instances evidence of paired burial in the late Bronze Age at Deir el-Balah and Megiddo.

Family membership determines tomb occupancy, and in cultures in which association with the leading family or dynasty defined the political community, then such tombs also identified the clan or state. Such a concern hugely reinforces the masculine hegemony of tomb life: political and military leaders were men. Bloch-Smith notes that she found not a single example of adult women buried alone (1992a: 68): they were always accompanied, mostly by children and adolescents, often by men.

In 1982 workmen inadvertently broke into an Ammonite tomb near Amman, Jordan (Hadidi 1987: 101–2). The tomb, originally a natural cave and perhaps once used as a reservoir, appears to have been in use from the eighth to the fourth century BCE. Benches had been chiselled out of the natural rock and a dome-shaped ceiling provided a height of nearly two metres. There were two rough stone graves on one of the stone benches, and their skeletons were oriented east–west, heads to the east. Skeletal remains of many other people were scattered about, along with rich grave goods, some dating to the Achaemenian period of the fifth century BCE. The presence of Greek vases indicated trade between Jordan and Greece. In the centuries up to 586 BCE, Levy (1995: 422) notes the presence in Israelite graves near Hebron of goods imported from Cyprus and Egypt.

These tombs were adaptations of caves and natural openings in the rocks. There is, though, as revealed by Bloch-Smith and the extraordinary digging effort at Bronze Age Jericho, a very strong drive to 'denature' tombs – to make them places clearly made by human hand, so accommodation for the dead is put on a par with accommodation for the living. In the grave goods mentioned by Levy (1995) and Hadidi (1987) is evidence that the commerce and trade which was so important to the living was 'important' also for the dead.

There is, in the Ancient Near East, little evidence for cremation, or of embalming. Martin Noth (1966: 168) states that 'cremation of corpses has not been customary in Palestine since the ancient Oriental period', thereby almost casually highlighting how common was inhumation, whether straight into the ground, in a shroud, in various forms of coffin, or in one of several styles of secondary burial. Noth emphasises also the fact that burial took place away from inhabited settlements, either in isolated family sites, or in necropoli or cemeteries where the size of the settlement justified it. Palumbo (1987: 43–59) analyses the grave structures, layouts and corpse arrangements of Bronze Age Jericho, noting that the variety of interment practices indicated the use of the cemetery by different ethnic groups, as well as by groups defined in terms of social status. While the tombs themselves are those of families, the method of corpse-arrangement ('primary extended, primary crouched, secondary disarticulated'), the presence or otherwise of grave goods, and the size, type and location of the tomb, all indicate that the social and ethnic hierarchies of the living were carried over into the cemetery.

Elizabeth Bloch-Smith points out the importance (although not the over-riding importance) of geology and topography, with simple pit-graves predominating in the coastal sandy areas, and caves and rock-cut tombs in the highlands. In the coastal areas, the graves were usually of single individuals, lying supine, clad in cloaks: here, as in so many of the interments of common people, much of the record has simply disappeared. We do not know whether or not such burials were, once made, ignored, or whether they were the location for ritual revisiting. In more hospitable topographies are to be found a variety of tomb-types, but Bloch-Smith is of the opinion that: 'By the eighth century BCE, the bench tomb (and perhaps the cave tomb) constituted the standard Judahite form of burial' (1992a: 51).

Excavations at Jerusalem reveal the steady elaboration of this type of tomb to keep up with the growth of the city's population. The extramural cemetery at Silwan sufficed until the eighth and seventh centuries BCE, but in the seventh and sixth centuries new rock-cut tombs spread into the older 'illicit' burial ground of the Ben Hinnom Valley, the Tophet so excoriated by Jeremiah (Jeremiah 7: 32) and associated with Gehenna. These new tombs were both 'collective' and lavish. Bloch-Smith notes that they were 'exceptional in the quality of their workmanship, the value of the provisions, the number of individuals accommodated and the adoption of foreign features' (1992a: 139). The Jerusalem cemetery had, for example, sunken panels, sculpted cornices, shaped headrests, individual sarcophagi with no 'overspill' provision (indicating a disinclination to reuse) and Egyptian and Phoenician inscriptions and decorations – all making the Jerusalem cemetery a far cry from simple rock-cut tombs or communal pit-burials.

Grave goods, of various types associated with age and gender, as well as with status, accompanied the dead; and Hachlili and Killebrew (1983) note one of the earliest (first century CE) appearances of Jewish tomb decoration, in the form of a wall painting of a vine and associated bird life, probably derived from similar Greco-Roman practices. At the Beth Shearim Necropolis, ornament and epigraphy (again of Hellenic as well as Jewish nature) is well attested. This was clearly a developing burial practice, since the very simple late Second Temple rock-cut tomb at Jerusalem reported by Joseph Zias (see the end of this chapter) demonstrates that lavishness in burial practice had not yet become the norm.

Hachlili and Killebrew are sure that by the first century BCE burials are primarily of individuals in wooden coffins, a practice which 'first appears among Jews at this time' (1983: 128). The authors point out that the term 'coffin' appears earlier only in the 'Egyptian' context of Joseph, while the dominant impulse was, as we have seen, to collective or tribal burial, to sleep with or be gathered to the ancestors. Hachlili and Killebrew take the view that there is a clear association between the burial practices they identify and a particular ideology and thanatology:

> individual burial for the entire population and not just for the upper classes, as in the Israelite period, is probably related to the increasing importance placed on the individual in contemporary Hellenistic society as a whole ... and *to the Jewish belief in individual resurrection of the body*.
> (Hachlili and Killebrew 1983: 128–9; emphasis added)

Was this development associated with an attempt by 'the authorities' to diminish the attractions of family-based cults of the dead? The most useful analyses of the archaeology of burial of the Jewish people, in particular in the land conquered by Joshua and his successors, is the work already referred to by Elizabeth Bloch-Smith and by Theodore Lewis. Bloch-Smith's account of 850 burials in the area of the southern Levant covers the Iron Age and the early historical period. She is clear that the archaeological record shows that the cult of the dead was flourishing, and that the 'official' policy to 'discredit the dead'

> testifies to the degree that the cult [of the dead] was integrated into Judahite social, religious and economic fabric. The lack of change during this period in the material remains uncovered through archaeological fieldwork, including in Jerusalem, supports the interpretation that there was no general shift in practices or attitudes regarding the dead. If common practice is to be labelled 'popular' then Jerusalem residents including Judahite national and religious authorities also followed 'popular' practice. The divine ancestors

continued as vital entities in Judahite religion and society
as long as the kingdom existed.

(Bloch-Smith 1992a: 150–1)

Bloch-Smith is supported in this view by Theodore Lewis (1989),
who is clear that the archaeological record demonstrates a high
degree of similarity between the cults of the dead of ancient Ugarit
and ancient Israel. Tombs in both cultures are equipped with such
things as doors, libation tubes, jugs, food receptacles and other
grave goods, all of which indicate the continued 'reality' of the dead
as part of the society of the living. Lewis points out that *some* of the
textual evidence (such as Qoheleth and Deuteronomy) oppose such a
cult: there is, simply, a tension in Israelite thanatology:

> The Wisdom authors give no credence to necromancy. The
> deceased are not knowledgeable about the affairs of humans
> and thus simply do not have the ability to grant favours or
> oracles to the living. The picture we get from most of the
> texts ... is that there was an ongoing battle by the
> Yahwism which emerges as normative against the practice
> of necromancy and other death cult rituals such as self-
> laceration and presenting offerings to the deceased. ... The
> legal material we find in the Deuteronomistic and Priestly
> literature is decidedly against cults of the dead and from
> this we may infer that such laws were formulated in reac-
> tion to existing death cult practices. ... Death cult rituals
> were common in some forms of 'popular religion'. ...
> Ancient Israel shared a solidarity with the other cultures of
> the ancient Near East and it should not be surprising to
> find cults of the dead such as we have in the Ugaritic and
> Mesopotamian literature.

(Lewis 1989: 176–7)

Lewis quotes Qoheleth to sum up 'official' disdain for cults of the
dead: 'a live dog is better than a dead lion!' (ibid.: 169).

There are other aspects of the archaeological record which indicate that the matter of 'cults of the dead' cannot be easily dismissed
or relegated to a distant part of Israel's history. For the archaeology
of the later Second Temple period (first century BCE–first century
CE), we have the work of Hachlili and Killebrew (1983), already
referred to, and that of Eric Meyers (1971; 1983). Meyers provides
further evidence of the continuation of the tension in Judaism

between 'normative' authority, concerned with Yahwistic proprieties, and a 'popular' inclination to maintain an intense relationship with the dead.

The issue focuses on the matter of 'secondary burial', since such practices involve opening tombs, repeated corpse-handling and the re-storage of disarticulated bones in ossuaries or pits, all of this being a practice hard to reconcile with the status of the corpse as pollutant. The over-riding of such a very strong tabu would indicate a degree of cultic activity at the tomb site.

Hachlili and Killebrew analyse the style and contents of 150 tombs in the Second Temple Jericho Necropolis, and in all the welter of artefacts claim to discover an historical sequence in which the 'customary' practice of primary burial in wooden coffins of the first century BCE is disturbed for about eighty years (in the first century CE) by a practice of secondary burial either in ossuaries or simply as collected bones. The ossuary burials of either type were, say Hachlili and Killebrew, a deviation 'short-lived and unique to Jews of this period' (1983: 127). They do not know what caused this short-lived (to them) deviation, suggesting 'turmoil in a society, perhaps the result of historical events which affected the religious beliefs of this period' (ibid.: 129). Their data on Jericho indicate a more customary tradition of individual, encoffined, undisturbed, primary burial – the 'normal' method of burial.

In their general thesis they are clearly at odds with Meyers who, for example, insists that burial practices which he holds to be normative for the earlier periods, i.e. secondary burial, disarticulation and the use of ossuaria, are also to be found both *much earlier and much later*, such as at the third century CE important necropolis of Beth Shearim where 'secondary burial was the dominant mode of inhumation' (Meyers 1983: 108). Hachlili and Killebrew tend rather to dismiss Beth Shearim (the major Jewish necropolis of the first centuries of the Common Era) as a necropolis where 'the matter of burial had become a commercialised public enterprise, and was apparently directed by the Burial Society (Hevrah Kadishah) which sold burial places to any purchaser' (Hachlili and Killebrew 1983: 127). We shall return to Beth Shearim later.

Meyers clearly demonstrates the longevity of the secondary burial tradition and the compatibility of it with the physical layout of tombs of various types. Bloch-Smith's data and semi-asides (see, for example, 1992a: 37: 'secondary burial may also have been practised') would at least support the view that post-mortem bone-handling was a 'matter of fact' practice in Judaism of the Iron

Age and early Biblical Age. Meyers insists that 'from the turn of the common era until the 4th century AD, Diaspora Jews buried the remains of their dead in Palestine' (Meyers 1983: 110), and that it was the ancient practice of disincarnation and secondary burial in ossuaries which enabled Diaspora Jews to do exactly that. He sees in this the basis of a 'cult of the dead' of remarkable longevity and of great flexibility, continuing, indeed, into Christianity:

> In a secondary burial the emphasis is on the keeping of the remains within the precincts of the family tomb, and this seems to be in close harmony with the Semitic conception of the nature of man. In the light of this the biblical idioms for death and burial are quite apt. Despite the apparent silence of the New Testament in regard to ossilegeum, the preservation of a martyr's remains or the veneration of a Christian saint in a relic chest seems best explained as an outgrowth of ancient Near Eastern burial customs.
>
> (Meyers 1983: 112)

In this conflict in the archaeological record lies a very considerable tension, a tension which occurs time and time again in the subject of 'the dead' and their burial. Meyers is implying that at least some version of the ancient cults of the dead persisted over thousands of years and retained its hold on both Judaism and Christianity. Such cults invoke ancestors as active participants in the lives of their descendants. The use of ossuaries, individual or collective, symbolises these transactions. Cults of the dead depend for their efficacy on the dead having some kind of intercessory relationship with the deity, a relationship adamantly denounced as idolatrous by 'normative' Judaism. Cults of the dead are generally 'dynastic', and the biblical approval of 'being buried with your people' may actually increase the dangers of idolatry. The development of loculi tombs facilitated the merging of two styles of burial, the individual with the collective, and this indeed is attested by Hachlili and Killebrew (1983) for the Jericho necropolis. Individual interments, in coffin or ossuary, can be placed in the several *kokhim* of the loculus, producing a kind of mini-catacomb, available for both primary and secondary burial. The quotations at the beginning of this chapter demonstrate both the extraordinary longevity of burial practices, in this case of Israelites-Jews, and the adaptive capacity of a variety of types of tombs. Flexibility, of course, does not 'solve' the problem: are the dead, in their varied tombs, safely and mutely dead, or are they merely waiting, more rather than less than human because they are dead only to this world? Are the dead, dead? Are they housed, or buried? The archaeological record of Israelite and Jewish burial practices seems to leave the answer open. What became 'normative' Judaism was hugely concerned with the opportunities for idolatry which any enlivening of the dead would entail. Equally, there was a very ancient tradition which located individual, dynastic and communal well-being in an appropriate, ritualised communion with the dead. Around both of these perspectives was wrapped a sense that the dead were 'active', either as allies or as potential enemies.

Before turning to an examination of Jewish texts and early funerary 'liturgy' to see how this tension was dealt with, I would like to end this chapter with the story of one burial which points the way to a consideration of the ideational, ritual, theological and demotic changes in Jewish *attitudes* to the dead, as they developed from biblical times and as they were expressed in authoritative Jewish literature such as the Bible, the Mishnah and the Apocrypha, as well as in Jewish folklore such as Bialik and Ravnitzky's collection *Sefer Ha-Aggadah* (1992).

In 1982 Joseph Zias reported on a 'Rock-Cut Tomb in Jerusalem' (Zias 1982: 53–5). The late Second Temple tomb was cut into the limestone. The central chamber had a dip in the centre, a 'repository pit' in one corner, and four *kokhim*, three of them still sealed off when discovered (in the course of building operations), the fourth having collapsed. Skeletal remains of nine humans (three males, three females, three infants/children) were divided unequally between the four *kokhim*. Zias makes several interesting comments. He notes that the grave goods were remarkably poor, indicating a disinclination to lavishness rather than poverty, as the cost of constructing the grave itself indicated wealthy ownership. Zias is particularly interested in the corpse of a young male (18–21), on whose abdominal cavity had been placed a heavy stone. In an aside which rather contradicts Hachlili and Killebrew, Zias notes that placing such a stone directly on top of a corpse was practicable because 'coffins were rarely used in Jerusalem' (1982: 45). More interestingly, though, the 'abdominal rock' was geologically quite unlike the local rock, and had therefore been deliberately imported for its purpose. What was its purpose? To answer Zias refers to both Jewish and Roman history and thanatology.

In the story of the war – a holy war – against Jericho, Achan, son of Carmi, is revealed as the man who had broken the ban which had reserved for Yahweh all of the material wealth of the captured

Jericho: Achan had hidden and appropriated for his own use a robe, and gold and silver. Achan is taken by Joshua to the Vale of Achor: 'All Israel went with him; and all Israel stoned him: a great cairn was reared over him' (Joshua 7: 25–6). On some readings (Hastings 1914: 7) Achan's entire family was killed and their bodies burned, before being covered by stones, the mark of the grave of a criminal or outlaw. The entire valley was named, after Achan, the Valley of Misfortune. The young man in Zias' tomb may have been under a ban and this fact was announced by the presence on his corpse of a single stone. Zias goes on to say that there was, in the Roman world of the time, a general superstition that the dead could be trouble-some and vengeful, and that the excessive size and weight of the stone also suggests a strong desire to protect the living by very firmly holding down the young man so heavily pressed down in his burial. Jewish burial liturgies and practices were much concerned to 'keep the dead in their place'. It is doubtful that there was general agreement as to where this was.

6

JUDAISM

Towards the common era

We have in the story of Achan an example of the interpenetration of Jewish history and treatment of the dead, set in the wider context of the Greco-Roman world. Graves may have been 'markers' of collective presence, or cultic places for ritualised, individualised and personalised remembrances, or of quarantining the dead, or of punishing the dead, or of opening sites of access to other post-mortem worlds, or evidence of a return to roots – or all of these and more.

In order to get some idea as to how the death and burial practices of Biblical and early Rabbinic Judaism evolved out of the worlds of the Ancient Near East, we will need to look in considerable detail at the Bible stories and commentaries on or elucidations of them such as the Mishnah, the Targums and other (noncanonical) texts which Nickelsburg calls 'apocalypses, narrative fiction, testaments, history, and the like' (1981: 6).

This approach, endeavouring to cover a very large period, will inevitably be more synchronic and episodic than diachronic and sequential, a form of illustrative synthesis and analysis rather than conventional or even telescoped history. Generally, I will take the Jewish Bible as the *symbolic* basis of the 'orthodox' or authoritative view of death, and then rely upon other sources to provide more detail as to actual behaviour and development. I will deal first of all with the relationship between Jewish cosmology and notions of a moralised and differentiated afterlife; then with the nature and organisation of Jewish funerary customs, and conclude with an examination of Jewish views on resurrection as these views developed in response to the increasingly tragic story of military defeat and societal destruction.

The records of Jewish practice and behaviour over these centuries demonstrate (again!) how many common elements there are in human response to the fact of death. Because everyone dies, everyone has a view on death. Unlike, say, religious art or textual analysis, death is always subject to both an authoritative 'official' set of rules and to demotic construction and reconstruction. Perhaps for this same reason, but also because a theology without a thanatology is thin gruel indeed, the political and intellectual elites of a religious movement (sometimes associated with a state or other political entity) will assiduously seek to elaborate and enforce an orthodoxy (including an orthodoxy of silence) about death and burial, while just as assiduously (and often enough in opposition) ordinary people will elaborate and broadcast their own. There is a perpetual dialectic in such matters, reflected in the existence, side by side, of official or 'closed' canonical versions of God and more 'open' and discursive thanatologies, which seek to keep God accessible and communicable with, either by the dead or by the living on behalf of the dead. Thus, for example, the Jewish Bible treats the deaths of the Patriarchs with what appears to be an abrupt and formulaic terseness, in keeping with a determination to maintain the integrity of the *Shekinah*, and to avoid the danger of any discussion or questioning of death which may tend to 'force' God to reply and justify himself. Canonically, death is silence:

> For in death there is no remembrance of thee: in the grave who shall give thee thanks?
>
> (Psalm 6: 5)

> For we needs must die, and are as water spilt on the ground, which cannot be gathered up again; neither doth God respect *any* person.
>
> (2 Samuel 14: 14)

> I am counted with them that go down into the pit: I am as a man that hath no strength: Free among the dead, like the slain that lie in the grave, whom thou rememberest no more: and they are cut off from thy hand.
>
> (Psalm 88: 4–5)

Other and perhaps more popular or populist Jewish writings – such as the Apocrypha, Pseudepigrapha, Targums, the *Book of Legends, Sefer Ha-Aggadah* (compiled by Hayim Bialik and Yehoshua Ravnitzky), or Louis Ginzberg's *Legends of the Jews*, or tomb and wall decorations and epitaphs – are simply not satisfied with the mute acceptance of death which logically follows from such a view. In, for example, the first century CE Testament of Abraham, there is an insistence on an amplification of the sparse official offerings, and this is done in the most discursive and imaginative ways, in an expostulatory conversation with the Almighty. The Testament of Abraham is a prolonged, highly personal and occasionally querulous discussion, argument even, between Abraham and God (through the medium of God's messenger Michael) about the circumstances under which Abraham will, or will not, accept God's decision that he is to die. God sends Michael to tell Abraham that he is to die, to point out that he has many possessions and has lived a virtuous life, but that he should now put his affairs in order. Michael is to conclude this message by giving Abraham the assurance that 'at this time you are going to depart this vain world and leave the body, and you shall go to your own Master among the good' (Testament of Abraham 1972: 5).

In the actual presence of Abraham, and with the evidence of his goodness and hospitality, Michael begins to weep because such a man has to die and he begs God to relieve him of the task of giving him the bad tidings. God agrees to relieve Michael of the task of giving Abraham the news, and instead says that he will tell Abraham through Isaac his son, via a dream, a dream which Michael is to

> interpret appropriately ... so that Abraham may know the sickle of death and the uncertain end of life, and so that he may make disposition concerning all his possessions, for I have blessed him more than the sand of the sea and like the stars of heaven.
>
> (ibid.: 11)

The dream is experienced and interpreted, and Abraham learns that he is to 'depart to God' – but Abraham refuses! On hearing this, God (still using Michael as a messenger) replies in a long speech, drawing attention to the blessings he has conferred on Abraham, and saying:

> As for you, tell me, why have you set yourself up against me, and why is there grief in you? ... Do you not know that all who have come from Adam and Eve have died, and none of the prophets have escaped death, and none of the rulers has been immortal, and none of the forefathers has escaped the mystery of death? All have died; all have gone

to Hades; all have been gathered by the sickle of death. To you I did not send Death; I did not permit a deadly disease to come upon you; I did not permit the sickle of death to encounter you; I did not allow the nets of Hades to ensnare you, nor did I wish you to meet any evil. ... Do you not know that if I permit Death to come to you, then I would be able to see whether you would come or not come?

(ibid.: 20–1)

The story and the conversation go on for some time. The Testament includes a world tour and a visit to heaven, as well as a judgement scene very like that to be found in Egyptian texts, and there are other (possible) Egyptian similarities. Eventually, Death is sent to replace the dithering Michael, and tells Abraham to stop all his questioning:

And Death said to Abraham, 'Come, kiss my right hand and cheerfulness and life and power will come to you'. For Death received Abraham and he kissed his hand and at once his soul adhered to the hand of Death. And at once the archangel Michael came with a multitude of angels, and they took his precious soul in their hands in divinely woven linen. And they tended righteous Abraham's body with divine ointments and perfumes until the third day after his death, and they buried him in the promised land at the oak of Mamre. And the angels escorted his precious soul and ascended to the heavens singing the trishagion hymn [short invocatory prayer] to the Master of all, to God, and they set it in obeisance to God and Father ... and the undefiled voice of God [said] 'Take my friend Abraham to the garden [paradise], where the tabernacles of my righteous ones and the abodes of holy ones Isaac and Jacob are in his bosom, where there is no toil, no sadness, no sighing, but peace and joy and endless life.

(ibid.: 56–7)

This is a far cry from 'Abraham gave up the ghost, and died in a good old age, an old man, and full of years, and was gathered to his people' (Genesis 25: 8), a comment which does not even occur as the climax to the chapter in which it occurs. It is at the level of writing such as the Testament of Abraham which complements (and often enough embroiders) but at times seemingly contradicts the

Him to account. To question God was idolatry – and highly dangerous. 'Can a man be profitable unto God?', expostulates Eliphaz to Job. 'Is it any pleasure to the Almighty that thou art righteous, or is it gain to him that thou makest thy ways perfect? Will he reprove thee for fear of thee? Will he enter with thee into judgement?' (Job 22: 3–4), and the bewildered and much put-upon Job replies:

> I go forward, but he is not there; and backward, but I cannot perceive him. On the left hand where he doth work, but I cannot behold him; he hideth himself on the right hand, that I cannot see him. ... But he is in one mind, and who can turn him? and what His soul desireth, even that he doeth.
>
> (Job 23: 8–13)

Job is described as 'perfect and upright' at the *beginning* of his Book (Job 1: 1) and, after his extraordinary troubles, as being more blessed by the Lord at the 'latter end' of his life than at the beginning (Job 42: 12). He still dies with no scriptural comment other than: 'So Job died, being old and full of days' (Job 42: 17). His blessings are the very earth-bound ones of the prosperity of his sons and the beauty of his daughters. There is no comment on his post-mortem reception by God. Elisha, the teacher of R. Meir (second century CE), denied that God blessed Job more at the end of his life than at the beginning, saying to R. Meir that R. Akiva had construed the story as meaning that 'the Lord blessed the latter end of Job because of the beginning' (Bialik and Ravnitzky 1992: 243.191). R. Akiva is saying that nothing in Job's constancy had had any effect on the Lord. Job was as perfect at the beginning of his trials as when he died at the end: there is little sense that God was affected by either his perfection or his death.

Job's story, R. Akiva's comment and the verses from Psalms and 2 Samuel quoted above, may be construed as indicating the biblical afterworld was undifferentiated, i.e. that there were (in the early books anyway) no separate fates ('heaven') for those who were good and those who were bad ('hell'); that at death everyone went to the morally neutral Sheol, a kind of storehouse of the not-alive, into which all went and from which none emerged. This seems to be the message of Job 3: 19 ('the small and the great are there') and associated verses, and of Job 10: 21, where Job rather desperately asks God to leave him unmolested, in a way preferring the nullity of 'the land of darkness' to the company of his God:

Before I go whence I shall not return, even to the land of
darkness and the shadow of death; a land of darkness, as
darkness itself; and of the shadow of death, without any
order, and where the light is as darkness.

In the entire Hebrew Bible only two humans go to heaven: Elijah,
arguably while still alive, is taken up in a whirlwind (2 Kings 2: 11),
and Enoch (see Genesis 5: 24: 'Enoch walked with God; and he was
not; for God took him'), apparently also while still alive.

For everyone else, death involves being 'gathered to one's fathers'
in a never-specified post-mortem place. For these reasons, Sheol has
been offered up as the obvious place for everyone who has died.
Heaven is empty, so is hell; the dead are neither alive in this life as
they once were, nor are they reincarnated (a totally alien concept),
and that leaves Sheol, the place of shades, the pale slow forms of all
the dead, shadows of what they once were (Isaiah 14: 10). Until
recently many scholars held to this 'undifferentiated' view of the
afterlife, seeing in a general 'Sheol' a congruency with a biblical
indifference to ideas of 'resurrection' (ideas generally related to a
differentiated afterlife and to access to heaven in particular), as well
as with respect for the inscrutability of God. (This idea, of a neutral
'grey' place for all the dead, was fairly widespread in the Ancient
Near East, and indeed in the Greco-Roman world. Inevitably, it
coexisted with other views of a differentiated afterlife).

Yet it is noteworthy that while the deaths of, for example, the
Patriarchs are reported tersely, *they are at least reported*. A proper
burial (see below) is in itself approval. Lesser people simply appear
and disappear, and the deaths of morally dubious or positively evil
people in the Bible are either unreported or quite clearly involve
forms of punishment. The 'King of Babylon' is promised a fate
much worse than simply being 'gathered to his fathers':

But thou art cast out of thy grave like an abominable
branch, and as the raiment of those that are slain, thrust
through with a sword, that go down to the stones of the
pit; as a carcase trodden under feet. Thou shalt not be
joined with them in burial, because thou hast destroyed thy
land, and slain thy people; the seed of evildoers shall never
be renowned. Prepare slaughter for his children for the
iniquity of their fathers, that they do not rise, nor possess
the land, nor fill the face of the world with cities.

(Isaiah 14: 19 ff.)

Ruth Rosenberg (1981) and indeed, in an earlier work, Alexander Heidel (1975) use such texts to indicate that Sheol is perhaps not the general 'pit' or storehouse of the shades that it seems to be. The inferences drawn from the relative silence about heaven and hell in some biblical passages, combined with the loquacity about what happens to the positively wicked on this earth, may be misleading. Other evidence from the Apocrypha and Pseudepigrapha supports this view, as does the Testament of Abraham referred to above. Ruth Rosenberg gives the following 'statistics' on Sheol:

> Four times does the Bible mention a disciplined way of life as being counterparallel to being remanded to Sheol. Explicitly it is ten times stated that the wicked are remanded to Sheol, and may be so inferred eight more times. Eighteen times is it explicitly mentioned that those who descend to Sheol die a violent death, by the sword, and three more times they die 'in blood.' In four instances those who are remanded to Sheol descend there alive. Five times severe affliction is the cause. Twice intense anguish is the cause, once mourning, and twice 'evil' appears. *In all instances the common denominator is premature death.*
>
> (Rosenberg 1981: 174–5; emphasis added)

Rosenberg adds that the common factor – premature death – applies also to the equivalent terms 'pit' and 'netherworld'. Sheol, argues Rosenberg, is the place to which humans are sent when they are in some way or other to be judged. In support of this, both she and other commentators have for example noted the recurring water-images of Sheol (in particular in the story of Jonah), which indicates among other things an 'ordeal', a place of testing and of the concomitant judgement. The use of terms for gates and gate-keepers, paralleled in Egyptian and Mesopotamian views of the underworld, also imply jailing, prior to or after judgement (see, for example, 3 Maccabees 5: 51).

Rosenberg comes to the conclusion that deaths which were 'untimely' or 'unnatural' (of which see more below) were in general seen as morally problematic. Those who suffered such a death were likely therefore to be sent down to Sheol. *Sudden* death was the problem, both evidence for and consequence of malpractice, and therefore incurring the wrath of God.

Among those who die unnaturally, or 'evilly', are (states Rosenberg) two groups – the *Rephaim* and the *Belial* – who are particularly problematic in the eyes of the guardians of both biblical and other religious beliefs of the Ancient Near East. The *Rephaim* are a group of complex origin, but in the Bible seen as overly potent in death – a challenge to the omnipotence of God and therefore in need of a firm, Sheol-permanent punishment: 'thou hast visited them with destruction and wiped out all remembrance of them' (Isaiah 26: 14). The group referred to in the term *Belial*, i.e. a positively evil group, will under no circumstances come up from Sheol. For others in Sheol, notes Rosenberg, the Bible provides ample evidence of the inclination (his ability being taken for granted) of God to raise up individuals, or individual souls from Sheol. See, for instance, Jonah 2: 3–8:

> Out of the belly of hell cried I,
> And thou heardest my voice.
> I went down to the bottoms of the mountains;
> The earth with her bars closed upon me for ever;
> Yet thou has brought me up from the pit, O Lord my God.

Sheol then is not the place for the permanent storage of all the dead. It is the case that biblical references to heaven, and of the translation to it of the good and the virtuous, are relatively sparse and undemonstrative, and there is little in the way of detail about the delights of that place. Wherever it is, though, it is never mentioned in connection with Sheol:

> This gathering place ... is never specified in space ... but it is never jointly mentioned with Sheol. Correspondingly, in the more than sixty Biblical passages in which Sheol is mentioned, it is never portrayed as a peaceful ancestral gathering place. ... The Bible's differentiation seems to be consequential. Natural death is accompanied by unification with kin and Sheol is never mentioned. In counterpart, evil death is followed by sundrance from all kin ... and results in delegation to Sheol, which is never described as an ancestral meeting place.
>
> (Rosenberg 1981: 192–3)

In comparison with later Christianity, for example, references to 'resurrection' (to heaven) are nuanced and oblique, although they are certainly there and gradually became more explicit (see Sawyer 1973: 218–34; Segal 1997: 90–125). The same is true of 'hell'.

Reticence, combined with a recourse to standardised, formulaic comments on actual deaths, serves a distinct purpose. In their preferred taciturnity, the writers and compilers of the early books of the Bible were concerned to avoid the dangers of invoking those 'cults of the dead' which they saw in the tempting pagan religions which surrounded them. The 'cult of the dead', the apparent ease of access to and manipulability of the gods that could be seen as characterising Egyptian and cultic polytheism, would have been anathema to a large section of monotheistic Jews. There were, though, other Jews who, all too humanly, sought to invoke a morally differentiated afterworld, a moral universe paralleling the material one. Judaism developed in a perpetual tension between the need to locate people's deaths in such a moral universe, while at the same time avoiding the dangers and idolatries of a cult of the dead which would challenge and offend their jealous God, which would challenge, that is, the very basis of their adamant monotheism. In a perpetually precarious world, 'chosen' by a most jealous God, surrounded by an endless eruption of enemies (who, militarily, eventually won) and struggling to turn a rough Iron Age tribe into a society based on law and restraint, Jewish leaders had to create a thanatology which expressed and proclaimed the social solidarity without which the enterprise was doomed – as it perhaps was. 'Burial' was not an extraneous bit of existence, a mere disposal of the dead: it was the endless but risky opportunity to define and emphasise, to ritualise and to explicate the 'chosen' nature of the Jewish people – but having to do so without creating a cult around (if not of) the dead.

By insisting on regarding the dead as polluting, *and by therefore creating the necessity for death rituals*, Jewish orthodoxy sought to find a way between the twin dangers of an idolatry which would offend God and an indifference which would offend everyone else. This may perhaps be best shown by a more detailed analysis of actual burial practices, insofar as these can be recreated from biblical and other references.

7

BURYING THE JEWISH DEAD

The corpse is, in 'canonical' Judaism, unclean, a collective Father of Uncleanness:

> Fathers of uncleanness in a corpse are: (1) the whole corpse; (2) an olive's bulk of a corpse or of corpse-dregs; (3) a ladleful of corpse mould; (4) the backbone or the skull; (5) a member from the corpse; (6) a member severed from a living man; (7) a quarter-kab [a few square inches] from the greatest in bulk or the greatest in number of the bones of a corpse, or from the greater part of the corpse, or from the greater number of its parts; (8) a quarter-log [a liquid measure] of blood or mingled blood; (9) more than a ladleful of grave dust.
>
> These all convey uncleanness by contact, by carrying, and by overshadowing. ... A sepulchre-stone and its buttressing stone convey uncleanness by contact and by overshadowing but not by carrying; and the same applies to a closed grave. ... If a man who has touched a corpse touches vessels and these vessels touch a man, they are all alike Fathers of Uncleanness.
>
> (The Mishnah 1967: The Rules of Uncleaness; 4, 7: 801)

Corpses are not the only source of uncleanness, but they play a very large part in such a concept. The rules of burial, as they evolve, are an elaboration of meticulous behavioural rules designed to protect the living from contamination at the same time as they carry out the serious obligation on all Jews to participate in the burial procedures. Indeed, the uncleanness of the corpse and the correlated rules of corpse-disposal, have precisely the effect of heightening the importance of death and the funeral. There was until well into the Common Era, as far as we know, no formal Jewish funeral liturgy (as we understand the term) and therefore no Jewish 'burial service'. It is the Bible, and later the various commentaries, which provides indicators of the existence of a Jewish funerary ritual.

Abraham, dying at the ripe old age of 175, was buried in the cave at Machpelah, together with his wife Sarah. Before he died, he handed on his property to Isaac, giving only gifts to sons (and only sons are listed) by his concubines and, it would seem, by his wife Keturah (who is not mentioned in the distribution of property). These children are sent away by Abraham:

> And these are the days of the years of Abraham's life which he lived, an hundred three score and fifteen years. Then Abraham gave up the ghost, and died in a good old age, an old man, and full of years, and was gathered to his people. And his sons Isaac and Ishmael buried him in the cave of Machpelah. ... The field which Abraham purchased ... there was Abraham buried, and Sarah his wife. And it came to pass after the death of Abraham that God blessed his son Isaac.
>
> (Genesis 25: 7–11)

In its very terseness, this is a 'good death', exemplifying the significance of the fact of death and the act of burial to this society. In a way, the burial is more important, getting more dramatisation than the death. Abraham's death, for example, takes up five verses in the middle of a chapter otherwise concerned with his sons by Keturah and then with Isaac's troubles with Esau and Jacob. By contrast, Genesis 23 is devoted *entirely* to the story of Abraham's purchase of the cave-site from 'the people of the land, the sons of Heth'. As the first Patriarch, Abraham, in choosing a burial site unconnected with his actual origins, is at one and the same time emphasising his own status as the founder of a people and religion, and of the possession (by proprietary interment) of a particular territory by that people. Initially, the sons of Heth had offered to *give* Abraham one of their own tombs: 'My lord, you are God's prince amongst us: bury your dead in the best of our tombs; not one of us would refuse you his tomb and keep you from burying your dead' (Genesis 23: 6).

Abraham persists, for gifts are not ownership perhaps, and asks for the cave at Machpelah. He is offered it, *free*, but again persists in buying it outright, and:

Ephron's field at Machpelah opposite Mamre, the field and
the cave that was on it, the whole of its extent in every direction, passed into Abraham's possession in the sight of the sons
of Heth and all the citizens of the town. After this Abraham
buried his wife Sarah in the cave of the field of Machpelah
opposite Mamre, in the country of Canaan. And so the field
and the cave that was on it passed from the sons of Heth into
Abraham's possession to be owned as a burial plot.

(Genesis 23: 17–20)

From then on Abraham-Machpelah locates Israel in the world: it is
surely significant that this seems to be the main concern of the text,
there being *no discussion whatsoever* as to Abraham's likely fate in the next
world, if there is such a thing. It is only centuries later that this 'defect' is
made good in commentaries such as the Testament of Abraham. The
Mishnah also refers to Abraham as one of the five possessions that the
Holy One 'took to himself in his world', and quotes in apparent approval
Genesis 15: 19: 'Blessed be Abram of the most high God, possessor of
heaven and earth' (The Mishnah 1967: Aboth 6: 10; 461; the abbrevi-
ation of the name is an additional commendation.)

In his rejection of the kind offer of a free tomb from the children
of Heth, as well as in his insistence on ownership of the burial site,
Abraham marks the distinctiveness of the people of Israel, their
adamant separation from all other people. In 'after the death of
Abraham God blessed Isaac' is the message of approval of Abraham's
seed, *part of Abraham's 'good death'*. Material, as well as spiritual
advantages inhered in this connection and approval. So, for example,
in discussing the question of legal status and citizenship, R. Judah
and R. Akiba say: 'All is in accordance with a person's honour. Even
the poorest in Israel are looked upon as freemen who have lost their
possessions, for they are the sons of Abraham, Isaac and Jacob' (The
Mishnah 1967: Baba Kamma 8, 6, 343). Later, Isaac was buried ('gathered to his people'; Genesis 35: 29) at Machpelah also, together with
his wife Rebekah. Jacob, who had already buried his wife Leah (though
not his wife Rachel) at Machpelah, told his sons that he was:

To be gathered unto my people: bury me with my fathers
in the cave that is in the field of Ephron the Hittite. ...
And when Jacob had made an end of commanding his sons,
he gathered up his feet into the bed, and yielded up the
ghost, and was gathered unto his people.

(Genesis 49: 30, 33)

Again, Jacob is gathered 'unto his people', not explicitly unto his God. On the orders of his son Joseph, Jacob was embalmed (a rare occurrence of this practice in Judaism) and carried, in a great procession, out of Egypt to Canaan and buried, in accordance with Jacob's instructions, at Machpelah. Joseph too was embalmed and 'put in a coffin in Egypt', to be taken by Moses (Genesis 50: 26) and buried in Shechem in a parcel of ground which became 'the inheritance of the children of Joseph' (Joshua 24: 32). Joshua was buried 'in the border of his inheritance' (Joshua 24: 30) near Mount Ephraim, in an oddly imprecise location. Burial is the title to the land, and the tomb the proclamation of its extent. Indeed, the Hebrew word for the place of burial is also the word for dwelling.

The embalmings of Jacob and Joseph were unusual, and occur nowhere else in the Jewish record: they are probably a reflection of the 'Egyptian' location of the deaths. Apart from this, these are the exemplary and quintessential death events of late Iron Age, semi-nomadic Israelite society – its thanatological and historical monuments. There is the concern for 'inheritance', that is the staking out (in the most sacred way) of perpetual rights of occupation, an occupation more firmly established by inhumance than by any other form of corpse-disposal. Indeed, so important was this that it almost inevitably gave rise, as Bloch-Smith has shown, to a veritable 'cult of the dead' in Iron Age Judah, in which part of the function of the dynastic Patriarchs was to exercise their privilege of access to the deity in defence of the very patrimony they had established. The dead were spoken to and fed; figurines and other intermediaries, such as prophets (see Isaiah 8: 19), were used to contact the dead. Tombs were equipped with foodstuffs, water-jugs, lamps, oils, perfumes and spices. 'In sum', writes Bloch-Smith,

> The ancestral dead with supernatural powers, residing in the tomb which constituted a physical claim to the patrimony, made the cult of the dead an integral aspect of Judahite and probably also Israelite society.
>
> (1992b: 222)

This 'use' of the dead, no matter how 'idolatrous' it appeared to strict monotheists, remained a permanent source of tension in the development of Jewish thanatology.

The role of 'the ancestors' (i.e. the dead) also determined, or reflected, gender relationships in the developing Jewish society. It is of course the male kin who are regarded as the proper custodians of the body and the overseers of a proper disposal of the dead; there is generally an indifference in the matter of death to the role of women, about whose deaths considerably less concern is exhibited. Ancestors are men. The burials of the Patriarchs are, however, couple-burials. All three Patriarchs are accompanied by their wives, although Jacob's favourite wife Rachel is, in some accounts, buried at Ramah among the 'Graves of the Children of Israel' where, unusually for either men or women, her grave was marked by a stone pillar erected by Jacob (Hastings 1914: 783; Genesis 48: 7; Genesis 35: 20). Absalom (2 Samuel 18: 18) erected a pillar – in Hebrew a 'hand-phallus' – for himself because he had no son to keep his name in remembrance. Over and above the honouring of the wife and mother is, in the tomb-proclamation of marriage, the expression of heirs and fruitfulness, of progeny and therefore of ownership and possession – of the importance, therefore, of proper relations between the generations, which required an identifiable burial place.

Much earlier Yahweh had been unforgiving about two of Aaron's sons (Nadab and Abihu) who had offended him. They had interfered with the sacrifice and were immediately burned to death by Yahweh for so doing. They were then, on Moses' command, taken 'from before the sanctuary out of the camp ... in their coats', and Moses forbade Aaron and his two other sons from mourning for them: 'and Aaron held his peace' (Leviticus 10: 1–6). These two sons of Aaron were denied a proper burial or even a burial at all, the worst of all fates. To be unburied is to be totally cast out, both out of the company of men (born and unborn) and out of the company of God. It is the punishment for only the greatest of sins: the *Sefer Ha-Aggadah* sees in this story a further emphasis on the importance of kinship in establishing the proper moral community. The behaviour of the sons was a threat to the entire society: 'Woe unto the wicked! They render not only themselves guilty, they bestow guilt upon their children and their children's children unto the end of all generations' (Bialik and Ravnitzky 1992: 548.116).

There is in the positive exemplary deaths of the Patriarchs, and *per contra* in the negative exemplary deaths of Nadab and Abihu, a sense of the absolute necessity of preparation and good timing, of avoiding death through illness, offence or accident. Jacob, for example, knew that he was about to die (Genesis 47: 29), and had time to make Joseph promise to take him to his burying place at Mamre and to deliver himself of a very detailed account of the qualities and destinies of his numerous sons. Only then did he gather 'up his feet into the bed and yield up his ghost' (Genesis 48–9). Moses, too, is given ample warning about his approaching death (Deuteronomy 31: 14), giving him plenty of time to write an admonitory song, to finish his Five Books, and to prepare Joshua and Israel for what was to come and himself for the perhaps ungenerous treatment by the God who had known him 'face to face' (Deuteronomy 34: 10). Moses is indeed buried, by God, within sight of the land he is not to enter, and at 120 years old 'his eye was not dim, nor his natural force abated' (Deuteronomy 34: 10). He seems to have died, that is, according to plan – God's plan – and it is entirely appropriate that there followed thirty days of mourning by the children of Israel encamped on the plains of Moab. The death of Moses is unique, certainly in the fact that he was buried by God. Neither was he 'gathered to his fathers' (as he clearly could have been) but has no known grave. This, though, gives the territory-claiming competence of his burial a very great scope indeed: the Promised Land, all of it. In that sense his death and burial share with those of the Patriarchs the character of individual deaths with a collective purpose, the creation of a record of occupancy and ownership, of a moral as well as a geographical journey, of a people as well as of their leaders.

The complicated story of Saul's death and eventual burial makes the point. Saul had been denied the dignified death, a proper 'gathering in' to his people. Saul and three of his sons were found, by the Philistines, dead upon the battlefield. They cut off his head, stripped him, advertised the fact of his death and fastened his body (and those of his sons) to the city walls of Beth-Shan. From here they were stolen by the people of Jabesh-Gilead. David recovered the bodies, burnt them and buried the bones under a tree, fasting then for seven days (1 Samuel 31: 8–13). Another version (2 Samuel 21: 13–14) has the eventual burial of Saul, by David, taking place in a sepulchre, after which 'God was entreated for the land' which was suffering from a drought. In this rather confused story, God makes it clear that the drought is a consequence of the inappropriate manner of Saul's death and burial: the *Sefer Ha-Aggadah* comments on the way in which this problem was solved:

> And the Lord said: 'It is because of Saul, because he was not mourned in the manner required by law' (2 Sam. 21:1). The Holy One asked David: 'David, is he not the Saul who was anointed with the oil of anointing? Is he not the Saul in whose day no idolatry was practised in Israel? Is he not the Saul whose portion in Heaven is with Samuel the Prophet? Yet you are in the Land and he is outside it.' At

once David got busy and gathered all the elders and notables of Israel. They crossed the Jordan, came to Jabesh-Gilead, and found the bones of Saul and his son Jonathan – bones over which worms had exercised no power. They took the bones, put them in a coffin, and went back across the Jordan. Then David commanded that Saul's coffin be borne through the territory of each and every tribe. Upon the coffin's arrival in a tribe's territory, the entire tribe – men, their sons and daughters as well as their wives – came out and paid affectionate tribute to Saul and his sons, thus discharging the obligation of loving-kindness to the dead. When the Holy One saw that Israel had shown such loving-kindness, he, immediately filled with compassion, sent down rain.

(Bialik and Ravnitzky 1992: 117.80)

It is perhaps possible to see in this parade of the body of Saul a 'cult of the dead' – it would certainly have seemed to be efficacious, and Saul was himself familiar with summoning up spirits for assistance. Equally, and perhaps more importantly, the episode shows the importance of proper burial for the solidity of Jewish society, and for the strength of its relationship with its cosmos-controlling God. This was a matter neither of a 'cult of the dead' nor of a 'cult of the monarch'. At every level, the proprieties of death and interment were the foundation of the moral and material welfare of individual, kinsfolk and tribe. There would be no Israel without the proper burial of the Patriarchs of Israel and the acceptance by God of their properly attested heirs.

We are told, indirectly, a great deal about the actual funerals and burials of the Patriarchs and others. It is possible to construct, from biblical and other sources, a picture of early Jewish funerary practice. In Jeremiah 16, in which God is denouncing his unfaithful people, we have (in the negation) an account of the nature of Israelite burial:

Thus saith the Lord concerning the sons and concerning the daughters that are born in this place, and concerning their mothers that bare them, and concerning their fathers that begat them in this land: They shall die of grievous deaths; they shall not be lamented; neither shall they be buried; but they shall be as dung upon the face of the earth; and they shall be consumed by the sword, and by famine; and their carcases shall be meat for the fowls of heaven, and for the beasts of the earth.

For thus saith the Lord, Enter not into the house of mourning, neither go to lament nor bemoan them; for I have taken away my peace from this people. ... Both the great and the small shall die in this land: they shall not be buried, neither shall men lament for them, nor cut themselves, nor make themselves bald for them: Neither shall men tear themselves for them in mourning, to comfort them for the dead; neither shall men give them the cup of consolation to drink for their father or for their mother. ... Therefore will I cast you out of this land into a land that ye know not, neither ye nor your fathers; and there shall ye serve other gods day and night; where I will not show you favour.

(Jeremiah 16: 3–7, 13)

Jeremiah's furious anguish is perhaps exceptional, but numerous texts in the Bible assert, for example, the overwhelming imperative to bury the dead and to do so quickly. Deuteronomy 21: 23 insists that: 'Thou shalt bury him on that day' (i.e. the day of the death). The Mishnah confirms this (in the context of a criminal put to death) and adds:

everyone that suffers his dead to remain overnight transgresses a negative command; but if he had suffered it to remain by reason of the honour due to it, to bring for it a coffin and burial clothes, he does not thereby commit transgression.

(The Mishnah 1967: Sanh. 6.5, 391)

The tomb was not immediately closed, there being a three-day visiting period to ensure that death had in fact taken place (*Jewish Encyclopaedia* 1916: vol. 3, 434). The grave, if in the ground, was to be marked 'by whiting mingled with water and poured over the grave (to give warning of uncleanness)' (The Mishnah 1967: Maaser Sheni, 5.1, 80). This was re-done every year. In an interesting remark on the rights and responsibilities of an executed criminal's relatives, the Mishnah (in what seems to be an interpolation) makes the following rather moving comment:

When the flesh had wasted away they gathered together the bones and buried them in their own place [the family burial place]. ... [After he was put to death] the kinsmen came and greeted the judges and the witnesses as if to say: 'We have naught against you in our hearts, for you have judged the judgement of truth'. And they used not to make open lamentation but they went mourning, for mourning has place in the heart alone.

(The Mishnah 1967: Sanh. 6.6, 391)

The *behaviour* (lamentation) had to be regulated (in this case forbidden), but the Rabbis were humane and sensible enough to know that *mourning* was a private concern. To be unburied was the ultimate disgrace – hence Jeremiah's violent threats ('dung upon the face of the earth'), and hence the provision in the Mishnah for burial of even those who had been judicially executed and for a decent respect for the feelings (as well as the responsibilities) of the deceased criminal's kinsfolk.

The same concern applied to the bodies of enemies killed in war. They were buried, partly out of compassion, partly because the unburied body polluted the earth, partly because there was some thought that the process of decay in the earth was painful to the corpse, and for that reason a means of atonement (*Jewish Encyclopaedia* 1916: vol. 3, 432). Jewish attitudes to their own military 'heroes', such as David and Joshua, are quite distinctive: military leaders are accepted, rather than venerated – they are denied the status conferred upon statesmen and, especially, religious prophets and sages. David, for example, though beloved of the Lord, is not allowed to build the Temple because he has killed in war (see below).

The requirement of quick burial, as well as the nature of the tombs, pointed to the need for tomb preparation well before any death. In the Mishnah we read, as part of a list of prohibitions during festivals:

They may not hew out tomb-niches or tombs during mid-festival, but old niches may be re-fashioned during mid-festival. During mid-festival they may dig a grave [this being less work than a rock-tomb] and make a coffin while the corpse lies in the self-same courtyard [proving that the work is urgent]. R. Judah forbids it unless a man has the boards sawn in readiness.

(The Mishnah 1967: Moed Katan 1.6, 208)

Whether with criminals or with ordinary people, the task of organising the burial belongs to the kin. The father of Judas Maccabeus, Mattathias, 'died in the hundred and sixth year, and his sons buried him in the sepulchres of his fathers at Modin, and all Israel made great lamentation for him' (1 Maccabees 2: 70). The synagogue-based Burial Societies are probably a feature of Talmudic times, and are to some extent a rationalisation of the general injunction on all Jews to participate in the burial of the dead. Thus, for example, R. Judah argues:

> A man who sees a corpse on the way to burial and does not accompany it shows no concern for the assertion 'He that mocketh the poor blasphemeth his Maker' (Proverbs 15: 5). And if he accompanies it, what is his reward? To him apply the words 'He that is gracious unto the poor lendeth unto the Lord' (Proverbs 19: 7) and 'He that is gracious unto the needy honoreth Him' (Proverbs 14: 31).
>
> (Bialik and Ravnitzky 1992: 685.411)

The task of burial, incumbent upon the whole community, was a particular duty of the family, and this extended to an obligation to note when a person was about to 'go the way of all the earth' (Joshua 23: 14) and to elicit from him a confession of his sins (Bender 1894: 664) and to give him time to make proper disposal of his property and patrimony. The 'last words' were crucial, as the dying man prepared to go to eternity; and custom required that where possible he be attended by ten males. Under no circumstances was a dying man to be left alone (ibid.: 669). The dying man became unclean (i.e. a corpse) only after his soul had gone (The Mishnah 1967: Ohol. 1.6). Care had to be taken in the necessary closing of the eyes at death (Genesis 46: 4; Bender 1895: 101):

> Our masters taught: He who closes [the eyes of a dying man] at the point of death is a murderer, as may be understood by analogy with a lamp that is flickering out; if one presses one's finger upon it, the lamp goes out at once. We have been taught that R. Simeon ben Gamaliel said: He who wishes the eyes of a dead man to close should blow wine into his nostrils, apply oil between his eyelids, or take hold of his two big toes, and the eyes will close of themselves.
>
> (Bialik and Ravnitzky 1992: 405.684; The Mishnah 1967: Shab. 23.5, 120)

The corpse is embraced or kissed (Genesis 50: 1). The body of the mourner might be 'mortified' (i.e. lacerated) and more usually clothes rent, and the *Shouphar* sounded to announce the death so that everyone could begin to plan for the obsequies. For three days close relatives were forbidden to work and were to weep. The home of the dead person became, in particular for seven days after the funeral, a house of mourning. Consolation was offered, as were mourning gestures (such as crying and wailing or face-veiling or putting earth on the head or sleeping on the floor) as witness of grief and sympathy (Joshua 7: 6 and elsewhere). Men would cut their hair and shave their beards (Job 1: 20), although Leviticus (19: 27–8) regards such things as tainted with paganism and forbids them. The 'cup of consolation' referred to in Jeremiah, above, was part of the food brought to the relatives of the deceased, as their own house was unclean and could not therefore be used to cook food.

The body was cleansed, sometimes with water infused with the spices which were also carried in the funeral procession, and dressed in white, unornamented linen. The Mishnah, in commenting on rules for the Sabbath, says:

> They may make ready [on the Sabbath] all that is needful for the dead, and anoint it and wash it, provided that they do not move any member of it. They may draw the mattress away from beneath it and let it lie on the sand that it may be the longer preserved; they may bind up the chin, not in order to raise it but that it may not sink lower. … They may not close a corpse's eyes on the Sabbath; nor may they do so on a weekday when the soul is departing; and he that closes the eyes [of the dying man] at the moment when the soul is departing is a shedder of blood.
>
> (The Mishnah 1967: Shab. 23.5, 120)

Like all societies, the Jews experienced problems with the cost of funerals, and there was a problem of bodies being abandoned by their kin because of the burden of the burial. Rabbi Gamaliel dealt with this very effectively: he had himself carried out in cheap linen shrouds and 'thereafter, all the people followed his practice by carrying out their dead in inexpensive linen shrouds'. In this way the biers of the rich and the poor were standardised so that the poor did not feel humiliated (Bialik and Ravnitzky 1992: 686.418).

The corpse was then taken on a bier carried by 'shoulderers', in bare feet so that they would not trip. The shoulderers had the right to trample over sown fields (The Mishnah 1967: Baba Bathra, 6.7, n.2, 375). The 'shoulderers' changed frequently, so as to give as many as possible the chance to share in the honour of carrying the dead. The conventional number of stops (or 'stations') was seven, and the burial places had a field to which the mourners would direct their procession (The Mishnah 1967: Meg. 4.3, 206). As they walked, they recited Psalm 91. Such work justified an exemption from saying the *Shema* and the *Tefilah*:

> They that bear the bier and they that relieve them, and they that relieve these, they that go before and they that follow after the bier – they that are needful for the bier are exempt, but they that are not needful are not exempt. When they have buried the dead and returned, if they can begin [the *Shema*] and finish it before reaching the Row they begin it. ... Of them that stand in the Row, they of the inner line are exempt, but they of the outer line are not exempt.
>
> (The Mishnah 1967: Berakoth 3.1–2, 4)

The Row was the double line of friends of the mourners, between whom the mourners passed on returning from the burial.

There would be no recourse to 'the synagogue' for a burial service, if only because at this time synagogues were places for reading scripture rather than for accommodating religious or liturgical practices. Mishnah Megillah 3.3, 205 seems to specifically exclude synagogues from being used in the funeral process: with some exception for the corpses of scholars (whose place of study would have been the synagogue), the corpse on its bier would have been taken direct to the cemetery. The procession was accompanied by trumpets and lamentations from wailing women. Mourners, some of them 'professional', and the people follow. Lamentations, sometimes also becoming 'professionalised' or formalised, were sung by men or women, although relatives (such as, for example, a father for a son) were always expected to carry out this task themselves. As the lament became more formalised, it became the particular task of women, who would then teach their daughters. R. Judah was of the view that even the poorest man should provide for his wife's funeral 'no less than two flutes and at least one professional female mourner' (Bialik and Ravnitzky 1992: 687.430). Pieter Van der Horst, in a study of ancient Jewish epitaphs, states that 40 per cent of them were of women; while this is still statistically 'skewed', it would appear to be a much higher proportion than in funerary cultures of Greece and Rome (Van der Horst 1991: 102; Pomeroy 1997). Women were certainly central to the mourning side of funerals.

De Vaux, from whom some of the above is taken, takes the view that in these laments there is little in the way of religious feeling, simply 'deep human emotion' (De Vaux 1974: 61). The laments are, he says, eulogies, a tradition reaching its finest expression in the book of Lamentations.

For close kin of the deceased, the period of seven days intense mourning was followed by twenty-three days of less intense mourning. In the case of burial in a rock-sepulchre, the bones were after one year gathered together and placed in a stone or earthenware box (The Mishnah 1967: Pesahim 8 n., 148. Opinions (see The Mishnah 1967: Moed Katan 1.5, 208) differed as to whether, in the case of one's mother and father, this gathering of the bones was an occasion for rejoicing (R. Meir) or mourning (R. Jose). The lengthy process of the burial and mourning could cause complications. In the Mishnah (1967: Moed Katan 3.5, 7, 210) we read of problems caused by a burial taking place during a (religious) festival. Again, this passage is instructive in what it implies about the ordinary processes of grief and lamentation:

> If a man buried his dead three days before the Feast, the rule of seven days mourning is annulled for him. ... During a Feast none save the near of kin may rend their garments and bare the shoulder and be given the food of the mourners; and food of the mourners must be taken with the couches set up [in the usual way, i.e. not 'turned up' as for mourning]. ... And they may not say the Benediction of the Mourners during the Feast, but they stand in the Row and offer consolation.
>
> (The Mishnah 1967: Moed Katan 3.7, 210)

From time to time concern arose about possible abuses arising out of over-lavish eating and drinking in the grieving process. Zechariah (most likely Deutero-Zechariah) is insistent that family mourning should avoid the problem of the mixing of the sexes by keeping female and male mourners apart. Bialik and Ravnitzky (1992: 426.687) describe the unfortunate result of a relaxation of the limit on the number of glasses of wine to be drunk in the house of a mourner: the mourning party became drunk. Such problems to do with food and burial had exercised Isaiah, who complained about and agrees to do so, thereby allowing God to draw his soul to heaven. This is no longer the inscrutable, unenquirable God. The Abraham of the Testament is no Job.

There are, inevitably, various views on the standing of this apocryphon, but it is part of a very large body of Jewish and early Christian apocrypha and pseudepigrapha which indicate a substantially altered view of the relationships between God and his suffering humans. Descriptions of heaven and of angels, and of the ends of worlds, for example, make graphic appearances in writings such as the Testaments of the Twelve Patriarchs and the Sibylline Oracles. God's promise of both collective and individual resurrection is made very explicit:

> And after these things shall Abraham and Isaac and Jacob arise
> unto life, and I and my brethren shall be chiefs of the tribes of
> Israel ... all in order. ... And the Lord blessed Levi, and the
> Angel of the Presence, me; the powers of glory, Simeon;
> the heaven, Reuben; the earth, Issachar; the sea, Zebulun; the
> mountains, Joseph; the tabernacle, Benjamin; the luminaries,
> Dan; Eden, Naphtali; the sun, Gad; the moon, Asher.
> And ye shall be the people of the Lord, and have one tongue;
> And there shall be no spirit of deceit of Beliar,
> For he shall be cast into the fire forever.
> And they who have died in grief shall arise in joy,
> And they who were made poor for the Lord's sake shall be made
> rich,
> And they who are put to death for the Lord's sake shall awake
> to life.
> And the harts of Jacob shall run in joyfulness,
> And the eagles of Israel shall fly in gladness;
> And all the people shall glorify the Lord for ever.
> (The Testaments of the Twelve Patriarchs: Testament of Judah,
> in Charles 1908: 324)

Authors such as John Sawyer, Gila Shmueli, Chris Rowland and Alan Segal see a radical change in the tone and tenor of life in the 800 years or so bisected by the birth of Christ. These years see a series of Jewish revolts, short-lived victories and long-term defeats. What to Aristides was the Pax Romana, was to the Jews in their several Judaisms the tyranny of an alien empire which oppressed and eventually destroyed the Jewish way of life – or perhaps the Jewish *ways* of life. Jewish history becomes a tragedy of such enormity that the rationality and sedateness of the biblical barriers to an extended discussion of death, of its place in creation and in the role and the very point or purpose ('the Face') of God, are shattered. Jewish society is fragmented by war, destroyed by defeat in war, and when some kind of peace descends it is of a type that creates yet further problems of identity and orthodoxy, problems of fission as much as of fusion. A community which sees so many of its people killed in war cannot unquestioningly accept Job's 'though he slay me, yet will I trust in him' (Job 13: 15).

Emerging out of the wars and killings of these early centuries is that most extraordinarily enduring and potent icon, that of the martyr-hero, the person who, in giving rather than taking life, in suffering rather than in inflicting suffering, attains a degree of exemplary salvific competence well in excess of 'ordinary' martyrs and of 'ordinary' heroes. Such a figure becomes the symbolic pole around which all deaths are measured and around which a whole new dimension of salvific living and sacrificial dying is constructed. This icon comes to be the moral code through which the oldest texts are read and re-read, and becomes one of the dominant figures of the centuries under discussion, for both Jews and Christians. The martyr-hero, in various permutations, can be read in, or into, the most ancient stories and traditions, such as those of Isis and Osiris, of Enkidu and Gilgamesh, and of Abraham and Isaac, the elaboration of the story of sacrifice that is known as the Akedah. The martyr-hero is a figure familiar to us in the twentieth century, through the tragedies of the Great War of 1914–18, a topic to which I will return at the end of this book. The Great War's reformulation of attitudes to death can be seen and read in the hundreds of thousands of European war memorials, the genuinely demotic texts of twentieth-century CE thanatology. These memorials, in epigraphy and iconography, reach back into very ancient symbols and mythologies, so that for example the words of Pericles at the annual Athenian public funeral for the war dead in 431–0 BCE were used by the Public Orator at Gettysburg and are to be found inscribed on the Scottish National War Memorial in Edinburgh Castle. At times of war and conflict, we see the mobilisation or remobilisation of the martyr-hero, probably the single most potent (male) icon to come out of our common culture, dominating the thanatology and soteriology of Western or Euro-Christendom (see Davies 1995).

Wars and conflict, whether in the Roman centuries or in our own, do not simply add something to an ordinarily pacific culture. They reveal the pre-existing patterns of power and violence within that 'ordinary' culture, and explode them into a new synthesis of life and death. As Susan Niditch puts it:

> Portrayals of war reveal a culture's fundamental values. ... Attitudes to war are a cultural map of sorts, war a world in itself in which relationships between life and death, god and human, one's own group and the other, and men and women all hang in the balance.
>
> (Niditch 1993b: 43)

To most of us, even 'ordinary' Jewish history – with its actively jealous God, its punitive Nature, its berating prophets and its endless avalanche of ravening enemies – seems tragic enough: it is extraordinary that in the face of such experience Jewish 'orthodoxy' could maintain a belief in monotheism, and its consequent and necessary denial of the existence of dualism or of a 'God of Death'. Dualism is one answer to the problems of a society destroyed by war and killing, of a society experiencing the end of collective and individual flourishing. It is, however, an answer vetoed by strict monotheism: there is no Jewish pantheon, no malevolent Jewish 'Mot' on whom can be placed the responsibility for (collective and individual) pain, disaster and death. The tension therefore remains, the huge tension between the human experience of war, death and suffering and the postulated existence of a beneficent and all-powerful God. One answer, retaining monotheism, is the one resolutely insisted upon in the 'official' Bible, which accepts the unquestionable taciturnity and opacity of God, his sheer unavailability to human questioning: 'The Lord gave, and the Lord hath taken away; blessed be the name of the Lord' (Job 1: 21) and 'Though he slay me, yet will I trust in him' (Job 13: 15). This is a tolerable (if remarkably stoic-heroic) posture *for an individual* as long as the purposes of this freely acting God do indeed, in their own inscrutable way, seem to be aimed at providing security, a land flowing with milk and honey, *for the collectivity* – his chosen people. In essence, this was (and is) the 'official' message of the Jewish Bible.

This 'reticence' was unable to hold against historical realities. For at least some Jews – faced by the Seleucid, Antiochian and Roman destruction of the Jewish world – resurrection at the hands of God, in and into his world, became one way of retaining a belief in monotheism along with a belief in the justice of God and in a just salvation. Another way, that of collective salvation on this earth *or the next* (there is functionally not much to choose between them) can remain in place, for thanatologies have generally been a mixture of alternatives rather than a logical choice of one of them. What tends to produce an inclination to the first option, of individual resurrection, is the historical experience and example of war and martyrdom, experienced collectively perhaps, but symbolised most adamantly in the exemplary iconic deaths and resurrections of particular soldiers and particular martyrs. These icons can be kept separate through a parallel proclamation of self-assertion on the one hand (the victorious soldier) and of self-sacrifice on the other (the self-giving martyr), but it is when they are conflated that the two icons carry the most powerful eschatological charge. The conflation also makes it possible to cross the gender lines, and indeed some of the most potent martyr-heroes are women.

Jewish traditions about war, death in war and appropriate behaviour at such times differ in certain very important ways from the later-developing Christian tradition – the Christian tradition, when fully developed, is closer to that of the State of Israel than to that of the Rabbis. True, the making of war is a large part of the Hebrew Bible. The Torah can be read as a record of military actions, war and killing, and of lives given and taken in both aggressive and defensive military action. Jewish history, not to mention the history of the post-1948 State of Israel, can be similarly constructed. The interpretation of this record, an interpretation which is in practice part and parcel of its very telling, reveals a complex attitude to both the 'hero' and to the 'martyr' tradition. Soldiers, even successful generals and leaders, are not the major carriers of the Biblical-Rabbinic story. The whole trope of king/priest/prophet can be seen as an effort to locate real virtue elsewhere than in a military tradition, that is to say in 'righteousness'. The Midrash tells us that:

> The entire reward of the righteous is kept ready for them
> for the Hereafter, and the Holy One, blessed be He, shows
> them while yet in the world the reward He is to give them
> in the future: their souls are satisfied and they fall asleep.
> (The Midrash Rabbah, 1977: vol.1, Genesis 549)

Military heroes, in the sense that their exploits and deaths acquire a salvific competence, are *not* a major feature of the Torah. Such heroes, no matter how successful militarily, are always evaluated within the framework of 'righteousness'. Righteousness itself, in the military sphere, is seen as an adjunct of the Lord, 'the Lord who *is* a man of war' (Exodus 15: 3). Louis Feldman, for example, notes that while for

Josephus, Abraham's attack on the Five Kings of Sodom is 'a human victory of a masterful general with lessons in it for the student of military science', the Rabbis are 'utterly divergent from this picture ... Abraham's victory is really a victory for God' (Feldman 1984: 47). Similarly, the newly chosen Joshua is required to subject himself to divine control, the only way to victory: 'and he shall stand before Eleazer the priest, who shall ask counsel for him after the judgement of Urim before the Lord' (Numbers 27: 21). Joshua is buried in a rather laconic way, the Rabbis later asserting that this was because, post-conquest, the tribes of Israel were so preoccupied with sorting out land boundaries and property shares to be too concerned with a proper burial for their dead military leader: military prowess is not highly valued in Judaism (Bialik and Ravnitzky 1992: 107, 12). The super-hero and perhaps martyr Samson is a man driven more by his penis than by a sense of honour, and his self-sacrificial death is but small return for a wasted life. David, greatest of the military leaders of Israel, is explicitly denied the privilege of building the Temple because he had been a soldier. Sadly, David tells his son Solomon (*shelemo*, *shalom*, peaceful one) that:

> The Lord came to me saying, 'Thou hast shed blood abundantly, and hast made great wars: thou shalt not build a house unto my name, because thou hast shed much blood upon the earth in my sight'.
>
> (1 Chronicles 22: 8)

The second-century CE hero Bar Kokhba ('Son of a Star'), in what was until 1948 the last attempt to restore an independent Jewish state, was cursed by God because he assaulted and killed R. Eleazar (The Midrash Rabbah 1977: vol. 3, Lamentations 159). The collective suicide of Eleazar ben Yair and his followers at Masada, commemorated every year by the IDF Armoured Regiments, is passed over in silence in the Talmud and Mishnah, and in the Midrash Rabbah. This may be because the Rabbis regarded Eleazar as a terrorist, but more likely we see in this attitude a reflection and emphasis on the Jewish insistence on the sanctity of life, an insistence which only grudgingly provides legitimisation for killing, be it of others or of oneself in 'martyrdom'. 'To live' (and not to kill) is a *mitzvah*, so that suicide and killing others is permitted only when murder, incest (including adultery) and idolatry are the alternatives. The Ten Martyrs, all of them rabbis killed in the Common Era for practising their faith, die to avoid idolatry. Eleazar ben Yair and his followers at Masada lacked this legitimisation.

There is running through all of this the Jewish treatment of the story of Abraham and Isaac, the Akedah, to which we will return. There is also another tradition, that of sensible compromise or even of creative 'tricking', in which heroic and possibly fatal posturing is shunned in exchange for a more practical, if less heroic, survival, or in which some level of subterfuge may be employed to obtain victory. 'Transgress', states the Talmud, 'and suffer not death' (The Midrash Rabbah 1977: Sanhedrin 502–6), although the text which follows makes this a most difficult doctrine to understand.

In order to see how the later-developing Christian attitude to war differs from that of Rabbinic Judaism, it is perhaps sufficient to note that in Jewish teaching killing defiles, as Numbers 31 makes very clear. The soldier-killer-heroes, however well-intentioned, must be purified by a sacrificial ritual which propitiates Yahweh by locating war within his rules and purpose. They must be saved from their acts, rather than by them.

It is the case, however, that the wars and massacres inflicted by the Romans on the Jews effected a substantial change in emphasis, if not a major reformulation of Jewish attitudes to the afterlife. John J. Collins and G.W.E. Nickelsburg, in *Ideal Figures in Ancient Judaism* (1980), endeavour to construct for the period between Alexander and Hadrian, and from the literature originating in the Jewish homeland, a set of 'ideal' or exemplary Jewish figures. Inevitably, no general typology is advanced, but the authors and editors note the predominance of *righteous men* from the past such as Noah, Daniel and those in Pseud-Philo; of *messiahs*, that is to say men from the future, and of *'contemporaneous' carriers of the Jewish experience*, such as the scribes Daniel and Aaron in Ben Sira. In all of this, the texts move back and forth between old and new tradition, recreating the ideal figures for the felt exigencies of the time as well as in terms of respect for the Jewish story. Military men are not a dominant type. The martyr does however make an emphatic appearance, in the shape of the mother and her seven sons in 2 and 4 Maccabees. In this story, the very real and graphic physical destruction of the bodies of the young men is explicitly compensated for by the promise of a physical reassembly and resurrection (2 Maccabees 7: 14–30). In addition, writes Alan Segal, it is in this text that God is first described as having the capacity to create *ex nihilo*: Segal comments that

At the end of this war, the victorious Judas Maccabeus rededicated the Temple and instituted the Day of Nicanor, the Antiochan general whose head (or thumbs and big toes, in one version) he had hung upon the wall of the citadel (2 Maccabees: 32–6). The head (or thumbs and toes) and the Day of Nicanor are war memorials – commemorating a national victory – of heroes and of martyrs. In the light of the later defeat, martyrs rather than military heroes become the more consolatory of exemplary figures.

The four centuries between 200 BCE and 200 CE provided the symbolic material for the creation of the martyr-hero, for a resolute view of death as resurrection, as triumph through and over death. The tradition, as lived and remembered history, became a reservoir of ideas and aspirations, of images of the virtuous life and the good death. As icon, as literary trope, the four centuries produced a common language of exemplary death. These examples rapidly became myth, as sects, messianic groups and congeries of demoralised and hunted people ('living in the mountains in the manner of beasts', 2 Maccabees 5: 27) sought to find in apocalypses and eschatologies, in suicidal heroisms and sanguinary martyrdoms, a form of revenge upon their enemies and a form of solace for their suffering. 'Judaism', always problematically conceived and never politically well-founded, became a dispute about orthodoxy, giving rise to a set of disparate and often competing groups: Sadducees, Pharisees, Essenes, Zealots, Gnostics, Charismatics, Miracle-workers – and 'Christians'. These mental and political struggles find written expression in a flood of extra-canonical texts, Testaments and Ascensions, Apocalypses and War Scrolls, in which the sedate formularies of conventional religious writing are overwhelmed by what Freud would perhaps call the return of the repressed, as the martyr-heroes of a defeated and ground-down world sought, in and through their victorious martyrdom, to proclaim the terrible risen glory of the world that was to come. Chris Rowland puts it well:

> Once the contrast between social and political realities stood in the sharpest possible contrast to the glorious future promised in the Scriptures and echoed in writings of the period, the situation led to disillusionment, a narrowing of religious vision or the conviction that change was needed. That hopes were entertained not merely as articles of faith but also as part of a programme of action is confirmed by the Dead Sea Scrolls. In the War Scroll from Qumran (1QM) we find there the belief that the might of God's enemies

would be overthrown in a battle in which the angelic legions would come to the aid of the sons of light. The fantastic detail of the preparations outlined in the War Scroll gives some indication of the frame of mind of some groups as they entertained hopes of participating in an armed struggle against the enemies of Israel.

(Rowland 1985: 18)

Recently, under the impact of the discovery of the Dead Sea Scrolls, a lot has been written about 'eschatology'; it is clear that these texts, together with their re-reading of older received texts, represent an enhanced moral dramatisation of the world and the cosmos, of life and the meaning of death. Richard Horsley and John Hanson (1985) have described in considerable detail the extraordinary variety of popular movements, violent sects and messianic groups that assembled and struggled around this cultural, religious and political furore. One has simply to contrast, for example, the biblical description of the death of the Patriarch Abraham with the Testament of Abraham quoted above, the terse comment on the death of Joshua in Joshua 24 with 2 Maccabees 12 (above), or read the description in Josephus of the death of the martyr-hero Eleazer at Masada, or read the War Scroll of the Essenes, to see how the moral framework of death is pulled out of a modesty towards God and an almost secular concern for a good long life and steady build-up of heirs and property into the world-denying, cosmos-claiming eschatological once-and-for-all self-killing gesture of the martyr-heroes, now become ordinary. Resurrection was no longer a matter of 'luck', as the Beth Shearim epitaph would have us believe. It was a matter of necessity if the injustice of the Roman world was to be transcended. Jewish apocalypticism and Christ and Christianity were part of the response to this world of violent and powerful empires.

At this point we have to step away from the world of Syria Palaestina into the larger world and world-empire of which it was but a small part. As Elisabeth Schussler Fiorenza puts it:

Whereas the Jesus movement in Palestine was an alternative prophetic renewal movement within Israel, the Christian movement was a religious missionary movement within the Greco-Roman world, preaching an alternative religious vision and practising a counter-cultural lifestyle. Both movements created tensions and conflicts with respect to the dominant cultural ethos. But where the Jesus movement could appeal to Israel's tradition as its very own religious tradition over and against certain practices within Israel, the Christian movement as a new religious group intruded as an alien element into the dominant cultural-religious ethos of the Greco-Roman world.

(Fiorenza 1983: 100)

It is to this dominant ethos that I will now turn.

Figure 1 'Hail and farewell, Dionysius! Hail and farewell, Paramon!':
*c.*fourth century BCE grave slab, depicting a funeral meal, placed
in the entrance to the thirteenth century BCE tomb at
Orchomenos, Boeotia. Inside the main tomb is a second or third
century BCE Macedonian altar.

Figure 2 Termessos, Lycian-Galatia. Fifth to first century BCE necropolis, sarcophagi with roof-shaped lids used for primary burial.

Figure 3 Telmessos, Lycia (now Fethiye, Turkey). Fourth century BCE extramural necropolis. The tombs, all for men, are cut into the rock-face. Upper right is the tomb of Amytas, whose name is incised inside a benched chamber behind the façade.

Figure 4 Beth Shearim, near Tel Aviv, Israel. Jewish catacomb-necropolis, second to fourth centuries CE.

Figure 5 Jericho, Second Temple. Monumental tomb, together with ritual bath supplied with water by aqueduct. The courtyard was probably used for mourning and memorial services.

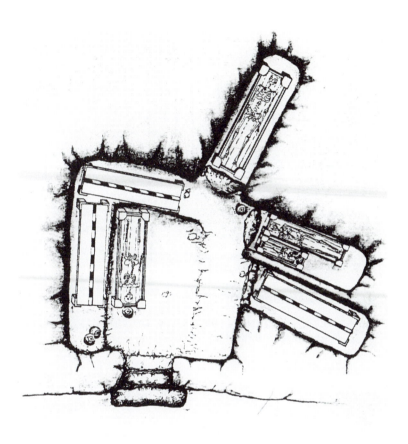

Figure 6 Jericho, Second Temple. Primary coffin burials in loculi, with one coffin in the 'pit' of the sealed tomb.

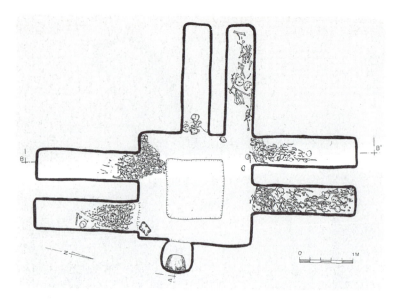

Figure 7 Jericho, Second Temple. Secondary burial with no trace of coffins or ossuaries, with the skulls placed on top of the piles of bones.

Figure 8 Alexandria, Tegran tomb, second century CE. Representation of a mummified corpse, under the winged sun-disc and attended by Isis and Nephthys.

Figure 9 Aphroditopolis (Atfih) Cemetery, south of Memphis. Roman-
period mummies with gold masks.

Figure 10 Hellenistic necropolis, near Ayios Philion, North Cyprus, with graves 'converted' by the addition of the Christian symbol, the fish.

Figure 11 'To his daughter Pervica': late second century CE Romano-Celtic gravestone, found at Great Chesters, Northern England.

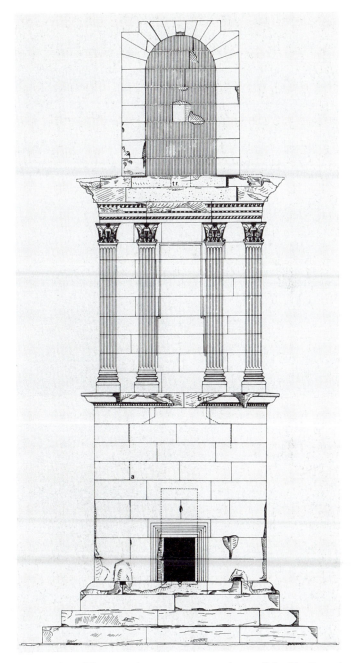

Figures 12 and 13 The second century CE mausoleum of the Flavii, at the Roman 'new town' of Cillium (now Kasserine, Tunisia).

Figure 14 Roman, second century CE. White marble cinerarium (ash container) in the form of a tomb. The gable shows a reclining sphinx, symbol of death, one paw resting on a basket with comic male and tragic female masks.

Part III

ROMANS AND GREEKS
A theodicy of good fortune?

> Before your empire everything was in confusion, topsy-
> turvy, and completely disorganised, but when you took
> charge, the confusion and faction ceased and there entered
> in universal order and a glorious light. ... Total security,
> universal and clear to all, has been given to the earth itself
> and those who inhabit it.
>
> (Aristides 1981: 96)

> There exists no idea of 'the sacred' in Rome.
>
> (Hornblower and Spawforth 1996: 1,307)

In this section, I will discuss 'death in the Greco-Roman world',
approaching it mainly through 'Roman' sources, i.e. the culture of the
Roman Empire, which of course includes much that is 'Hellenistic'
or 'Greek'. There is simply too much material to be able to 'track',
in any meaningful way, the evolution of Archaic and Classical Greek
or early Republican Roman thanatologies back to their Mycenean
and Etrurian origins and then forward into the Augustan and post-
Augustan era. My point of departure will be the world of the Late
Republic and the early Roman Empire, the world in which 'Hellenism'
was being moulded and reconfigured to the serious purposes of the
Roman world empire. 'The Greeks', then, will be essentially Greeks
within the Roman orbit, although the strength and competence of
the inheritance from the Greeks makes it seem more often than not
as if the Romans (like us!) were in *their* orbit.

9

ROMAN AND GREEK
PHILOSOPHIES OF DEATH

Parched with thirst am I, and dying.
Nay, drink of Me, the ever-flowing Spring
Where on the right is a fair cypress.
Who art thou? where art thou? – I am the son of Earth
and of star-filled Heaven,
But from Heaven alone is my house.
                    (A Greek prayer, in Breslin, undated: 4)

According to Hesiod, human beings in the Age of Gold lived a carefree, never-ageing life. The earth bore food automatically and there was no death, merely a falling asleep. However, quarrels with the gods, and indeed quarrels and killings amongst the gods, result in a radical deterioration of human life. The gods send floods, disease and earthquakes – and women (Pandora), created as a special evil for men, a punishment for Prometheus' stealing of fire, the symbol of power and creativity. Death comes also: human beings must die and go as shadows to the underworld (Grant and Kitzinger 1988: 870 ff.).

The quotation opening this chapter is from one of sixteen *lamellae* (tiny rectangular gold sheets placed along with other grave goods in cinerary urns) dating from the fourth century BCE to (the only Roman example) the third century CE. On them are to be found a kind of guidance for the soul as it seeks to locate itself in its new environment, the underworld, with new companions – and new dangers. The guidance varies in poetic style, but the lines 'I am the son of Earth/and of star-filled Heaven,/But from Heaven alone is my house' and the reference to thirst are clearly formulaic, rather like the standard exculpatory spells to be found in the Egyptian *Books of the Dead*. On the *lamellae* the soul is instructed to avoid the oblivion that would arise from over-indulgence in the spring by the cypress, for that spring is Lethe, the waters of forgetfulness, and to turn instead to the lake of Mnemosyne (Memory), whose waters, the waters of life, will elicit a favourable reception from the lords of the underworld. There are *two* paths in the underworld, one leading to oblivion, one to 'life'. The arriving 'person' has to make choices: the uncertainty of life, that is, continues after death. A version of the story is told in Plato's *Republic* when the soldier Er, dead in battle, returns from the Plain of Oblivion to this world. His return persuades Socrates and Glaucon that there is *hope for, but no guarantee* of immortality (Plato 1959: 387–401). If the formulae on the *lamellae* are correct, then hope lies in the acceptance by Mnemosyne of the dual nature of humanity, 'Son of Earth and the star-filled Heaven'.

'The universe', wrote Cicero optimistically, 'is a kind of city state belonging jointly to gods and men' (Cicero 1991: 65). Greek and Roman culture provided an almost endless series of myths and stories in which both the gods and humanity seem to be persistently testing the nature and strength of the boundaries between them. Of these boundaries, none was more important than that between mortality (the human condition) and immortality (the god condition). There is simply no let up in the efforts by human beings to transcend this boundary, no matter how poignantly each failure seemed to reinforce it. In this sense of the human condition, the myths of Hades, Persephone and Demeter, of Orpheus and Eurydice, of Adonis and Aphrodite, of Selene and Endymion, of Herakles and Dionysus, are myths of death and rebirth, of journeys into and out of the underworld, of transactions and transformations between gods and humans. In a variety of forms these ancient stories were reinvented and reinvigorated in the Roman Empire which subsumed both Classical and Hellenistic Greece, and added its own traditions to them.

It should be stressed that this Roman 'annexation' of ancient Greek myths was *a very deliberate affair*. In terms of funerary architecture and ornament, for example, whether on great mausolea or altars or on humbler sarcophagi, funerary urns or tombstones, the myths of gods and humans and their myriad entrances and exits into and out of worlds, overworlds and underworlds, reflect official Roman concern to regulate the mind-sets of the populace. So insistent was this concern that Paul Zanker is able to say that even on essentially private or familial funerary objects such as ash urns:

> It became impossible to find a means of individual expression. Sculptors and patrons had to try to formulate personal sentiments, if this was the goal at all, using the language of

imperial politics. Thus the scene of Aeneas and his family is employed on grave monuments as a symbol of personal piety and devotion, while the she-wolf with the infants Romulus and Remus, the embodiment of Roman pride and self-assurance, is transferred to funerary altars as a symbol of selflessness and love within the family.

(Zanker 1988: 278)

Did the Greeks Believe in their Myths?, asks Paul Veyne, and we, confronted by what seems to be Augustus' attempt to manipulate private emotions, may perhaps ask the same of the Romans. To Veyne and to the late fourth century BCE mythographer Palaephatus, we owe the view that:

> If they have not been educated, men believe everything that is told them; but wise men believe in nothing. The latter are wrong, for everything that has been spoken of has existed, otherwise how could one speak of it?
>
> (Veyne 1988: 67)

Greek and Roman society contained a variety of traditions about the nature of death, of the afterlife and of the relations between men and gods which underlay those traditions. The late Republic and early Empire were rather diffident about post-mortem survival, let alone post-mortem flourishing.

In Epicureanism there was an outright repudiation of the idea of individual post-mortem survival. 'Death', wrote the Epicurean Lucretius in the first century BCE, 'is nothing to us and no concern of ours, since the nature of the mind is now held to be mortal' (Lucretius 1994: 87). He insisted that it was not possible to separate the body from the 'soul' or 'vital spirit':

> The vital spirit is present in the whole body ... body by itself never experiences birth or growth, and we can see that it does not persist after death. ... The minds of living things and the light fabric of their spirits are neither birthless nor deathless ... the mind is mortal ... when the whole bodily envelope crumbles after the expulsion of the vital breath, the senses of the mind and spirit likewise disintegrate, since body and mind can only exist when joined together.
>
> (Lucretius 1994: 75–81)

This Roman philosopher (born *c*.100 BCE) was following his teacher the Greek Epicurus (born on Samos about 341 BCE) in the view that at death, the particular assemblage, the human individual, breaks up into its constituent atoms which fly off into the 'gusty air ... the air itself will be a body' (Lucretius 1994: 81). Through re-entry into the haphazard cosmic dance of the atoms, this air-body becomes some kind of immortality, some endless random life, the physics of the stars. From this Lucretius derived strength:

> So the war of the elements that has raged throughout eternity continues on equal terms. Now here, now there, the forces of life are victorious and in turn vanquished. With the voice of mourning mingles the cry that infants raise when their eyes open on the sunlit world. Never has day given place to night nor night to dawn that has not heard, blent with these infant wailings, the lamentation that attends on death and solemn obsequies.
>
> (Lucretius 1994: 51–2)

Seneca, a Stoic rather than an Epicurean and writing about 100 years later, wrote to his friend Lucilius recommending the value of Virgil's lines:

> Life's finest days, for us poor human beings,
> Fly first: the sickness and the sufferings,
> A bleak old age, the snatching hand
> Implacable of merciless death, creep near.
> (Seneca 1969: 208)

'What is to come', advises Seneca, 'is uncertain', though he was sure that 'old age is itself a kind of incurable sickness' (ibid.: 209). He himself had, he said, for some time been a vegetarian, having been converted by Pythagoras (born, like Epicurus, in Samos in the middle of the sixth century BCE) and Sotion (second century BCE, born in Alexandria) to a belief in the doctrine of the transmigration of souls. To his correspondent, Seneca quoted Sotion: 'what we call death is only a move to another home ... nothing ever perishes on this earth, instead merely undergoing a change in its whereabouts' (ibid.: 206). The inference was that a meat-eater of, say, a pig, might inadvertently 'eat', in the pig, the soul of a dead ancestor, the soul having 'changed its whereabouts' and become lodged in the pig. Seneca gave up his vegetarianism, he says, at the request of his father because at some point in the reign of Tiberias 'certain religious cults of foreign origin ... [taught that] abstinence from certain kinds of animal food was regarded as evidence of adherence to superstitions' (ibid.: 206–7). The rather snobbish Senecas did not wish to be seen to be part of such a foreign crowd.

In keeping with Stoic views, Seneca maintained a resolute impassivity in the face of death. In commenting, in a consoling way, on the death of a mutual friend, he wrote:

> Let us reflect then, my dearest Lucilius, that we ourselves shall not be long in reaching the place we mourn his having reached. Perhaps, too, if only there is truth in the story told by sages and some welcoming abode awaits us, he whom we suppose dead and gone has merely been sent on ahead.
>
> (ibid.: 117)

Note the 'perhaps' and the 'if only'. Seneca goes on to say that:

> Life is the gift of the immortal gods. ... Death has an evil reputation. Yet none of the people who malign it has put it to the test. Until one does it's rather rash to condemn a thing one knows nothing about. And yet one thing you do know and that is this, how many people it's a blessing to, how many people it frees from torture, want, maladies, suffering, weariness. And no one has power over us when death is within our own power.
>
> (ibid.: 161, 183)

Seneca was instructed to commit suicide by Nero, and did so, rather painfully. His wife, who against his wishes chose to die with him, tried to commit suicide, but was 'rescued' on Nero's orders. Death and death's pain were closer to a Roman life than they have, generally, been to ours: Seneca was not merely theorising.

The religious records that have come down to us are generally rather portentous and serious, especially when they have to do with death and the commemoration of death, the associated doings of gods and heroes, and the civic and political affairs of Rome. It may well be, of course, that the huge difficulties of translating and understanding, say, Ancient Egyptian or Ugaritic texts simply mask nuances of wit and scepticism and irony which are and will probably for ever remain beyond our comprehension. In the second century CE however we get, in Lucian of Samosata (born about 120

CE, in Samosata on the Euphrates), a humorous and satirical treatment of the beliefs which his fellow Romans held about the gods and the afterlife.

Lucian's native tongue was probably Aramaic, but he spent his most active years in Athens and his last years in Egypt, having visited Gaul in the meantime. In several essays he poked fun at what he considers to be popular illogicality and sentimentality about contemporary burial and mourning practices, and about the alleged role and purposes of both Olympian and chthonic deities. In so doing, he provides some clues as to the nature of popular belief about death, which is, he says, 'guided solely by custom and convention ... taking as text-book the fictions of Homer and Hesiod and other poets' (from 'On Mourning'; Lucian 1905: vol. 3, 212). In his 'Dialogues of the Gods', 'Dialogues of the Sea-Gods', 'Dialogues of the Dead' and shorter essays on 'Charon', 'Voyage to the Underworld' and others, all in vol. 1, Lucian ridicules the full range of Greco-Roman beliefs about the gods and death.

Charon, allowed by Zeus to visit the upper world to see why men are so sad when they go down to him, asks his guide and co-worker Hermes to explain why human beings put corpses into 'receptacles' called (says Hermes) 'sepulchres or tombs or graves ... mounds, columns and pyramids, outside the various city walls, the store chambers of the dead'. Charon expostulates:

> Why, they are putting flowers on the stones, and pouring costly essences upon them! And in front of some of the mounds they have piled up faggots, and dug trenches. Look: there is a splendid banquet laid out, and they are burning it all; and pouring wine and mead, I suppose it is, into the trenches! What does it all mean? [Hermes replies:] What satisfaction it affords to their friends in Hades, I am unable to say. But the idea is that the shades come up and get as close as they can, and feed upon the savoury steam of the meat and drink the mead in the trench. Eat and drink, when their skulls are dry bones? [says Charon], Oh, fools and blockheads! You little know how we arrange matters, and what a gulf is set betwixt the living and the dead!
>
> (from 'Charon'; Lucian 1905: vol. 1, 181–2)

In a kind of Greco-Roman version of Kipling's 'Recessional', Hermes and Charon discuss 'the great cities that we hear talked about in Hades' – Nineveh, Babylon, Mycenae, Cleonae, Troy – now 'gone the way of all flesh. Cities die just like men', says Hermes; Charon responds with 'Oh Homer, Homer! You and your "holy Troy", and your "city of broad streets", and your "strong-walled Cleonae"!' (op. cit.). This essay ends with a comment on the futility of war, since the heroes contending for occupation of the whole Peloponnesus will, by Aeacus (one of the judges of the underworld) be given barely a foot of ground in the underworld. In 'Dialogues of the Dead', Hermes and Charon discuss the problems of the peaceful nature of the Roman Empire, because Charon's operating costs are up while his custom is down because of peace:

> After all, though, Charon, in old days men were men; you remember the state they used to come down in – all blood and wounds generally. Nowadays, a man is poisoned by his slave or his wife; or gets dropsy from over-feeding; a pale spiritless lot, nothing like the men of old. Most of them seem to meet their end in some plot that has money for its object.
>
> (from 'Dialogues of the Dead'; Lucian 1905: vol. 1, 112)

In an extended treatment of mourning and beliefs about the after-life, Lucian concludes with the comment that such 'are the absurdities that may be observed in mourners. ... And all springs from the vulgar error, that Death is the worst thing that can befall a man' (from 'Of Mourning'; Lucian 1905: vol. 3, 218). 'The vulgar', he writes, taking 'as their text-book the fictions of Homer and Hesiod and other poets', believe in a Hades where the king is Pluto, brother of Zeus. Hades is a 'spacious, murky and sunless' subterranean hole, from which no one is allowed to return (though there were two or three exceptions). The dead are kept in unbreakable shackles. Vast rivers surround Hades. The first obstacle is Acheron, a lake passable only in Charon's boat, it being so big that not even deceased birds can fly across it. Near a gate of adamant stands the judge Aeacus, and a three-headed dog (fifty-headed in Hesiod), who is friendly enough to newcomers but who, with 'the yawning horror of his jaws', makes sure there are no runaways. On the inner shore of the lake Acheron is a meadow on which grows asphodel, and a fountain, the fountain of Lethe, which 'makes war on memory'. Lucian makes some acid comments about the alleged source of all this information, i.e. 'witnesses' such as Theseus and Odysseus who were among the few who had visited and escaped from Hades. From them the Greco-Romans would have learnt that Pluto and Persephone

rule in Hades with the assistance of 'a host of underlings', such as the
Furies, the Pains, the Fears and Hermes who is 'not always in attendance'. Two judges sort out the just men from the evildoers. The
former are sent to form colonies in the Elysian fields, 'there to lead
the perfect life', while the latter are punished by the Furies 'in due
proportion to their iniquities ... the rack, the fire, the gnawing
vultures'. There is then a third class of 'neutral characters', who are
'formless phantoms that evade the touch like smoke':

> It seems that they depend for their nourishment upon the
> libations and victims offered by us upon their tombs:
> accordingly, a Shade who has no surviving friends or rela-
> tions passes a hungry time of it in the lower world.
>   (in 'Of Mourning'; Lucian 1905: vol. 3, 214)

Lucian then lists, with commentary, the funeral practices of the
'common people': the coin for Charon for the ferry over the Stygian
lake, the washing and anointing and dressing of the corpse, the provision of flowers and garlands. In the funeral procession, the women
wail, and men and women weep and beat their breasts, lacerate their
cheeks, tear their clothes, rend their hair and sprinkle dust on their
heads, putting them in a worse condition, according to Lucian, than
the deceased who 'reposes gracefully on his lofty bier, adorned as it
were for some pageant'. A professional mourner, 'an artist in grief,
with a fine repertoire of cut-and-dried sorrows at his command,
assumes the direction of this inane choir', and the mother or more
usually the father then falls upon the bier ('to heighten the effect we
will suppose its occupant to be young and handsome') and 'utters
wild and meaningless ejaculations', referring to his son, taken out of
his time, never married, childless, never had a job or reached old
age, never again to enjoy drinking or making love, never to eat and
drink with his friends. Sometimes, says Lucian, men have been
known to slaughter horses, concubines and pages on the tombs, and
to burn clothes and other finery, or to bury such things, on the
assumption that the deceased will find use for them in the lower
world.

'Tomfoolery!', says Lucian, all this 'fluting and beating of
breasts', when it is obvious that no one is the better for it, the sacrifices are mere waste, the dead are probably better off in Hades, free
from the problems of this life (among these problems Lucian
includes women and old age): 'can your sapience', asks the corpse of
his bewailing father, 'point to any single convenience of life, of

which we are deprived in the lower world?' (from 'Of Mourning';
Lucian 1905: vol. 3, 212–8). By contrast, Lucian abandons his usual
scatology when he commends the death (and the life) of his friend
Demonax, a man always quoting Homer to the effect that 'idle or
busy, death takes all alike'.

> When he found he was no longer able to take care of
> himself, he repeated to his friends the tag with which the
> heralds close the festival: 'The games are done, The crowns
> all won, No more delay, But haste away', and from that
> moment abstaining from food, left life as cheerfully as he
> had lived it, indifferent to questions of funeral preparation,
> saying that 'scent will summon my undertakers'.
>
> (from 'Life of Demonax'; Lucian 1905: vol. 3, 11–2)

Demonax's wishes were ignored by the Athenians, who insisted on a
lavish public funeral, even garlanding and sanctifying the stone seat
on which he used to sit.

While Lucian mocked the Greeks and their mythologies, Cicero
took them rather more seriously. Indeed, in writings such as his
Tusculan Disputations Cicero set himself the task of introducing
Romans to the best of Greek philosophy. He believed in the gods
and in divine providence, in which all men had a share. It was,
though, the responsibility of humans to deal with the detail of their
lives. From Plato, Cicero derived the idea, dismissed by Lucretius,
of the immortality of the soul, i.e. that it exists before birth and
after death; from Pythagoras the idea of the transmigration of souls,
the idea that had driven Seneca into vegetarianism. Cicero wrote in
words which invoke the 'son of Earth and star-filled Heaven'
formulae of the prayers on the *lamellae*, and in ways which influenced several early Christian Fathers – and, indirectly, many more
Christian martyrs:

> As long as we remain within these bodily frames of ours,
> we are undergoing a heavy labour imposed upon us by fate.
> For our human souls have come into our bodies from
> heaven: they have been sent down from their lofty abode
> and plunged, so to speak, into the earth, which is alien to their
> divine and eternal nature. As I believe, the reason why the
> immortal gods implanted souls in human beings was to
> provide the earth with guardians who should reflect their

contemplation of the divine order in the orderly discipline of their own lives.

(Cicero 1971b: 244)

This is, of course, one way of dealing with one of the fundamental problems of death, that of transcending the god/human separation, where the gods are immortal (as Greeks and Romans believed) and *per contra* humans are not. If the souls of humans are heaven-derived, and the body can be seen as an earth-based prison from which to escape, then death is a restoration of the soul to its prior and immortal order. Indeed, Cicero goes on to make precisely that point in reporting Xenophon's account of the death of Cyrus the Elder: Cyrus is speaking to his sons,

> If I am right in believing in eternal life, then I am now turning into a god for you to worship! If, on the other hand my soul is going to die with my body, still I know you will keep me in dutiful memory, reserving your worship for the gods who rule and watch over the beauties of the Universe.
>
> (ibid.: 245)

Cyrus has an element of sensible doubt – '*If* I am right'. Cicero seems to be in less doubt as to his own post-mortem fate:

> What a great day it will be when I set out to join that divine assemblage and concourse of souls, and depart from the confusion and corruption of this world! I shall be going to meet not only those of whom I have spoken, but also my own son. No better, no more devoted man was ever born. He should have cremated my body: but I had to cremate his. Yet his soul has not gone from me, but looks back and fastens upon me its regard – and the destination to which that soul has departed is surely the place where it knew I too must come. To the world I have seemed to bear the loss bravely. That does not mean that I found it easy to bear, but I comforted myself with the belief that our parting and separation would be of short duration.
>
> (ibid.: 246–7)

Cicero's sorrowful 'belief' (or perhaps hope) was shared by a father of the first century CE, grieving on an epitaph for his nine-year-old daughter:

The cruel Fates have left me a sad old age.
I shall always be searching for you, my darling Asiatica.
Sadly shall I often imagine your face
to comfort myself. My consolation will be that soon
I shall see you, when my own life is done,
and my shadow is joined with yours.

(Hopkins 1983: 227)

The joining of 'shadows' is clearly nothing like so strong a sense of an afterlife as Christians were to develop, but is probably indicative of the most general Roman construct of the afterlife: it was shadowy and the dead had no real existence, no potency to maintain contact with the living. The grieving father can only rejoin his daughter by dying himself.

The poet Horace has even lower expectations of the afterlife, although offering perhaps a degree of posthumous consolation to the poor:

> Whether thou be rich and sprung from ancient Inachus, or dwell beneath the canopy of heaven poor and of lowly birth, it makes no difference: thou art pitiless Orcus' victim. We are all being gathered together to one and the same fold. The lot of every one of us is tossing about in the urn, destined sooner, later, to come forth and place us in Charon's skiff for everlasting exile.
>
> (from 'Enjoy the Fleeting Hour!'; Horace 1968: 115)

Like many members of the Roman elite, Horace found such optimism as he had in the strength and stability of the Roman state and in the person and position of its Emperor: 'While Caesar guards the state, not civil rage, nor violence, nor wrath that forges swords, embroiling hapless towns, shall banish peace' (from 'Augustus'; Horace 1968: 345–7). He emphasised the inability of the enemies of Rome to challenge the security of its society – as long as 'Caesar guards the state' – and, within this peace,

> On common and on sacred days, amid the gifts of merry Bacchus, with wife and child we first will duly pray the gods; then after our fathers' wont, in measures joined to strains of Lydian flutes, we will hymn the glories of the heroic dead, Troy and Anchises and benign Venus' offspring.
>
> (ibid.)

Under Caesar, and in family worship, the gods and the heroic dead will provide whatever safety and security there is. It was Horace, of course, who gave us one of the most quoted (though quoted these days more in derision and disbelief) lines on the sacrifices necessary to secure the peace which made life possible and death tolerable: *dulce et decorum est pro patria mori* (from 'Endurance, and Fidelity to One's Trust'; Horace 1968: 175).

Horace, though, was aware of the dangers implicit in the success of an empire which had made itself by force of arms: 'Brute force bereft of wisdom falls to ruin by its own weight. Power with counsel tempered, even the gods make greater. But might that in its soul is bent on all impiety, they hate' (from 'Wisdom and Order'; Horace 1968: 191). There is an immanent Armageddon underlying what seems to be the 'theodicy of good fortune' of the Roman world, a counter-culture of war, famine and plague, and of day-to-day misery, illness, death and violence which insistently erupted into the patrician establishment – and did so in some measure because the patricians themselves, like Horace, were well aware of the precariousness of their civilisation.

Clearly, this was not the world of Jewish Palestine, where a very real Armageddon had actually happened and where apocalyptic styles of religion were a form of realism. Neither was it the world of early Christianity in which individualised notions of guilt, sin and salvation came to propel human beings into an intensely anxious soteriological preoccupation with the afterlife. The Roman world seemed stable, but only if all necessary forms of 'decorum' were mobilised to keep chaos and disorder at bay – 'at bay', never defeated, but, possibly, not always victorious. Roman thanatology was partly hopeful and largely fearful, fearful that human action, the gods being often otherwise concerned, could and would remove the only anti-death system that was available, the routine this-worldly competence of the Roman state and of Roman urbanity, Roman 'decorum'.

Roman funerals were part of this attempt at 'decorum', a series of large and small routines and ritual, incremental additions to or maintenance of the boundaries of a possible life.

10

ROMAN RELIGION AND ROMAN FUNERALS

> The Romans were not sure of survival after death, and the dead played no central role within organised religious belief.
>
> (Walker 1985: 13)

Cicero (see Chapter 9) clearly loved his son. In Roman legal theory, *patria potestas* allowed a father to execute his own children, and it was not until the year 374 CE that infanticide was placed on an equal footing with parricide (the killing of near relations). Yet, as Cicero shows and many epitaphs attest, Roman parents loved their children – although this was perhaps not always reciprocated. One of the most heartbreaking aspects of the martyrdom of Perpetua in early third century CE Roman Carthage is the frantic sorrow exhibited by the Roman father of the about-to-be martyr at his daughter's determination to die. Throwing himself at her feet, he weeps: 'Daughter, have pity on my grey hair, have pity on me your father'. Roman fathers did not normally so diminish themselves in front of their children. Neither did Roman daughters respond so coldly and independently. Perpetua noted that: 'This was the way my father spoke out of love for me, kissing my hands and throwing himself down before me'. She ignored her father's sorrow, and died for Christ in the arena at Carthage, abandoning not only her father but also her husband and her own infant son (Salisbury 1997: 89).

The Emperor Domitian seems to have had greater regard for his child than Perpetua did for hers. When he became Emperor in 81 CE (murdered in 96 CE), he immediately 'deified' his baby child who had died some years earlier (McDermott and Orentzel 1979). On coins issued during his reign, his wife Domitia appears as *Pietas*, holding out her hands to a child. On the reverse of the coins appears *Divus Caesar* as the infant Jove, described by Martial as throwing snow from the heavens upon the smiling Caesar. Domitian and his wife clearly loved their son – indeed, their marriage seems never to have recovered from this infant death, a not uncommon outcome in such cases. One has to ask, though: what solace lay, for Domitian and for Domitia, in the deification of their dead child?

When seeking the distinctively Roman (and to a large extent the Greek) view of death, dying and the next world, we should perhaps take into account Susan Walker's comment at the beginning of this chapter that: 'The Romans were not sure of survival after death, *and the dead played no central role within organised religious belief*' (Walker 1985: 13; my emphasis). Susan Walker goes on to say that: 'Permanent memorials were crucial to their hopes for immortality, serving a function of little relevance to Christian believers' (ibid.). Humphreys makes a related point for Greek funerary practice:

> What the Greeks hoped to achieve for the dead was perpetual remembrance, by strangers as well as kin. The dead did not become ancestors (they had no effect on the lives of their descendants and were not reincorporated into society to serve as focal points in the genealogical definition of social relationships): they became *monuments*.
>
> (Humphreys 1981: 270; author's emphasis)

Roman and Greek religion was essentially the public cults of cities and their protective deities, expressed in public, and therefore political processions and sacrifice, *in which priestly and political functions were integrated*. In deifying his dead child, Domitian, as *pontifex maximus*, was turning him into a public monument, heaping upon him as much positive monumentality as the Roman imperial cult could mobilise. In some sense, the whole pressure of Roman religion was to impose the supremacy of the imperial cult as the principle of order in the seemingly endless profusion of cults, native and foreign, new and old, which characterised the Ancient Near East and the other lands of the Empire. In this purpose, the funerals and funerary obsequies of the Emperor played a central part. From the imperial funeral descended a hierarchy of imitative rites, of varying degrees of splendour and solemnity.

For the Roman masses, living in 'the gloom of life' (Scheidel 1996: 153) in what was essentially a huge unhygienic slum, such funerals were objects of ambition rather than actuality. Hopkins quotes the first century CE official announcement which prohibited the burning of corpses beyond a certain line, and went on to reinforce a similar prohibition on the dumping of 'ordure or corpses' with the promise of 'trouble' if shit wasn't taken 'further on'. At times of pestilence, not uncommon in a city virtually without drainage in which the summer regularly saw an increase in mortality, the dead would find mass graves or cheap interment in bisected amphorae (Hopkins 1983: 210; Scheidel 1996: 153; Scobie 1986). Lucretius, relying on Thucydides, describes the consequences of plague in Athens in 430 BCE, a situation replicated in Rome in both the second century CE and the third century CE:

> Many corpses lay unburied on the ground, heaped one upon the other. ... Lonely funerals were raced without a mourner to the grave. ... Exposed in streets and public places you might see many a wasted frame with limbs half dead begrimed with filth, and huddled under rags, dying in squalor with nothing to cover the bones but skin ... every hallowed shrine of the gods had been tenanted by death with lifeless bodies ... occupied by crowds of corpses. ... The mode of burial that had hitherto been in vogue was no longer practised. ... Men would fling their blood-relatives amid violent outcry on the pyres built for others and set torches under them.
>
> (Lucretius 1994: 197–9)

For the dominant Roman citizens, such treatment of the dead would have been deeply shaming: vast sums of money were spent on ensuring that the *genius* of the family was both protected and proclaimed by a fittingly monumental death. For Ancient Egyptians (see Chapter 1) and for Christians (see Chapter 13) death was always and centrally religious, preoccupied with salvation. This was not the main priority of the Roman (or Greek) funeral – unless one redefines 'religious' for this purpose. Inevitably, in any culture religious language will flow around death, but essentially, for Romans and Greeks, religion was the series of public, political processions, calendars and rituals (including the Games) which emphasised the continuity, the immortality perhaps, of the city or state, that is of the collectivity. Roman citizens were expected to lead their lives, as well as construct their deaths, in this light:

> He who betrays his country is not more reprehensible than one who abandons the advantage and welfare of all for personal interest or security. That is why, seeing that our

> country is fittingly more precious to us than our selves, a man who suffers death for his community does indeed deserve to be praised. ... It is undoubtedly true that we should take thought also for those who will come after us, for their own sakes. This attitude of mind is the explanation for men at the hour of death making wills and appointing trustees.
>
> (Cicero 1991: 65–7)

It was the making of the will, the appointment of trustees and the fact of doing this at the hour of death, which represented life and continuity, a representation in which a good death could then take place as the sensible end of a life well lived. The heir, in proof of continuity, was expected to provide the funeral, this obligation being one of the few legally prescribed funerary stipulations. Naturally enough, funerals took place in public, but they were essentially family or 'collegial' events. Domitian, as Emperor, could enhance the significance of the death of his child by attaching the infant to the imperial cult, in which the familial limitation of death remembrance is transcended by the association of that one particular family with the central religious rite of the Empire. As *Divus Caesar* the child would attain a degree of publicly attested 'immortality' and monumentality. Domitian was a conscientious practitioner of Roman imperial religion, taking part in the Secular Games which marked the longevity of Rome and the birth of the new age. He executed three Vestal Virgins for breaking their vows of chastity, and entombed alive their superior for allowing this and other things to happen. The behaviour of these women jeopardised the security of the state for which the cult was responsible. On the occasion of his wife's adultery with an actor, Domitian not only executed the actor but removed all trace of his wife from the coinage, equating, it would seem, adultery with *blasphemy*, in the sense that adultery by the Emperor's wife undermined the dignity and therefore the stability of the Empire (McDermott and Orentzel 1979: 77).

The death of a Roman Emperor was the occasion for huge public spectacle, deifying the dead emperor and emphasising the stability and pedigree of the Roman state – all the more necessary, perhaps, because the very real circumstances of *dynastic* instability too often resulted in conspiracy and chaos at the top. Michael Koortbojian, using the writings of Herodian, Polybius and Suetonius, describes how a wax effigy of the deceased Emperor, lying on an ivory couch, would be displayed before his palace and surrounded by a seven-day re-enactment of his death, then carried through the mourners, to the funeral pyre. The mourners, the living, would be joined by the dead, in the form of charioteers or actors wearing masks or carrying portraits portraying the great generals and emperors of Roman history (Koortbojian 1995: 122).

The funeral procession of the Emperor Augustus was headed by the statue of Victory which stood before the Senate House. A wax image of Augustus, rather than his body, was dressed as for a military triumph. The real body was hidden behind an ornate funerary couch. Two 'images' of the Emperor – one of gold, one carried in a war-chariot – preceded the cortège, which was surrounded by images and portraits of Roman heroes, real and legendary (such as Romulus). Orations, by Tiberius (the successor) and by his son Drusus, were delivered from separate rostra, that of Drusus from the *rostra vetera* decorated with the prows of captured ships and statues of famous generals. The body was then carried by senators to the Field of Mars and placed on a pyre. Priests, cavalrymen and infantry surrounded it. Centurions set the pyre alight, and onto it went all the honours held by those in attendance, while an eagle was released to the heavens, signifying the flight of the Emperor's spirit upwards. The widow stayed by the pyre for five days. Then barefoot knights collected the bones, and took them to the mausoleum Augustus had built twenty years before (from Walker 1985).

In such ways, all Rome, living and dead, witnessed the death and apotheosis of the Emperor. Similar, if less elaborate, public (and publicly financed) displays attended the deaths of the great citizens. Again, the body itself would be carried to the forum and placed on the rostra. Seated upright, it would appear to deny death. The virtues and actions of the dead man would be proclaimed, in front of the dead man, sitting there, taking part in his own living dramatised obituary. Such eulogies would usually be spoken by a grown-up son or some other relative, and they would be kept and referred to as a kind of permanent obituary or moral pedigree. Polybius described the funeral procedures whereby family members took the ancestor masks from their own faces and put them on

> Men who seem to be the most similar in height and size to the men represented by the masks. These 'actors' put on a purple-bordered toga, if their 'character' was a consul or praetor, an entirely purple toga if he was a censor, and a gold-embroidered toga if he had celebrated a triumph or done some other such thing. They all ride in chariots, and

according to the respective rank of political office held by each 'character' in his lifetime, the 'actors' are preceded by the fasces, axes and other such things which usually accompany the magistrates. When they reach the Rostra they sit down on curule [ivory] seats. It would not be easy to find a more splendid sight for a young man who loves honour and virtue to behold. For who would not be moved by the sight of the images of men renowned for their excellence, all together in one place, portrayed as if still alive and breathing? What finer spectacle could there be than this? ... Since the renown of these noble men and their reputation for excellence is constantly being called to mind, the fame of men who have done great deeds is made immortal, and the glory of those who have faithfully served the fatherland becomes well known to the people and handed down as a model to future generations. The most important thing, however, is that young men are inspired to endure or suffer anything on behalf of the common good in order to achieve the glory that surrounds men who are brave.

(Shelton 1988: 99)

The imperial cult and the public funerals of the great citizens were the apex of a political-religious system which, in the eyes of its practitioners who were politicians as much as priests, would guarantee (if properly observed) the extraordinary success of Rome.

Plutarch, who would have been about forty years old when Domitian was assassinated, wrote in *De Fortuna Romanorum*:

While the mightiest powers and dominions among men were being driven about as Fortune willed, and were continuing to collide with one another because no one held the supreme power, but all wished to hold it, the continuous movement, drift, and change of all peoples remained without remedy, until such time as Rome acquired strength and growth, and had attached herself not only to the nations and peoples within her own borders, but also royal dominions of foreign powers beyond the seas, and thus the affairs of this vast empire gained stability and security, since the supreme government, which never knew reverse, was brought within an orderly and single cycle of peace; for though Virtue in every form was inborn in those who contrived these things,

yet great Good Fortune was also joined therewith, as it will
be possible to demonstrate.

(Plutarch, in Dillon 1997: 237)

Earlier, within five years of the assassination of Domitian, in *Precepts
of Statecraft* and in *Moral Essays*, Plutarch had rejoiced in the pacific
nature of the Empire and in the happy circumstance of the absence
of great issues of state, in particular of questions of war, as this
meant that people were now asking of the gods answers to 'purely
personal' questions such as 'should I marry?' or 'should I go on a
voyage?' – 'these things the wise man will ask the gods in his
prayers to grant his fellow-citizens' (ibid.: 235): there were no 'great
questions'.

In the *Acta* and in the *Fasti*, in deified emperors and imperial
families, in dedicated coinage, in the series of great altars such as
Augustus' *Ara Pacis*, the *Ara Pietatis Augustae*, and imitations, in
the public festivals and ceremonies which proclaimed and attended
these events and monuments, and in the deification (i.e. the monu-
mentalisation) of the *Emperor-Pontifex Maximus* are to be found the
serious purpose of Roman religion and of the Roman gods, the
maintenance of the Empire as the benign End of History. The life of
the Empire was celebrated; the death of the Empire was denied.

This is very different to the apocalyptic atmosphere of Palestine,
in which we saw the development of Jewish thanatology. Indeed it
is in many ways its antithesis; it gave to 'ordinary death' in the
Roman Empire a particular flavour, in which the emphasis is more
on the living and their concerns than on the deceased and their fate.
This is, it must be said, a difference which is always in danger of
conjuring up its opposite. Death breaks hearts, whether in the great
and stable empires of the world or in the most transient and precarious of human societies – and Rome was never as unambiguously
stable as Plutarch and others such as Aristides may have believed.
Yet as we shall see in the discussion of Roman epitaphs and
sarcophagi in particular, the Roman dead were treated in a way
emphasising not so much their own separate post-mortem fate as
their continuing responsibilities for and membership of their living
families and societies – and, concomitantly, of the continuing
reality to the living of a responsibility for the reputation of their
dead.

In keeping with its concern *for the living*, Roman society provided a set of 'official' religious festivals dealing with the dead: the
Parentalia, from 13–21 February, a festival of ancestors, involving the

dies parentales and ending in the Feralia; and the Lemuria, on 9, 11 and 13 May. While these were in the official calendar, they were legally classified as private rituals, the business of clubs and families. It should also be noticed that the licensing of such activities for and on certain days in the year implied, very clearly, that they were to be restricted to those days and those days *only*. The Roman authorities did not want the tumult of endless invocations of the dead, nor did they wish to vitiate the public-political nature of civic or imperial religion by too close an identification of it with the ordinary business of death and dying. In the laws governing the calendar, and in a series of sumptuary laws which (under both Greeks and Romans) regulated the public aspect of funerals, the state emphasised the relative separation of ordinary funerals from the mainstream politico-religious concerns of Roman, and indeed Greek, culture.

Within the laws and conventions, each family had its own devotional style (*sacra*), determined by the male household head. The household dead were part of the on-going concern of the household. As Toynbee puts it:

> All Roman funerary practice was influenced by two basic notions – first, that death brought pollution and demanded from the survivors acts of purification and expiation; secondly, that to leave a corpse unburied had unpleasant repercussions on the fate of the departed soul.
>
> (Toynbee 1971: 42)[1]

The Lemuria rites, for example, were aimed at propitiating (usually around midnight) apparently dangerous hungry ghosts (*lemuria*) prowling around the houses. *Di Penates* were spirits specifically connected with the innermost parts of the house, and as such regarded as a domestic concern. Note, again, that the concern is with the welfare of the living.

Roman 'spirits of the dead' were separated into various groups, about which there is still considerable disagreement. Tombstones, which in their nature do not permit of anything but the most laconic of comment, often carried the letters 'DMS' or 'DM': to the gods of the dead, *di manes*, sometimes *manes* appearing as a collective noun, the 'shades' perhaps of earlier cultures and like them problem-

---

1   Much of what follows this quotation is also taken from Toynbee.

atically undifferentiated. The *manes* were 'worshipped', collectively, at the three festivals of Parentalia, Feralia and Lemuria, and individually on the anniversary of a person's death. For them to be 'happy' and unthreatening, funerals had to be properly constituted and the post-interment rituals observed.

In both Greece and Rome, funerals were arranged and paid for by the family and/or by one of the numerous funeral clubs (*collegia funeraticia*) based usually upon cultic or occupational membership. Zanker states that Roman burial societies were originally formed by imperial freedmen as a way of providing, in collective columbaria, an alternative to the stand-alone, ostentatious mausolea and monuments which they themselves could not afford (Zanker 1988: 293). The constitution of the funeral club of 'Diana and Antinous' (the latter was a young lover of Hadrian, who semi-deified him as Apollo, Diana's brother) was laid down by the Roman Senate, anxious to avoid gatherings for political conspiracy. Club members were to meet once a month only, and then only to collect club dues. The club rules provided for the retrieval of members dying outside Rome, expenses of twenty sesterces being allowed for the three members who went to bring the body home. Slaves were members of this club:

> If any member of this club who was a slave should die, and if his body should not be handed over to us for interment because of the unfairness of his master or mistress, or if he has not left a will, a funeral will be held for an effigy of him. ... If any member of this club who was a slave should be manumitted, he should donate an amphora of good wine.
>
> (Shelton 1988: 101)

The reference to 'effigy' may seem odd to us, but it refers to standard Roman practice (see the description of the imperial funeral) of making wax images of the dead which were then carried in a funeral procession. Funerals could take place without a body.

In imperial Rome, the style of the funeral followed class and status divisions, which in essence decreed, in both procession and monument, the highest degree of 'publicity' (and therefore religiosity) to Emperors and other dignitaries, and a high degree of anonymity, again in procession and monument, to the very poor and faceless. Heralds would summon the citizens to the funerals of important people. For imperial funerals, such summonses were orders; for a *funus publicum*, a funeral of an important person, when the costs were paid out of the public purse, such summonses were invitations.

Soldiers who died in battle were collectively buried, while those who died in service received a funeral paid for by fellow soldiers out of a pay-packet levy. Military culture provided a powerful substratum of ritual for Roman burial. In ordinary times, the size of the Roman military establishment would see approximately 22 per cent of Roman males in their twenties and thirties in the army. If to this are added the service trades associated with the military, then probably one in four Roman male citizens was involved with army life and army culture. At the apex of this system stood the Emperor, whose life and death symbolised the security and 'virtue' of Roman life. The imperial *funus* was a military event, replicated through the ranks (see Toynbee 1971: 54–5; Scheidel 1996). For all other funerals, whose essentially private or domestic character was highlighted by the very existence of publicly funded funerals, the family was responsible, both for the actual interment and for the ensuing round of anniversaries and ceremonies.

Religion, the law (the Twelve Tables), a concern for public health and convention determined that corpses were not brought into the city 'lest the sacred places in the city be polluted' (Shelton 1988: 97). A similar concern for 'sacrilege' forbade the construction of sepulchres next to or near dwelling houses. This prohibition of intramural interment or cremation led not only to lengthy funeral processions, but also to the creation of 'cemeteries' – sometimes linear, along the main roads out of the city; sometimes (in the Etruscan fashion) in necropoli, walled cemeteries, funerary gardens and columbaria, these last being three- or four-storey structures (often favoured by the burial clubs of the middling classes) containing a large number of funerary urns. Undertakers, gravediggers and grave decorators, as well as sellers of plots and providers of sarcophagi, ensured a wide variety of necessary services. The very poor might end up in common pits (*puticuli*, or 'stench and rot' places) or in simple holes in the ground containing either a corpse or burnt remains and over which the top-end of an amphora would provide both grave marker and a means of pouring in libations of wine or flowers or incense at the relevant times.

The Roman extramural cemeteries normally consisted of lots of small family plots, used for two or three generations. Extramural burial came to an end in 567 CE, the date of the last known burial outside the walls of Rome and of the first recorded epitaph from within it (Hornblower and Spawforth 1996: 307). The Christian catacombs of the first four centuries CE were also located outside the walls, as well as under the ground.

Given that the death was polluting, and therefore potentially dangerous, the laws and conventions decreed a short period, generally about eight days, from the time of death, through the laying out and 'exposure' period, the cremation, and the funeral procession, to the actual disposal. After forty days, the person-corpse had been transformed into one of the community of the *manes*. This did not mean that the person-corpse was in some distinct other-world, either heavenly or hellish, but that they were now a dweller in those extramural plots of land to which the dead were sent and to which the family would pay regular visits. The family sent the deceased on their way, closing the eyes on death, providing the last kiss (a task usually performed by the mother, if she was alive), calling out the name of the dead, uttering the first lamentations, washing the body, laying it out, equipping it with Charon's coin, lamenting and following the bier, which was carried to the grave site by *vespilliones*. A series of specialists – undertakers, cremators, gravediggers – ensured that the disposal was handled correctly. Horns and pipes, and the cries of the mourners, some of them professional, female, mourners, would accompany the bier, the women of the family bringing up the rear. The family would throw earth on the corpse in its grave or collect the ashes in the case of a cremation, sacrificing the pig without whose ritual death the grave was not legally in being (Toynbee 1971: 50). The funeral procession usually took place at night, the processors being dressed in black. Cremation was generally the custom in the Latin Western Empire, with the ashes placed in funerary or 'Canopic' urns, or in house-shaped terracotta chests, with effigies on top. The ashes of the poor would be placed in open-mouthed amphorae. In the Greek Eastern Empire, inhumation in wooden or stone sarcophagi was the practice, the bodies being placed in family or chamber tombs, on stone shelves or free-standing. By the third century CE, inhumation spread from the east to become the favoured method of corpse-disposal in the Empire.

Roman memorial and funerary architecture, as with Roman monumental architecture in general, spread all over the Roman world. The library at Ephesus, dating from about 100 CE, was built by a son as a memorial to his father, who was placed inside the library in a marble sarcophagus (Walker 1985: 40). Susan Walker describes the discovery by John Turtle Wood of the Roman and early Byzantine cemeteries of Ephesus. On the road leading south to the city of Magnesia, Wood found 'substructures of monuments, some of which are of large proportions and very massive and are evidently raised over persons of distinction. These are to be traced for more than two miles beyond the gates' (ibid.: 13). This cemetery seems to have been reserved for Roman and native officials and soldiers, while in another cemetery, on the road to the building he was looking for, the lost Temple of Artemis, Wood found that the road was

> Lined with tombs of every description, but chiefly sarcophagi of white marble. ... On the side of the mountain near this road an upper road for foot passengers had been constructed with arched recesses where they were required by the irregularities of the natural formation. Many of these recesses had been used as columbaria, i.e. chamber-tombs with niches for ossuaries, cinerary chests and urns.
>
> (op. cit.)

The grave-monuments, some of which were cut out and shipped to London, record the travels and deeds of Roman soldiers, judges and imperial officials, the stones themselves often being raised, inscribed and paid for by their surviving colleagues and friends.

Susan Walker describes other burial-records in the possession of the British Museum. Before he died, Sextus Julius Aquila of Andemantunnum (now Langres, France) commissioned a memorial shrine for himself, on an island, in its own ground. The shrine was to include a statue of Aquila, set in an alcove, and equipped with marble seats and a permanent supply of cushions and rugs. In the altar in front of the statue were to be placed Aquila's bones, with the marble lid so constructed that it could be opened at the anniversary feasts and rededications. Money was set aside for ground and monument maintenance. Aquila's personal effects (hunting nets, spears, swords, traps and snares, sedan chair, rush-boat and medicines) were to be cremated with him.

An early fourth century sarcophagus from Aix-en-Provence containing the orator Proclus is totally Greek in style and sentiment: Susan Walker points out that this memorial dates from the time when Christianity was just about to become the official religion of the Empire, and there is no evidence whatsoever that funerary practice is affected by anything other than the powerful sway that Greek custom held over the Romans after Hadrian's espousal of Greek manners and habits (Walker 1985: 15–7).

An African-Roman example, the mausoleum of the Flavii at

Cillium, now Kasserine in Tunisia, demonstrates the extraordinary 'mix' of cultural influences which went into the construction of commemorative funerary architecture and literature. The mausoleum was built in the mid-second century of the Common Era by T. Flavius Secundus in memory and honour of his father and as proof of his own *pietas*. Cillium was a new town, planted by the Romans to incorporate its African colonies into the culture of the Empire. The Flavii were veterans, settled in Cillium, who became prosperous by introducing viticulture into the area. The tomb erected by T. Flavius Secundus was a tower-mausoleum, an architectural mixture of Punic, Hellenistic and 'Libyan' elements (Hitchener 1995). The long poem (see Appendix) which was inscribed on the mausoleum was a mixture of Latin verse, epigrams and Greek prayers, a genre

> Occurring initially on 1st Century AD epitaphs of slaves, freedmen and veterans from Italy and Spain, and newly-enfranchised Africans residing in the colonies and towns of northern Africa Proconsularis and eastern Numidia ... a 'popular' manifestation of 'Roman' culture representing a blend of non-elite Greco-Roman and African funerary epigraphic traditions ... [addressing] parallel or shared conceptions of life, death and the afterlife within both Greco-Roman and African culture.
>
> (Hitchener 1995: 496)

T. Flavius Secundus' poem is full of uncertainty about the afterlife – but of certainty about the function of the monument.

> May the Destinies and the King of Styx in his awesome might give me the power to express myself. Now is the time to maintain that your father is immortal, that he has left behind Dis and fled its sinister palace, since he prefers, until the end of time, to follow the fate of this monument and to live, thanks to these names inscribed here eternally, to inhabit these familiar woods, to contemplate from here with tenderness the hills of his fatherland and remain, one might say, the master of the household that he has passed on to his children.
> Many people think perhaps, that in making casual remarks about such things, one is inviting premature death by erecting, in one's own lifetime, a monument to the future. ... I believe on the contrary that those who have gone and

set up an eternal dwelling place, and have displayed an absolute rectitude in their lives, have built walls that will never fall down, and they are protected by them.[2]

(My translation)

It is very evident in the case of the Cillium mausoleum, that such tombs, in celebrating filial piety, celebrated the family. The 'mobile' bits of the funeral equipment, the masks which, for the more wealthy, had accompanied the procession, would be kept at home, evidence of piety and of a properly cared-for family ancestry: 'What cannot be achieved', the poem asks, 'by filial piety combined with learning?' (see Appendix).

It was the family who, on return from the graveside, had to begin the purification ceremonies and attend to the provision of the funerary feast, eaten at the graveside on the same day as the funeral. Another meal was held by the family on the ninth day and by others throughout the year, on the deceased's birthday and the annual festivals described above. Tombs might be opened so that the deceased could share in the family meal. Food and wine could be sent down into the tomb through the mouths of amphorae, or through holes specially cut in funerary chests and urns. The state tried to govern mourning practices, generally in the direction of controlling family mourning behaviour:

> Parents and children over six years of age can be mourned for a year, children under six for a month. A husband can be mourned for ten months, close blood relatives for eight months. Whoever acts contrary to these restrictions is placed in public disgrace. Whoever is in mourning ought to refrain from dinner parties, jewelry, and other adornments, and purple and white clothing.
>
> (Shelton 1988: 97)

Roman children died in large numbers. Behind the generally accepted figure for Romans at this time of an average life-expectancy at birth of between twenty and thirty years, lies the fact that (then as now) it is in the early years that humans are vulnerable. At birth, Roman babies would be examined by the midwife to

---

2 Flavius Secundus' poem is reproduced in full in the Appendix (trans. Ros and Dave Place).

see if they were worth saving (Hornblower and Spawforth 1996: 321). Within the limits of the data and analytical techniques, it would seem that nearly half of Roman children would die within ten years of birth (Saller 1994: 25). A Roman woman conforming to the necessary fertility rate to replace the population (2.1 live births is *today's* figure) would therefore have had to give birth to, on average, 5 children and watch about half of them die. Sometimes, of course, babies were killed, girls more often than boys. In the last year of the Common Era, Hilarion (a Roman husband working in Alexandria 200 miles down the River Nile from his pregnant wife Alis at Oxyrhynchus) wrote:

> I beg you and entreat you to take care of the child and, if I receive my pay soon, I will send it up to you. If you have the baby before I return, if it is a boy, let it live; if it is a girl, expose it. You sent a message with Aphrodisias, 'Don't forget me'. How can I forget you? I beg you, then, not to worry.
>
> (Shelton 1988: 28)

The Julian laws encouraging child-bearing may well have discouraged such practices, and Sarah Pomeroy thinks that Roman female infanticide was not on the same scale as that of the Greeks, where the imbalance in the genders in the cemeteries may indicate a rate of 20 per cent female infant-killing (Pomeroy 1997). Yet, in what is by no means the only evidence for parental grief at the death of a child, we have from Rome the following moving evidence of the sorrow of a mother for the death of her daughter – again, it is interesting how anxious the mother is to 'tell her story' to passers-by:

> Stop, traveller, and read what is written here. A mother was not allowed to enjoy her only daughter. Some god, I don't know which, begrudged her to me. Since I, her mother, was not allowed to dress her while she was alive, I performed this task as was fitting after she died, when her time on earth was over. A mother has honoured with this memorial the daughter whom she loved.
>
> (Shelton 1988: 205)[3]

---

3   The daughter seems to have been a slave and separated from her mother.

Like so many epitaphs, this one is very anxious to communicate to strangers or 'travellers' the details more of the family relationships than of the particular quality of the deceased. In this, Roman and Greek epitaphs are very different from our own, as indeed were their sarcophagi. The sarcophagi and the epitaphs constitute a major resource for the understanding of Roman and Greek attitudes to death: it is to these that I will now turn, regarding them as a 'bridge' between Rome and Greece, which together make up the 'classical' world.

11

OVID'S 'EVER-VARYING FORMS'

Greek mythologies, sarcophagi and the boundaries of mortality

From the arts of those centuries, remove everything that was not largely devoted to religion. The heart of culture then is gone.

(MacMullen 1981: 24)

> Everything changes; nothing dies; the soul
> Roams to and fro, now here, now there, and takes
> What frame it will, passing from beast to man,
> From our own form to beast and never dies.
> As yielding wax is stamped with new designs
> Yet is indeed the same, even so our souls
> Are still the same forever, but adopt
> In their migrations ever-varying forms.
> Therefore lest appetite and greed destroy
> The bonds of love and duty, heed my message!
> Abstain! Never by slaughter dispossess
> Souls that are kin and nourish blood with blood!
>
> (Ovid 1987: 357)

Immortals are mortal, mortals immortal, living the others' death, dead in the others' life.

(Heraclitus, in Lyons 1997: 69)

Funerary equipment is partly mere physical object – a box for a body or a marker for its location – and partly ornament, a repository of symbols and cultural messages, lapidary texts expressing reflections on the fixed but paradoxically always shifting boundary between the gods and humankind, between the immortals and the mortals. Nothing fascinated and preoccupied Greeks and Romans more than this boundary, towards which and occasionally over which gods and demi-gods were endlessly foraging, and over which

155

men and heroes were just as endlessly (but generally hopelessly) trying to climb. The words of the epitaphs and the mythology implicit in the ornament of the sarcophagi are centrally located in these shifting cosmogonies, these 'Metamorphoses', to use the title of one of their more celebrated poetical expressions, quoted above and again here:

> Everything changes; nothing dies; the soul
> Roams to and fro, now here, now there, and takes
> What frame it will ...
>
> ... our souls
>
> Are still the same forever, but adopt
> In their migrations ever-varying forms.
> Therefore lest appetite and greed destroy
> The bonds of love and duty, heed my message!
> Abstain! Never by slaughter dispossess
> Souls that are kin and nourish blood with blood!
>
> (Ovid 1987: 357)

In a way these lines sum up the sense there is in Greco-Roman thought of the dual nature of death, or (just as truly) of life. There is endless and unavoidable change, the 'migrations of ever-varying forms' of Ovid's lines, and there are the this-worldly matters which, in the middle of all this change, are permanently important − 'the bonds of love and duty' which tie men, women and their generations to each other. Greek and Roman *epitaphs*, the subject of the next chapter, tend to be concerned with 'the bonds of love and duty'. The *sarcophagi* and their related mythologies, the subject of this chapter, tend to express the 'ever-varying forms'.

Sarcophagi are an ancient form of corpse-container. The Egyptians used them frequently: a large (2,000 lbs) terracotta sarcophagus, decorated inside and out, of the sixth century BCE (now in the British Museum), is one of over 200 attested similar great tombs manufactured in and around Smyrna (Izmir). From about the second century CE there was a substantial growth in the Roman use of lavish, expensive, marble and highly decorated sarcophagi. Sarcophagi were a Greek funerary style, as were the *osteothekai*, the smaller chests or boxes made to receive the bones which survived from cremation. In 'origin' such funerary artefacts probably come from the Etruscan and Minoan (and perhaps even Egyptian) cultures which preceded and lay behind Greek and Roman societies. The quarrying, carving and transport of heavy marble sarcophagi made them expensive objects, although economies of scale, standardisation of ornament and a degree of 'finishing work' carried out at the point of sale to 'customise' the sarcophagus may have made them available to more and more 'ordinary' Romans (Walker 1985: 18). The use of Greek marble from the quarry at Proconnesus in the sea of Marmara is attested in a tombstone in the Ephesian cemeteries described above. Greece had for centuries used, and exported, marble of various types from this and other quarries at the Phrygian city of Docimeum (the Phrygian sepulchral speciality was a tombstone carved out as a door), at Belevi, near Ephesus; and at Mount Pentelicus, near Athens. This marble had been imported by several emperors to rebuild Rome itself: Greek sculptors and funerary masons found their skills in great demand in the Early and Middle Empire.

Sarcophagi and their ornamentation formed a large part of the successful attempt by Augustus and his successors to impress a ubiquitous imperial culture upon their sprawling empire, and they mobilised as full a repertoire of myths and stories as can be found in Ovid's *Metamorphoses* and *Fasti*. They are lapidary 'texts' presenting to a largely illiterate Roman 'readership' the full sense of the great and successful pedigree of their empire, in which (as Koortbojian puts it) 'the myths evolved along with the people who had recourse to them' (Koortbojian 1995: 3).

There is, inevitably, some disagreement about the reasons for the great expansion in the sarcophagi trade in the second and third centuries CE, although it may be associated with a move away from cremation towards inhumation. Anna McCann believes that:

> By the mid-second century, a deepening belief in life beyond the grave seems to have led to an increased interest in the care of the dead and to a desire for more elaborate personal memorials ... and the growing belief in the immortality of the soul and the resurrection of the body, emphasized especially by the oriental mystery cults and Christianity.
>
> (McCann 1978: 20)

In contrast, we have the comment of Susan Walker (see Chapter 10) that Proclus' early fourth century CE sarcophagus at Aix-en-Provence was totally Greek and unaffected by Christianity (Walker 1985: 15–7).

Koortbojian (1995), while surmising that the move to inhumation was perhaps a revival of older Etruscan and Asia Minor practices, points out that on the 'new' Roman sarcophagi the importation and utilisation of ornament and symbolism was selective and purposeful: the traditions of the past were to be used *for Rome*. Koortbojian concentrates on one aspect of the Romanisation of myth on Roman sarcophagi: the attempt to approach questions of death and life, of mortality and immortality, through the stories of sexual relations between the gods and humans. In Greek mythology, one of the ways whereby the gulf between the gods (the immortals) and men (the mortals) was (albeit with trouble and usually with dangerous consequence) on occasion almost transcended was by sexual union and love between female deities and mortal men and between male deities and human women. The men and women were, naturally, beautiful, and usually in the prime of youth. The death of such men (and indeed of young and beautiful women) was to the Romans particularly tragic, it being the death (*mors immatura*) of young people who had survived the perils of early childhood but who were then denied the *virtus* of maturity. Greek mythology has several stories of the love of a goddess for a male mortal, but the Roman sculptors, funerary masons and their customers adopted only two, the stories of Aphrodite and Adonis and of Selene and Endymion.

Koortbojian shows how the sarcophagi depict the story of Adonis, the beloved of Aphrodite, who rather foolishly perhaps entrusts him to Persephone, goddess of the underworld and niece/wife of Hades, lord of the underworld. Adonis and Aphrodite are shown, in love, on the sarcophagi, but Adonis, in pursuit of the life of manly 'virtue' taken so seriously by the Greeks and Romans (and, millennia before, by Gilgamesh and Enkidu), has to do what young men have to do: risk his life in manly activities, in this case the hunt. On the hunt, he is attacked and wounded (in the groin) by a wild boar. Typically, the last scene on the sarcophagi is the arrival of Aphrodite to try to save Adonis, through her love or through sex, the life-force. Koortbojian comments that the sedate French scholar Cumont actually expurgated an explicitly sexual sarcophagus on which the goddess revives Adonis through sexual intercourse (Koortbojian 1995: 68), even though on numerous other Roman sarcophagi the sexual motif is very clearly rendered in depictions of the lovemaking of Dionysus and Aphrodite (Henrichs 1982: 148).

The Adonis sarcophagi illustrate the ideals of mature Roman (male) life: Adonis as hunter; Adonis the *exemplum virtutis*, representing 'a challenge to the awesome powers of ineluctable fate' (Koortbojian 1995: 38); and a nude Adonis, 'heroically nude' perhaps,

but for that reason the object of desire, of overpowering and therefore doomed sexual attraction. The Cult of Adonis (see Turcan 1996;
Hornblower and Spawforth 1996) may well have celebrated, in the
germination of seeds, more positive 'life-force' elements, the botan-
ical metamorphosis and rebirth or resurrection of Adonis – but the
sarcophagi ignore this completely:

> Each of these scenes [on the sarcophagi] suggests the
> inescapability of Adonis' fate. Just as Aphrodite was unable
> to prevent Adonis' departure for the hunt, so too she was
> helpless to prevent his 'departure' from life. ... The
> imagery evokes the tragic reality that even *heroes* die: to be
> loved by the gods is not enough to save them. ... The three
> scenes of the Aphrodite repertory collectively render a story
> of heroic *virtus*, the *amor* of the gods, and the conquest of
> both by the power of Fate.
>
> (Koortbojian 1995: 41, 48)

Lyons refers to the comment that heroes have an 'obligatory relationship with death' (Lyons 1997: 69), which is to say that they
must suffer death to become a hero. It is the characteristic of Greco-
Roman heroes (as indeed of Mesopotamian heroes) that they must
die as a dignified alternative to a failed attempt at immortality and
divinisation. The Adonis sarcophagi depict this judgement on the
human predicament.

The Selene/Endymion story depicted on the sarcophagi is in a
sense more optimistic. Endymion does not actually die: he sleeps
eternally and is visited regularly by Selene, and is on some
sarcophagi attended by Hypnos (Sleep) and Thanatos (Death). He is,
in his endless sleep, 'immortal' in some sense, and Koortbojian
(1995: 67) notes that he is often represented as much larger than
the visiting Selene and that his genitals are prominently displayed,
indicating that the picture on the sarcophagus is but stage one of
yet another story of anticipated sexual intercourse. A series of Roman
stelae locate the sexual triumph of the 'celestial marriage' in minia-
ture temples which form the pediments of the stelae, that is 'in an
architectural context that was symbolically conceived as the province
of the gods and as a symbol of the celestial realm' (Koortbojian
1995: 78).

The Endymion story, then, would appear to contradict or at least
qualify the Adonis story in envisaging the possibility of something close
to 'immortality', something denied Adonis. Koortbojian however

nature and understanding of the boundaries of life and death, immortality or extinction. There was, of course, no Greek medicine to challenge the hold the gods had on matters of life and death. As Amundsen (1996) shows, Greek medicine was concerned with health, not with prolonging life, an alien idea. As soon as Asklepios' patients looked as if they were going to die, they were asked to leave the Asklepion. Zeus killed Asklepios for presuming to challenge the monopoly and power of the gods, and their determination that men must die.

It is, in Greco-Roman and other Ancient Near Eastern stories, *men* who seek most anxiously to attain immortality. It seems to be a particularly male concern. In the myths and the sarcophagi, and in the metamorphoses of flesh and spirit, of life and death that they symbolise, we do however find myths of heroines *as recipients of*, rather than seekers after immortality. Lyons makes the interesting point that many more mortal *women*, the heroines, achieve apotheosis than do men, but in a way peculiar to the female sex, related to their restricted, depersonalised and 'unnamed' social status, and usually associated with circumstances of actual or attempted rape and abduction. Such women do not achieve *individual* immortality. They become stars or animals, attaining species or orbital immortality. Io, for example, becomes a cow, Kallisto a she-bear and Cassiopeia a constellation. Lyons sums up the style and function of such specifically female transcendence of the boundary between mortal/ immortal:

> In such contexts the solution to the problem of mortality is translation into the animal or vegetable world, with species-continuity replacing the continuing life of the individual, or transformation into astronomical phenomena whose enduring nature is obvious. ... Cut off from mortal or heroic spheres of action, these heroines are far less likely to achieve *kleos* [fame or glory] through any action of their own but are paradoxically more likely to achieve it by making the leap to immortality. ... Heroines have unique powers, related to their ability to transcend death. Acting in sympathy with gods, they mediate symbolically between the remoteness of divinity and the direct experience of mortals.
>
> (Lyons 1997: 27, 58, 171)

Few men can be seen settling for such non-individual forms of immortality! Indeed there are only two male-mortals who, in all the heavenwards effort, actually appear to have made it and become immortal: Herakles and Dionysus.

The world of Greek religion and mythology – flourishing in cultic centres in the Hellenic world, and being endlessly refreshed or overwhelmed by Egyptian, Babylonian and Roman notions of gods and men, of mortals and immortals, of heroes and heroines – has indeed the flexibility and capacity for innovation on which Sourvinou-Inwood commented. When the Romans and Greeks needed a new god, they got one, and the Hellenistic world is full of extraordinary innovatory attempts to 'jump the boundary' between the gods and humans, to comprehend and transcend the brute fact of human mortality. This spirit found its institutional reflection in the numerous cults and rites of the Roman Empire as described by contemporary writers such as Ovid in the *Fasti* or, somewhat later and in different style, by Lucius Apuleius in *The Golden Ass*. Lucius, Apuleius' namesake and hero, undergoes a radical metamorphosis – he becomes an ass – and after a series of adventures encounters Isis 'natural mother of all things, chief of the powers divine, queen of all that are in hell, the principal of them that dwell in heaven, manifested alone and in one form of all the gods and goddesses' (Apuleius 1996: 187). She takes Lucius under her protection, promising him:

> You shall live blessed in this world, glorious by my guide
> and protection, and when after thine allotted span of life
> thou descendest to hell, there thou shalt see me in that
> subterranean firmament shining in the darkness of
> Acheron, and reigning in the deep profundity of Styx, and
> thou shalt worship me.
>
> (ibid.: 189)

Isis was, of course, the major Egyptian deity, absorbed as readily into the Greco-Roman pantheon as were so many others. Even she, however, does not offer immunity to death or an avoidance of the underworld.

To Plutarch, the genius of Greco-Roman religion lay precisely in this ability to absorb the gods of other places:

> Isis and the gods related to her belong to all men and are
> known to them. ... There is nothing wrong with this if in

the first place they preserve the gods as our common
heritage, and do not make them the peculiar property of
the Egyptians.

(Plutarch 1970: 221–3)

It was, however, this very resourcefulness and inventiveness which,
in the first Christian centuries, earned the contempt of Christian
apologists such as Clement of Alexandria, who dismissed such cultic
competence as the work of 'raving poets' full of 'maimed, wrinkled,
squinting divinities' (Clement 1909: 18, 60). He poured scorn on
the ability of the Greco-Roman cultic system to answer human
questions about death. He ridiculed statues made of gold or covered
with gold leaf, and the depictions on walls of houses and on tombstones of 'Aphrodite locked in the embrace of her paramour' or of
men 'entombed with a lifeless paramour' (ibid.: 63, 62). The
temples where the Greeks kept their gods and demi-gods he refers
to as 'tombs', saying that the cults are 'audacious impieties',
showing that the 'heathens' to whom he is speaking are 'completely
dead, putting as you do your trust in the dead' (ibid.: 51). Clement
asks:

> How, then, can shades and demons be still reckoned gods,
> being in reality unclean and impure spirits, acknowledged
> to be of an earthy and watery nature, sinking downwards
> by their own weight; and flitting about graves and tombs,
> about which they appear dimly, being but shadowy phan-
> toms? Such things are your gods – shades and shadows ...
> maimed, wrinkled, squinting divinities.
>
> (ibid.: 60)

Clement, originally a pagan philosopher, was very familiar with the
works of Homer and Hesiod, as well as those of the other great
Greek and Roman writers; indeed one of his favourite polemical
tricks is to use, say, Homer to debunk beliefs in sacrifice and various
other god-propitiating activities: 'God', he writes in a single
dismissive phrase, 'needs nothing', by which he means that there is
nothing that human beings can do *for* God (ibid.: 102). Nothing
could be more unlike the gods of Greece and Rome, endlessly
surrounded by cultic propitiatory and calendrical rites, expressing
and insisting on their active relevance in day-to-day life and death.

Setting aside Clement for now, there is, in this mythology and
thanatology, a permanent and usually futile but never abandoned

'boundary dispute' going on in the minds of men, as they push the limits of their mortality as far as they can into the realm of the gods – and then retreat, with little reward but pain and humiliation. Heraclitus (500 BCE), already quoted, probably best captures this rather terrible and always tragic expression of the human condition:

> Immortals are mortal, mortals immortal, living the others' death, dead in the others' life (Lyons 1997: 68)

Is there, over these many centuries and cultures, a 'trend' in the nature of these boundary transactions, a linear development in Greek and Hellenistic attitudes to the possibility of transcending death? Sourvinou-Inwood argues (very tentatively) that as the Homeric and associated tales achieved some degree of 'closure' in the eighth century BCE, they became for many centuries, and perhaps remain, among the central foundation documents of a culture containing within itself a tension between the deeply rooted conviction that 'everyone must die' and a developing, but uncertain and tentative, subscription to the idea of a special dispensation at least for an elite and exemplary pioneering few – the human lovers of goddesses, for example, or great soldiers and heroes, or heroines, or emperors (Sourvinou-Inwood 1995: 52–3).

This was no sudden or even very clear development. The architectural demonstration on the sarcophagi and on the face of the myths of the essential 'unknowability' of what the gods would do, especially at death, and even for the chosen few, remained powerful and pervasive. The old wisdom of 'all men must die' would endlessly correct and qualify whatever trend there might have been towards a belief that it *was* possible to bridge the terrible division between the gods and humans. This division lay in creation itself: humans die and gods do not. Asklepios met this barrier full-on, as did the fifth century BCE Greek-Sicilian polymath Empedocles when he claimed to have descended to the underworld to fetch back the vital soul of a human. 'The idea of trying to bring someone back from the dead was, in the framework of normal Greek morality, almost unthinkable' and was essentially, says Kingsley, a Babylonian-Zoroastrian idea, not a Greek one (Kingsley 1995: 226). Yet neither the derision heaped on Empedocles, nor the death of Asklepios (a god, after all) could end the effort, especially by and on behalf of various kinds of 'hero', to transcend the boundary. Where the Ancient Egyptians became Osiris, where biblical Jews sought to approach God and his heaven through the Covenant, and where

Christians would later seek everlasting life through their own reborn saviour, Greeks and Romans sought to address the problem of death through a world of heroic metamorphoses, mythically amply in evidence around them, but never finalised because almost by definition they could not be. Lucius is saved by meeting Isis, but he still has to die – albeit to a somewhat better Styx.

We will conclude this part of the book with a return to the perennial and central concern of both Greeks and Romans for 'feeling out the boundary' between gods and men, between extinction and immortality, between mortal supplicant and the immortal gods. At this point, however, I would like to look at the mirror-image of the extraordinarily volatile world of metamorphoses, the very down-to-earth workmanlike practicalities of Greco-Roman epitaphs and funeral orations. The same world which gave us Ovid also gave us Plutarch and Aristides, as sure as anyone could be of the permanence of the Roman world, a world grounded in urbanity and self-confidence, sceptical and contemptuous of 'superstition', especially superstition about death, but insistent on proper familial decorum in funerals and funerary arrangements.

12

OVID'S 'BONDS OF LOVE AND DUTY'

Funerals, epitaphs, orations and death in the arena

At the risk of huge over-simplification, I will deal only briefly with Greek funerals. Most of what we know is about Athens. As with Rome, there was a high degree of public regulation, operating through both 'customary practices' (in a highly tradition-bound society) and specific sumptuary laws. Evidence for the archaic period indicates that funerary monuments were resorted to in the event of 'untimely' death – of children, of young men in war, of unmarried women (Humphreys 1980: 104). Pomeroy and others note that the main rationale for classical and Hellenistic burial customs and law was to reinforce the solidity and social position of the family group through the enactment of appropriate forms of interment, sculpture, ornament and commemoration (Pomeroy 1997). Greek burials were family affairs using extramural cemeteries and family plots, usually with single burials. The family focus included considerable concern for inheritance: in cases of disputed inheritance the person actually organising the burial would, for that reason, have a good claim on the property. A family which left its dead unburied (practically unthinkable) or not properly disposed of and commemorated through set rites and post-mortem remembrance, incurred enormous human disapproval and divine revenge. Endowments, together with slaves freed on condition of looking after the tomb, would fill in for any family default or dereliction, should this occur.

The extramural nature of Greek burial, as with Roman, arose out of a sense of the 'pollution' of death and a desire to keep the world of the dead and that of the living away from each other. Paradoxically, however, it enhanced the status of the dead. The (day time) funeral and the visits and processions to the places of the dead, given that the dead were some distance away, in a place dedicated solely to them, increased the consequentiality of the funeral and remembrance.

The processional activity, at death and at times of anniversary and remembrance, was the liturgy, the way of managing death. The following rather lengthy quotation provides a graphic account of a first century CE death: the public burial and the civic commemoration of a citizen of the city of Kyzikos, located on what is now called the Sea of Marmara, then the Propontis.

> The *demos* and the Romans engaged in business in the city honoured Apollonis, daughter of Prokles, because of her parents' virtue and that of her husband, and because of her own moderation. ... In view of these things the citizens instructed all the magistrates to inaugurate appropriate honours for her. As a result, indeed, the *demos* has resolved: the totality of all men and women who live in the *polis* are to be in mourning. The temples, sacred areas and all the shrines are to be closed ... until her burial. The presidents and the eponymous magistrates are to follow the cortege, as also are the boys, ephebes, citizens, and all the free males who live in the city; likewise unmarried girls, female citizens, and the remaining free women who live in the city. Since she has been granted the privilege of a funeral dressed in beautiful (clothes [i.e. dressed in purple]), she is to be interred in her husband's ancestral vault, near the Great Harbour. The presidents who hold the presidency for the month of Anthesterion are to crown her (i.e. her statue) annually with a gold crown at the Anthesteria festival on the twelfth and thirteenth days, while the sacred herald proclaims, after those who have been previously honoured, 'The *demos* crowns Apollonis, daughter of Prokles, because of her parents' virtue and that of her husband, and because of her own moderation, with this perpetual crown'. A place for her statue is to be provided at the Charitesion, on the right side where people enter from the Sacred Agora in which also stands her statue. And in view of the fact that she held the priesthood of Artemis amongst the Pythaistrides, as a testimony of her piety concerning religion, on the seventh day of Artemision annually when the priestesses, the Pythaistrides, and the temple overseers assemble in the Charitesion, they are to crown her statue. Additionally, in order that the remembrance of her moderation may be visible to all the city, a statue of her is to be erected in one of the rooms on the Square Agora on its eastern portico, which

lies between the office of the *timetai* and the *Agoranomion*. The *kosmophylax* and his successors in the magistracy are to have the use of this office in perpetuity once it has been decorated. Those who register with the *kosmophylax* the formalisation of their marriage are required to garland the statue of Apollonis which is dedicated in the office. And other statues of her are to be set up ... [in the shrine?] of Aphrodite ... in the shrine of Artemis ... and a statue in. ... A gilded statue is to be set up in whatever location her relatives choose. Beneath the statues the following inscription is to be recorded: 'The *demos* and the Romans engaged in business in the city honoured Apollonis because of her parents' virtue and that of her husband, and because of her own moderation'. The treasurer is to record this decree on her tomb. May the decree be for the safeguarding of the city.

(Horsley 1987: 12–13)

This is clearly a case where family reputation and concerns mesh with those of the *polis*, with a huge emphasis on maintaining the dead, 'active', in this world, and not on ideas of a 'return' of the dead or resurrection, to which the living had to attend.

Greek funerals (see Pomeroy 1997; Hornblower and Spawforth 1996; Garland 1985) followed a general pattern with which we are still familiar – with some differences. Dying and death were so strongly family affairs that after the funeral no one was allowed to visit the graveside other than family members. Priests were barred from taking part in funerals, to avoid pollution, i.e. the pollution *of the priest* by the potentially disruptive force of unleashed emotions. There is no record of any standard formal funeral liturgy. The funeral, together with sacrifices and funerary banquet, in effect became part of an individual and/or familial grave 'cult', the site of visits and libations (Pomeroy 1997: 102–4), with particular days (the *nekysia* or days of the dead, and the *genesia*, days of the forefathers) being set aside for such purposes. Libations and food offerings underwrote the belief that on one day, but only for one day, the *anthesteria* (the dead) would emerge and travel through the city. Libations poured into urns or open chambers were deemed to be a physical way of actually contacting the person-body interred in the ground. To what manner of existent these libations were being offered is problematic.

Ian Morris shows that tomb size and ornamentation and the specific location within the cemetery were determined by social status (of the male): 'burials', he writes, 'are the material remains of self-representations of social structure through the agency of ceremony' (Morris 1987: 8):

> The Greeks explicitly linked the spatial organisation of cemeteries with the membership of the corporate group and with landholding, and the exclusion of groups from the formal cemeteries, on the basis of age and rank, constituted a powerful statement about the ideal structure of the community.
>
> (ibid.: 44)

Wide conceptions of citizenship produced a less hierarchical burial practice; narrow conceptions of citizenship increased the hierarchy.

Pomeroy makes the very telling point that Greek cemeteries replicate gender hierarchies, as well as others. Women are statistically under-represented on individually identifiable grave markers, themselves a sign of high status: this, plus a high rate of female infanticide, produces an under-representation of women in Greek cemeteries of about 30 per cent (Pomeroy 1997: 120–1). Pomeroy points out that the laws which regulated funeral practices were aimed at controlling women, generally regarded as dangerous when appearing 'in public', for example at funerals, and particularly so when infused with the emotionality likely to be engendered at times of death and mourning. Women's 'emotionality' was generally felt to be most problematic on such occasions (Pomeroy 1997; Simms 1998).

By contrast male-controlled burials, in particular the burial of the war dead, were characterised by formal eulogising rather than by processions and lamentations. 'Great' men and heroes would be buried intramurally, itself a sign of great honour. Their intramural tombs would become cult centres, where civic rites became part of the overall politic-religious hierarchy of the *polis*. It should be noted that such practices would have been most suspect in the eyes of normative Judaism described above, although popular pressure would no doubt have pushed in the opposite direction. I will return to this aspect, the 'bond of duty', in the concluding section of this chapter.

Greek and Roman epitaphs have been extensively studied. The major student of Greek and Roman funerary inscriptions, Richmond Lattimore, is of the opinion that 'the belief of the ancients, both Greek and Roman, in immortality, was not widespread, nor clear, nor very strong' (Lattimore 1942: 342). Lattimore uses data from the seventh century BCE for Greece, through the Hellenistic and Roman periods, and coming well into the 'Christian centuries'. Of the inscriptions, epitaphs are a very large part, interesting precisely because of the 'criticism' made of them by Robert Garland when he sets out to write about *The Greek Way of Death*:

> Epitaphs are of limited value to this study since, with some signal exceptions, the majority record little more than the achievements and virtues of the deceased and the sense of loss he has bequeathed to his relatives.
>
> (Garland 1985: xi)

This, of course, is precisely why they are so fascinating! Why, above the place or 'home' of the dead, is there so little about death? To be fair to Garland, there is over the centuries covered by Lattimore a long slow trend away from the terse and relatively uninformative very early Greek inscriptions to the rather verbose productions of the Empire and Hellenism.

Epitaphs tend, though only tend, to get us a bit closer to the concerns of 'ordinary' Greeks and Romans, and indeed to those most invisible of all humans: women and children. Perhaps a supplicatory prayer, rather than an epitaph, may be allowed as introductory evidence that nothing much changes in the entanglements of children and their mothers with their fathers and husbands: it is noticeable how strongly the mother objects to what seems to be the father's failure to attend properly to his child's funeral. The prayer, of uncertain date, is from Hellenistic Egypt.

> O master Oserapis and the gods who sit with Oserapis, I pray to you, I, Artemisie, against my daughter's father, who robbed her of the funeral gift and tomb. So if he has not acted justly toward me and his own children – as indeed he has acted unjustly toward me and his own children – let Oserapis and the gods grant that he approach not the grave of his children, nor that he bury his own parents. As long as my cry for help is deposited here, he and what belongs to him should be utterly destroyed badly, both on earth and on sea, by Oserapis and the gods who sit together with Oserapis, nor should he attain propitiation from Oserapis nor from the gods who sit with Oserapis.
>
> (Kraemer 1988: 95)

Unlike such written depositions, epitaphs were not cheap to put onto stone, even at the lower end of the market: as with pre-eighteenth century CE English wooden grave markers, any wooden Greco-Roman 'memorials' will have rotted with the wood. Lattimore notes a tendency to use set formulae (Lattimore 1942: 18–19), and the degree of standardisation may reflect the existence of handbooks or lists of stock phrases and sentiments used by stone masons, a practice familiar today in the 'In Memoriam' poems and litanies to be found in the columns of nearly all local newspapers in Britain (Davies 1994: 36 ff.).

Epitaphs and tombstones were one of the ways in which Greeks and Romans (and, later, Christians) dealt with the business of actually commemorating, rather than attempting (and failing) to immortalise or revitalise the dead. More importantly, they tell us of the importance *to the family* (an entity extending over several generations) of the reputation of each individual member of it, each of whom were expected to live their lives with the reputation of their family in mind. Within the almost limitless variety of biography, this factor tended to produce a formulaic style, aimed at associating the deceased and their families with the values and stability of the *polis* and, later, the Empire. Around the tombstone inscriptions will be located the other appurtenances of 'monumental' burial such as busts, death masks, poems, '*imagines*' (funerary portraits of entire families) and, for the richer citizens, statues and mausolea, further evidence, as Zanker puts it, of the success of Augustus' 'moral revival ... a religious and spiritual renewal' (Zanker 1988: 3). It should perhaps be repeated that this 'renewal' was a renewal of life and faith in this world, not a subscription to a belief in an 'active' life after death (see Lattimore above). What Mikalson says of the Greeks is probably as true of the Romans: they 'expected neither rewards nor punishments in the afterlife for their deeds in this life. What mattered ... was this life' (Mikalson 1983: 82). Or, more laconically, in a widely used Lucretius-like formula: 'I was not, I was, I am not, I don't care' – i.e. 'First I was nothing, then I became something, now I am nothing again; and being nothing, I do not care' (Lattimore 1942: 84–5).

On Greco-Roman tombstones in particular the inscription records not only the name of the deceased but also the name and relationship to the deceased of the commemorator. Often enough this is the heir of the deceased. In Meyer's view this is evidence of the importance in the matter of death of establishing the stability and continuity of the family. In support of this, she quotes the dignified Cicero:

> What do the procreation of children, the propagation of the name, the adoption of sons, the care taken about wills, the very burial monuments and epitaphs mean, if not that we also think about the future – that is posterity?
>
> (Meyer 1990: 76)

When society is stable and the state powerful, then the appeal to posterity will be confident and proclamatory: societies and states in trouble do not build comfortable monuments, and neither do their citizens.

The statistical incidence of funerary memorials is by no means random, and seems to follow, in both Greece and Rome, changes in the fortunes of society, both internally and externally. Meyer analyses over 10,000 Athenian epitaphs, the number of which rose in the first half of the fourth century BCE, then fell away in the second century BCE, and then fluctuated until they petered out in the third century CE. This she explains by seeing them as 'assertions of citizenship', emerging to proclaim membership of the *polis* at times when such citizenship was 'valued and honoured' and diminishing together with that citizenship and the political and military standing of Athens in the Greek world (Meyer 1993).

She makes a somewhat similar point for Roman epitaphs, when the variation (large numbers in the first and second centuries CE, falling thereafter) is also explained by the changing potency and attraction of Roman power and prestige and the associated felt need of new citizens to use tombstones to proclaim their participation in the great imperial adventure (Meyer 1990). In different mode, post-Constantine Christian burials move from being underground to being 'in the open', above ground, a statement perhaps of a sense of security and indeed of triumph (see Shaw 1984; 1996).

Apart from its appearance on the actual tombstone (in imperial Rome in particular) the startlingly different form that so many of these epitaphs take (different, that is, from our own) is in their 'audience'. They speak, as it were, as from the tomb, and as from the tomb-occupier, to the general passer-by. They are anxious to broadcast 'virtue' to anyone who would stop to listen. It must have been the case, for all but the most prescient of souls, that the actual language and nature of the broadcast would emanate from survivors, usually family members. They represent, therefore, a kind of public announcement on behalf of the family, symbolised in the moral worth of the deceased *in this, secular, world*, and of the virtue flowing from the deceased's life for all his family members:

> For 39 years married to one husband, lived to her last day in the greatest concord, left three surviving children by him, a son who held the highest municipal posts through the favour of Augustus Caesar, another who in the army of the same A.C. has held the highest post of equestrian rank, and a most virtuous daughter, married to a most upright man, and through her, two grandchildren ...
>
> (Braund 1985: 271)[1]

This is an example of what Pomeroy would no doubt call, in the Greek context, 'the *polis* taking precedence' in matters of death (Pomeroy 1997: 126). The dead woman is anxious to locate her virtue in what she has produced for the state and for society – two sons in the public service, and a daughter married to an upright man. She dies a grandmother, a Roman matron. Lattimore reports a second century BCE Greek woman, dying in not quite such a confident mode:

> Nicandros was my father, my country was Paros, and my name Socratea. My husband Parmenion buried me when I died, granting me that favour so that my seemly life might be remembered even among those to come. The Erinys of bearing a child (which none can guard against) destroyed my pleasant life through a haemorrhage. Nor by my travail could I bring the baby into the light, but he lies here among the dead in my own womb.
>
> (Lattimore 1942: 270)

A major reason for high female mortality (Scheidel 1996) was of course the dangerous business of pregnancy, dangerous in this case it would seem for both mother and child. Socratea here implies that her husband had the right to refuse to bury her, but that he did in fact bury her, so her life, and evidently his decency, could be remembered: a 'seemly life'. Another, Roman, epitaph from the same century may serve to explicate further the nature of female seemliness:

> Friend, I have not much to say: stop and read it. This tomb, which is not fair, is for a fair woman. Her parents

---

1 An epitaph for a woman who died at Niger near Corfinium, 300 miles south-east of Rome.

174

gave her the name Claudia. She loved her husband in her heart. She bore two sons, one of whom she left on earth, the other beneath it. She was pleasant to talk with, and she walked with grace. She kept the house, and she worked in wool. That is all. You may go.

(Lattimore 1942: 271)

What, one has to wonder, would Socratea and Claudia, proud wives and mothers, and the equally proud anonymous grandmother above, have made of Euripides' *The Bacchae*, in which the mother, in the grip of Bacchic possession, tears out the arm of her own son and with her mob of bacchantes proceeds to pull him to bits? *The Bacchae* is a play designed to 'épater' precisely the kind of middle-class matrons that are proclaiming their virtues on these epitaphs. Perhaps the matrons concerned would have found their 'respectability' buttressed by the very real evidence the epitaphs give of spousal love and affection. Two further examples will be enough:

Chaerestrate lies in this tomb. Her husband loved her as long as she lived, and when she died he grieved for her.

(Lattimore 1942: 275)[2]

I, Nicon, who have written this was her husband, but am no longer. For I gave my lovely one over to the keeping of another who begrudged me, and I long for her, because of her goodness – as I have already written – and yet it avails me not at all. I lament, but she does not hear. I hold fast by my love, and shall remain even as I was. Yet it avails me not at all; for she has vanished, just like the wind.

(ibid.: 276)[3]

Lattimore notes that *sine ulla querella* ('never a day's quarrel') is the almost formulaic phrase found on many epitaphs, being the evaluation that the surviving partner (at least!) has of their marriage. No doubt our Greek and Roman ancestors would have been as anxious as we are to say nothing but good of their lives together at the time of death (but probably nowhere near as anxious to sneer at marriage

---

2   From Piraeus, fourth or third century BCE.
3   From Crete, third or fourth century CE.

and the realities of conjugal love). Pomeroy notes how often, on Greek epitaphs, women are identified in their domestic roles as wives and mothers, a pattern she finds present and indeed emphasised in Ptolemaic Egypt (Pomeroy 1997: 128). The epitaphs and other material quoted in Shelton (1988: 45 ff.) demonstrate how powerfully patriarchal Hellenistic society was, in death as in life. Yet the epitaphs also, it seems to me, demonstrate very clearly that Greek and Roman husbands and wives loved each other (why does this even need saying?), and that the death of a partner, or the death of a child, broke hearts then, as now. The epitaphs do show differences between then and now: the reputation of the family and mutual love are clearly bound up in each other – the public and the private intersect, although the pattern of dedications clearly shows that commemoration was a family, not a public matter (Saller 1994: 33 ff.).

The epitaphs also show both how vulnerable people were to illness and death, and how phlegmatic they were, in at least a portion of their being, in the face of the Fates or the Furies that took away a child or demanded the 'not fair' death that took Claudia. Lattimore has several examples of epitaphs objecting, but in a rather accepting way, to the way in which the Fates have snapped the 'strands of life' which have been spun for each of us, threads which are the same length as life itself: 'at fifteen the grievous thread of the Fates snatched you away' (Lattimore 1942: 159), an image Lattimore interprets as signifying that death 'completes' life. We have seen in Chapter 11 how Isis described Lucius' death in this way.

The sense of being in the hands of inscrutable gods, sometimes cruel gods, is to be found on the epitaphs, as is the image of life as a road with a fixed end: 'the road that is the due of all who live' (ibid.: 169). Shaw, in contrasting early Christian epitaphs with those of late paganism, states that the latter accept that the dead will never live again, and concentrate therefore on their secular, familial relationships, including those with the commemorator. The pagan tombstones and other funerary ornament *face into this world*, the deceased being concerned to build their status on a reputation in this world, and showing little sense of a retained 'life' in a world to come. By contrast, the Christian stones see the dead as only temporarily 'asleep', and concentrate on their impending, individual relationship with the God who awaits them and their resurrection (Shaw 1984). Pagans are permanently in the tomb, the 'eternal home'. Indeed, the tomb is on occasion seen as a hotel or as a residence:

All a person needs. Bones reposing sweetly, I am not anxious about suddenly being short of food. I do not suffer from arthritis, and I am not indebted because of being behind with my rent. In fact lodgings are permanent – and free!

(Jones and Sidwell 1997: 148)

Again there is here a direct 'address' to passers-by, almost casual in its tone, like Claudia, above, who ends her message to her readers with: 'That is all. You may go.' A third century CE Greek tombstone tells everyone that 'I, a small tomb, conceal no small man' (Lattimore 1942: 228), and another is very clear in its reason for existence: 'his wife inscribed the stele to keep his name so that mortals, even those yet to come, may learn of it' (ibid.: 230). Another, clearly assuming that the readers ('strangers') will be primarily men, or perhaps that it is the male readers who are most in need of advice, says: 'Farewell, stranger: go your way, and find no fault with your own wife' (ibid.: 236).

Whether expressed as example, perhaps in the 'seemliness' of wives and matrons, or as exhortation ('find no fault with your wife'), these are statements made to the passing public, to strangers, people who the dead are represented as wanting to keep on the path of civic and social virtue. The epitaphs also, as we have seen, give a voice to the relatively ordinary: I will conclude with one of those, a Roman tradesman anxious, it would appear, to maintain customer good-will even after he was dead!

I am now free from care, who once was well known in the Holy City for selling leather goods ... I displayed wares suitable to popular use. My exceptional good faith was praised everywhere. When doing work on a contract, I always kept my accounts straight, and was on the level in all my dealings, as fair to all as I could be, and sometimes a help to a persistently needy person, always generous and always going shares with my friends.

(Jones and Sidwell 1997: 143–4)[4]

These epitaphs, of small tradesmen and mothers of slaves, get us as close as we are ever going to get to the windows on to the death of

---

4   From a village epitaph, forty-five miles north of Rome.

our more ordinary ancestors. So, in a society of almost permanent war, do war memorials.

As far back as our history goes, war memorials have been among the most ubiquitous forms of 'Western' or European statuary and death monuments. Every country creates public monuments to its war dead. In style and ornament, contemporary war memorials often recapitulate Greek and Roman attitudes to war and the men (generally men) who die in war. The monument in northern France at Thiepval, for example, is a series of triumphal arches soaring over an empty sarcophagus, the arches from Rome, the empty tomb the Greek symbol for the missing in war. The range of emotions elicited by such memorials is not the same as the range of emotions elicited by ordinary funerals, although it is ordinary men they celebrate. The public burials of the Greek war dead, in collective tombs, in Athens in the Kerameikos, were specifically removed from a 'lamentation' atmosphere and from the family ambience. The funeral oration, by a public orator, and restricted to such occasions, was aimed at celebrating the memory of the dead, not at grieving for them, and at proclaiming the 'immortality' of the *polis* through their deaths. Such burials were political occasions, male-dominated, in which pride and praise, not sorrow and grief, were the dominant emotions. Loraux argues that in this way Athens actually 'invented' itself:

> To praise any Athenian in Athens amounts, then, to praising the Athenians, all Athenians, dead and alive, and above all 'we who are still living, those who coincide with the city's present'.
>
> (Loraux 1986: 2)

Deborah Lyons notes how such funeral orations record women only as an absence. Pericles ended what must be one of the greatest of all war orations by telling the women that 'the greatest glory of a woman is to be least talked about by men' (Thucydides 1972: 151; Lyons 1997: 57). The community that the orations 'invent' is the community of martial men and their attendant women. Indeed, in martial cultures such as Greece and Rome, it is around the commemorated deaths of men in war that are constructed the general pattern of gender relationships.

While the public burials of the Athenian war dead were indeed primarily about men, they were about *all* men. They were a contrast to the elitism of ordinary burial, which in spite of sumptuary laws would reflect the social hierarchy. So Humphreys can say:

> Sculptured monuments, like ostentatious funerals, loudly proclaimed that the dead belonged to the elite. Paying visits to the tombs of famous ancestors was not a pious duty, but a way of reminding contemporaries of the glory of one's own family. It was the state funerals for the war dead which first brought the honours of heroic burial within the range of every Athenian citizen, and I would suggest that it was this significant change which stimulated the development in the late fifth and fourth centuries of monuments commemorating the domestic virtues of ordinary citizens.
>
> (Humphreys 1980: 123)

As we have seen in the case of the Jewish wars, and as is certainly the case in our times with (in particular) World War I, war and death in war are major determinants of thanatology. Christian culture had little difficulty in adapting Greek (and Roman) military *funeraria*, including tomb-cults, to their own soldiers and heroes, the saints and martyrs of the Church, and, much later, to those millions of 'ordinary citizens' who 'gave their lives' so that the living might live.

War alters, for Greeks and Romans as well as for us, the nature of what it is (the 'soul' or some aspect of it) that is seen as 'surviving' death. It is the *psychē* which, in the Homeric poems, seems to survive death; two other parts of the person-body, the *thymos* and the *aion*, seem not to. The *psychē*, as *eidelon*, was that part of the person which survived to become the 'I', the discarded body simply rotting and the *thymos* and *aion* vanishing (Sourvinou-Inwood 1995: 56). The epitaph on the Athenian war dead at Poteidia in 432 BCE states that 'the ether received their *psychai*, but earth their bodies', and a fourth-century inscription from the Peirios also sent the body of Eurymachos to the grave but his '*psychē* and proud spirit to the ether' (Garland 1985: 75). Generally, the Greek dead were not 'proud', but lacking in vigour, witless, minus their personality, needing a libation of blood before they could 'recognise' anyone, and with little knowledge of what was going on in the upper world. Sourvinou-Inwood regards this view of the dead as changing, very gradually and only partially, towards a notion of a happy afterlife, if only for the chosen few. These 'few', she writes, were initially the war dead, whose public epitaphs indicate a process not only of civic immortality through glory, and of heroisation, but also of celestial immortality (Sourvinou-Inwood 1995: 54, 194). Mikalson quotes Hyperides on the afterlife of the war dead:

> If death is like non-existence, these men are freed from diseases and suffering and from the other things which beset the life of a human being. But if men have perception in the house of Hades and if they are cared for by the daimonic [element], as we suspect they are, then it is reasonable to assume that those who defended the abused honors of the gods find the greatest care from the daimonic.
>
> (Mikalson 1983: 78)

The war dead were 'heroes', men who most closely approached the gods. In the great epics, heroes contend more with the gods than with each other. The endless wars of Greece and Rome, however, provided a flow of heroes, located within battles and massacres which underpinned this construction of the essential male. Casualty rates in Greek and Roman wars were pretty much those of the wars of this century. Athens' wars were citizen wars, and even under the Empire, with a professional army, the scale of the army made military experience normative for men. Appropriate commemorative acts sat well with popular views: 'the funeral oration', writes Walters, 'was a true *vox populi*' (Walters 1980: 20). Cared for in the other world, such men had highest regard in this. Herodotus describes how Solon regarded the Athenian Tellus as the happiest man who ever lived because:

> His end was surpassing glorious. In a battle between Athenians and their neighbours near Eleusis, he came to the assistance of his countrymen, routed the foe, and died upon the field most gallantly. The Athenians gave him a public funeral on the spot where he fell, and paid him the highest honours.
>
> (Herodotus 1996: 17)

There is no need here to analyse the Greek and Roman eulogies to and for the war dead. They are too familiar. They represent the male counterpart of the matronly virtues expressed on the epitaphs, the virtues necessary for the stability and glory of the *polis* and the Empire, the virtues necessary for posterity. They were explicitly formulated in that way by Pericles in the classic statement of male military virtue, in Athens in 430 BCE. These were virtues readily taken into Roman civic culture, and later Christian eulogies for *their* martyred dead would to some extent amplify and echo the form and often the content of such statements: they did not have to rebut them. Indeed, the Greco-Roman 'hero cult' had some attractions to later popular Christianity. The Greek heroes had their own cultic practices which took place around the hero's tomb. The hero was a human. Yet this did not prevent him, once dead, from playing something of the role played by Christian martyrs and saints. The hero 'delivered oracles, effected cures, provided protection, and dealt out retribution' (Zaidman and Pantel 1992: 179).

I will, in Part IV, address at some length the matter of the 'character' or pedigree of the Christian martyr. I have already noted, in Part II, how the wars and martyrdoms of the Jewish resistance to Rome provided another, potent contribution to early and late Christian elaboration of the cult of the martyr-hero. In like manner, the power of Pericles' oration could be carried over many miles and many cultures and centuries to Gettysburg, where it was used by Edward Everett, the official orator, speaking before Lincoln. It can be found on the walls of the Scottish National War Memorial in Edinburgh Castle, where it eulogises the Scottish dead of the Great War:

> The whole earth is the tomb of heroic men, and their story
> is not graven in stone over their clay, but abides everywhere
> without visible symbol, woven into the stuff of other men's
> lives.

To repeat, funeral orations and commemorations for the war dead of a democracy, or even a democracy's posterity, be it Greek or Roman or American or European, must not be seen as some 'minority' interest or as reflecting some marginal theodicy. They are generally the absolute opposite of that, distilling out of a whole welter of religion and myth and grief, the genuinely religious feelings for the dead on the part both of their surviving comrades and the broader community for whom the dead died – and lived. Not all soldiers are martyrs, of course, nor all martyrs soldiers: in some respects Greeks and Romans kept the two concepts very far apart, being much more adulatory of military prowess and the joys of the 'triumph', the proof of the power and stability of the Empire.

The terrible paradox, of course, is that the martial virtues which are necessary for the well-being of the community are also those which most readily threaten it. Just as 'the seemly virtues' of the Roman matron were endlessly threatened by the spectres of maternal mortality and child mortality, the deadly results of domestic sex, so the male-dominated Roman state was under perpetual siege by war, both civil and foreign, and by its attendant famine and pestilence. 'War' was a part of the fabric of society, on a par with earthquakes, droughts, destructive storms and slavery' (Hornblower and Spawforth 1996: 1619). Pritchett is referring to Greece, but the comment applies to Rome. The Roman state existed in a condition of permanent crisis, whether due to internal dynastic struggles or external wars, or to natural calamities. It could live only by killing, in deadly wars abroad or in 'fatal charades' in the domestic arenas (Coleman 1990; Kyle 1998). The quiet good sense and humour of the epitaphs, especially of the women, and the firm pride and genuine accomplishment of the soldiers and their memorials may well add up to a 'theodicy of good fortune', as Max Weber described it (Weber 1970: 271). The 'metamorphoses' of Ovid, the shifting base on which the apparent solidity stood, may seem relatively benign when set alongside the stark images of Heraclitus or the apocalyptic satire of Lucan or the denunciatory violent triumphalism of the Christian author of the Book of Revelation. Even in these pessimistic writers there is a realisation that Augustus had achieved something outstanding. Perhaps it is the pride in this accomplishment that explains the absence in great texts and on humble epitaphs of expressions of *guilt* and *sin*, which came to be the hallmark of Christian culture. Robert Turcan comments that 'the idea of sin, and above all collective sin, was alien even to oriental paganisms, in which "penances" were the punishment for ritual misdeeds towards the divinity' (Turcan 1996: 338). The human accomplishment of the Empire was too self-evidently real to permit feelings of guilt or sin: yet the violent basis of the accomplishment was also self-evident, giving rise to fear and even terror, if not to guilt and sin. The phlegmatic Horace might be able to offer the view that 'a common night awaiteth every man, and Death's path must be trodden once for all' (from 'Death the Doom of All'; Horace 1968: 77); the singers of the Homeric 'Hymn to Demeter' could at Eleusis intone: 'we humans endure the gifts of the gods' and find no problem in the paradox (Rice and Stambaugh 1979: 176).

Heraclitus had seen the human condition as a game of dice played by the gods, with humans as the pieces, in which the players cannot die and in which the pieces can do nothing else but wait to die (Dilcher 1995: 145–57). If the disfavour of the gods is actually expressed as indifference or random cruelty, or if the hostility of the gods is incurred with little interest on their part as to whether the alleged human offence is either voluntary or involuntary, then how is one to know what is right and what is wrong? Indeed, what is the point of trying to find out?

True, men can be prudent and try to understand, by cultic activity and careful behaviour, the meaning of the communications from the gods: 'The gods', said Demosthenes, 'have made it impossible for human beings to prosper without knowing what they must do and without taking care that they must do what must be done' (Mikelson 1983: 17). Yet, as Heraclitus saw it, it was essential to the nature of the gods that they are *unwilling* to be clear and obvious in their messages and that man 'knows that any misunderstanding may be mortal to him' (Dilcher 1995: 151). The first century CE Roman writer Lucan was certain that human beings were of no interest to the gods. Lucan depicts the gods as turning a deaf ear to 'all the peoples, all the races' (Lucan 1992: 118). Humanity's concerns were not the concerns of the gods, however much seemly matrons and dutiful soldiers sought, in cult and in family life, to make them so.

The gods must have seemed even further away to the *humiliores* of the Empire, the non-persons whose tortured and humiliated death in the arena provided the most popular form of public entertainment. Roman 'criminals', the *humiliores*, as well as Christian martyrs, would learn too well how mortal their 'misunderstandings' were when they confronted, in a public arena, state officials and Roman crowds, and wild beasts, determined that they should die as painfully and as luridly as possible. 'For the state', writes Donald Kyle, 'the killing in the arena symbolised power, leadership and empire' (Kyle 1998: 3). The killings in the arena, which were on a huge and routine scale, were not the accidental by-products of otherwise ordinary 'games' but were deliberately staged to impress, through terror, the populace with the power of the Emperor and his hierarchy of officials over life and death. To the Romans the 'games' were, on some understanding, a way to immortality, as the gladiators (and maybe the martyrs) demonstrated victory over death either by winning or by dying indifferent to it: commentators such as Pliny the Younger and Livy felt that becoming inured to such bloody spectacles was the way to maintaining Roman military prowess, proper stoic virtues and respect for the Emperor. Indeed, the two major gates of the standard Roman arena were called the

'Gate of Life' and the 'Gate of Death', and the imperial control of these gates symbolised the awesome power of Caesar, a power 'over life and death' later assumed by a very different King in the Christian centuries. Both 'Gates' symbolised routine, official terror.

In the arena, mobs (including seemly matrons) would demand that mauled and near-dead 'criminals' and martyrs be killed in front of them 'so that their eyes could share the killing as the sword entered the flesh' (Coleman 1990: 59). Cultic figures were 'impersonated' by victims, to be castrated (or to castrate themselves) like Attis, or to be burnt alive like Hercules. In a re-enactment of the myth of Pasiphae, real bulls would somehow be made to copulate, in the arena, with female 'criminals', an activity which must have resulted in the deaths of the women concerned (Coleman 1990: 63). As Kyle puts it:

> Death in the arena was public, official, and communicative: and, when properly conducted, spectacles of death were comforting and entertaining for Romans of all classes. Spectacles played a major role in the festival calendar, the social life and the public space of ancient Rome for over a millennium. With industry and pride, Rome scoured the Empire for victims, built monumental facilities, orchestrated events and immortalised these performances in art, architecture and literature.
>
> (Kyle 1998: 2)

Often enough, these violent 'games' would be attached to the funerals of important men, a blood-tribute, a *munus* for the departed, in effect a human sacrifice. The bodies of those killed in the arena would, in deliberate and violent contravention of all Jewish, Ancient Near Eastern, Greek and Roman funerary proprieties, be either dumped in potters' fields to be eaten by dogs or simply thrown in the Tiber to bloat and rot (Kyle 1998). The dead bodies were abused as much, and as deliberately, as the living ones. Lucan, in what must be one of the most terrifying of all accounts of a society based on violence, picks up the sense of this total reversal of death customs when he describes the witch Erichtho:

> funerals she has brought back from the grave,
> reversing the procession; corpses have escaped from death ...
> But when dead bodies are preserved in stone, which draws the
>   inmost

moisture off, and once the marrow's fluid is absorbed and they
   grow hard,
then greedily she vents her rage upon the entire corpse:
she sinks her hands into the eyes, she gleefully digs out
the cold eyeballs and the pallid nails
on withered hand....
Every human death is to her advantage.
[She] bends over well-loved limbs and, while planting kisses,
   mutilates
the head and with her teeth she opens up the tight-closed
mouth and, biting off the tip of tongue which sticks
to parched throat, pours mumbles into icy lips
and sends a secret outrage to the Stygian shades.

(Lucan 1992: 120–1)

Lucan was, at the age of twenty-five, forced by Nero to commit suicide and did so by opening his own veins while reciting lines from his own writing. His civil war was neither allegory nor fiction: it was an account of the world he and those murdered in the arena lived and died in. Even at this remove, Lucan's vision terrifies as it insistently picks at the fatal flaw in Augustus' Pax Romana: that it killed, and had to kill, in order to succeed – and, if Donald Kyle is correct, it came to enjoy the killing. In Lucan's words 'blood, once tasted, never lets the defiled throat return to gentle ways' (ibid.: 11).

Bynum is of the view that it was to a large extent in reaction to the corpse-degrading, corpse-humiliating nature of these deaths, especially the deaths of martyrs, that we owe the elaboration of the Christian doctrine of resurrection. She quotes, with agreement, Rothkrug's suggestion that, to the physically abused Jews of the Maccabean period and to early Christians, 'resurrection was a substitute for the burial owed to the pious' (Bynum 1995: 48). This seems to have been one of the sources for the doctrine of resurrection, a source developing out of Jewish as well as Christian tradition and experience. This aspect, discussed in Part II above, will be further discussed below in Part IV. Yet at the same time there was also in the Empire an endless flow of 'oriental cults' of extraordinary variety, operating in an atmosphere halfway between happiness and terror, ecstasy indeed, and teaching ideas of less sanguinary and more other-worldly forms of salvation. Isis offered the long-suffering Lucius life 'above the time that the fates have appointed and ordained' (Apuleius 1996: 189); Artemis, in protecting parturient women, protected, in their offspring, their immortality (Strelan 1996: 83–4), and Mithras, in its astrology, perhaps provided a track to salvation for the journeying soul (Hornblower and Spawforth 1996: 992). Dionysus offered an ebullient cultic celebration of the power of life and of the soul over physical death. The cults were for the initiates, not simply for kings or heroes or philosophers: that is they offered some taste of immortality to 'ordinary people', not just a chosen few.

The cults were many and varied, yet in their concern for a providential, rather than an indifferent god perhaps had more in common with the new 'cult' of Christianity than they did with the imperial cults of Rome – and it was largely in competition with the cults that Christianity was forced to, or sought to define and establish itself. As Strelan puts it in his account of Paul's activities in Ephesus,

> In encountering Artemis and other gods and their cults, as well as the growing influence of the imperial cult, the cult of Jesus whom Christians worshipped *quasi deo* (Pliny Ep., 10.96.7) could at best hope to be considered as one among them.
>
> (Strelan 1996: 125)

To the particularly Christian contribution to the cultures of death, the various thanatologies of the cities and towns of the Roman Empire we will now turn.

Part IV

CHRISTIANS, MARTYRS, SOLDIERS, SAINTS

> The victory of Octavian ... yielded an era of unprecedented stability and opportunity for urban life which would last a century. ... It is remarkable that the former pagans who formed the new Christian congregation in the Macedonian city [Thessalonica] could have been persuaded that such apocalyptic images [in 1 Thess. 1:10] were an apt picture of their world and lives.
>
> (Meeks 1983: 11, 171)

> The New Testament gospels all place the story of Jesus in the context of global war.
>
> (Pagels 1994: 17)

Somewhere in between the quotidian routines of peaceful life, and the spasmodic terrors and millennial expectations of the Parousia and 'global war', small but growing groups of Christian converts had both to bury their ordinary dead and to consider the extraordinary witness of their martyrs, including their first one. Whether as Jewish or Gentile converts, they lived, in the first and then the ensuing decades of their faith, in situations of barely tolerated existence punctuated by periods of persecution and of what Eusebius called the general circumstances of 'famine, pestilence and war' (Eusebius 1986: 365). The Empire may indeed have seemed stable and even peaceful viewed from Rome or Capri. It may not have felt that way in cities like Sardis and Philadelphia, both destroyed by earthquake in 17 CE, or in 'Britannia', crushed by Roman armies, or in Jerusalem and Qumran, destroyed rather than merely defeated. It is hard to believe that the captives and prisoners of war brought in to be murdered in the arenas would have felt with Meeks that their lives and deaths were an 'opportunity for urban life'. The peace of the conqueror is never experienced as such by the conquered.

Eusebius, of course, chronicles the eventual triumph of Christianity: to some extent we must project ahead to see what that success looked like 'on the ground'. In this concluding part of the book, I will pick out two aspects of Christian death and burial: first, the steady establishment of 'ordinary', routine burial practices and, second, the associated but (from our perspective) quite extraordinary activities associated with the death and interment of Christian saints and martyrs. Together they provide some indication both of what Christians retained from their Jewish and Greco-Roman antecedents, and what they changed in this inheritance to make it 'ours'.

The cult of martyrs was a two-stage process: the initial 'proclamation', through martyrdom and associated suffering, of the Christian perspective on death, and then what Markus has called (1990: 53) the process of 'Christian mediocrity', whereby the exemplary elitism of the martyrs is both broadened and softened so that *all* Christians, in whatever dutiful, self-denying calling, can claim some measure of sanctity, able to die in the knowledge that they, too, have 'lived unto the Lord'. On the latitudes and longitudes of the lives and deaths of the long-buried martyrs in their martyries came to be transposed the self-denying lives of the nun in her celibacy, of the mother in her selflessness, of the worker in his faithfulness, of the scholar in his dedication, of the wife and husband in their chastity, of the pilgrim in his fortitude, of the child in its obedience, of the soldier in his self-sacrifice. The common theme is self-denial, self-sacrifice and a voluntary choosing of the (relatively) hard option:

> Not for ever by green pastures
> Do we ask our way to be;
> But the steep and rugged pathway
> May we tread rejoicingly.
> (*Hymns Ancient and Modern* 1983:
>   Hymn 113)

The soldier in particular came to be accorded a close identity with the martyr, not for the violence he deployed but for the life he 'laid down'; I shall conclude this book with a short epilogue containing a commentary on the way in which loss and suffering in war, at the beginning of our century, was able to call upon a very ancient Christian tradition, aeons-long, to provide a means of coping with death on a scale still scarcely imaginable.

13

CHRISTIAN BURIAL

We have no 'formal' Christian burial liturgy until about the year 900, though there are pieces of one in various forms (Paxton 1990; Rowell 1977). The activities and deaths of the martyrs are well chronicled, and provide the dramatic orchestration of and crescendo to more routine concerns. As Peter Brown puts it:

> The cult of the martyrs was the only form of popular devotion in the Early Church: and, in Africa, the accounts of how these 'prize-fighters of the Lord' had snubbed raging governors were read from the altar on innumerable anniversaries.
>
> (Brown 1972: 31)

In trying to keep these two strands running together it may be possible to reconcile the two quotations with which this part of the book begins. There was a 'global war' going on within the peaceful boundaries of the Augustan Empire, a 'peace' that was itself more obvious to highly placed patricians and to nineteenth century historians, perhaps, than to the average Jew in Palestina or to the prisoner in the arena.

The advent of Christianity, slowly but surely, became obvious in the funerary architecture and burial ecology of the cities and villages of the Roman Empire. As Fontaine puts it:

> We see, on the one hand, the continuation of the ancient practice of pagan necropoli located on the exit roads of the cities and the concomitant separation of the cities of the living and the cultic sites of the dead: and on the other hand we see the gradual introduction of what Saint Augustine called the *communio sanctorum*, in which the dead project

themselves into the lives of the living. The Christian dead, since their *dies natalis* alive in God, have a presence as real as the living, and they come to play a larger and larger part in the liturgies of the community. In this sense, what we see is 'the procession of the dead into the cities of the living', an interpenetration of the two cities, that of the dead and that of the living, a process which gives a new face to the cities of late antiquity and above all to the history of the Middle Ages.

(Fontaine 1989: 1,152)

These changes did not take place overnight. The chosen burial option of the early Christian and Jewish communities in Rome itself was the catacomb, located as were all Greco-Roman burial sites *outside* the city walls. If there was, among the general (pagan) population, a move in the late first and second centuries CE towards inhumation and away from cremation, this would merely have brought them into line with Jewish (and by extension Christian) practice, which had long favoured individual inhumation. Goodenough (1953) and Rutgers (1995), in their different ways, show how in late Ancient Rome itself, both Jews and Christians buried their dead in catacombs, located underground and outside the city walls. 'Underground' burials were, as we have seen, a feature of the Ancient Near East, and this tradition continued in, for example, the Galilean burial ground and catacomb of Beth Shearim, a burial site contemporaneous with the Roman catacombs.

The Roman catacombs varied in origin, being sometimes the 'linking-up' of smaller hypogea or smaller, older, underground burial sites, sometimes the adaptation of old watercourses, cisterns and quarries. There is evidence, for both Jews and Christians, that the larger catacombs were designed and purpose-built. Eventually, over a thousand kilometres of galleries extended under the outskirts of Rome, providing burial space for something in the order of six million people (Shaw 1996: 101). Construction, even underground, on this scale could not have been 'invisible' to either the authorities or the populace of Rome, so there cannot be much sense in the idea that the catacombs were dug to hide funerals and bodies.

The Jewish and Christian catacomb-galleries, the types of graves, the workforce of diggers and decorators employed, and the grave decorations are very traditional and in some senses similar (Rutgers 1995: xvi). Jews and Christians, in their respective catacombs, over the late second to early fifth century CE, buried their dead in either

192

loculi of about 6' by 2' by 2' cut into the walls of the galleries, giving a 'beehive' effect, or in *cubiculi*, chambers (with benches covering the actual graves) for two or more burials. Decorative effect might be enhanced by an arch over the benches, producing an *arcosolium*, a mini-temple effect (Shaw 1996: 101; Ferrua 1991: 19–21). The *loculi* were, *for both religious groups*, the most used form of interment, followed by the *arcosolia*, and then *forma* (straight into the ground), sarcophagi and amphora.

Rutgers, the major student of the Jews of late Ancient Rome, states that 'Jewish catacombs are identical to the Christian catacombs' (Rutgers 1995: 58), representing perhaps the persistence of the old burial practices of the Ancient Near East, imported into imperial Rome and adapted to the circumstances there. However, Rutgers picks out small but significant differences. The Christian catacombs were highly decorated, using biblical motifs. In contrast, the main Jewish catacombs were, until late on, relatively undecorated (no 'graven images') – although it is significant that mourners seem to have embellished them with graffiti and incised, hand-written messages: where formal decorations do appear, they tend to be simple representations of the menorah (Rutgers 1995: 56). Inscriptions, for both sects, were in Greek. Burials were of full-body cadavers: neither Jews nor Christians allowed cremation. While the catacombs of Jews and Christians looked very similar, they were exclusive: Jews in their tombs, Christians in theirs, more apart perhaps in death than they were in life; indeed, in death rebutting, to some extent, the inevitable interaction between the diverse faiths and ethnic groups of cosmopolitan Rome.

At the end of the fourth century CE Christians began to abandon the Roman catacombs, and above-ground Christian burial sites associated with churches or with mortuary chapels began to appear *within the city walls*, proclaiming the new and dominant status of Christianity. This move, architecturally very visible (where the catacombs were both hidden and extramural), is associated with two other aspects of Christian life in the late Ancient Roman Empire, the development of the cult of the martyred saints of the periods of persecution, and the exigencies of church government and administration in the periods of tolerance and eventual supremacy. The original name for Christian churches was 'martyries', and these buildings became the shrines and sites of civic, *localised* cultic worship and pilgrimage. (In this sense, and in this sense only, the cult provided some continuity with the civic and localised cults of paganism.) The second need, the need to provide buildings for church administration, saw the construction of large churches and later cathedrals, the symbolic spaces and official centres of bishops and other administrative leaders of the church. As Fontaine says in the quotation near the beginning of this chapter, the nature of Christian beliefs about death, as well as the two other factors, produces in late antiquity this 'image' of Christian witness, of the dead colonising the cities of the living. The dead of all other religious cultures had been kept outside the city walls. The urban 'proclamations' of death emphasised the Christian occupation of the symbolic spaces of the Empire, complementing the gradual translation into the languages of the Empire of the basic Christian texts (Fox 1988: 282). We see developing the (to us) familiar image of a Christian church (later a cathedral) or chapel, located at city or town or village centre, with attendant graveyard and, for the important or martyred or saintly Christians, burial within the church itself or in a shrine, the whole being frequently placed on top of older, defeated pagan religious and burial sites. By the end of the sixth century CE, for example, the ancient city and oracular site of Delphi had been occupied by three Christian churches, built from material used in the temples associated with the ancient site (Deroche 1989: 2713–26). At the other end of the Empire, in Britain, the martyrdom of St Alban in 304 CE saw the overbuilding of the Roman cemetery and the eventual shift of the entire town away from its Roman foundation to a new axis around the Christian buildings and the martyr's shrine, a pattern paralleled, says Painter, in many other cities such as Ephesus, Augsburg, Tours, Xanten and Bonn (Painter 1989: 2037). The *Proceedings of the 11th Conference on Christian Archaeology* (*ACTES*) provide ample evidence for this process of 'christianising' the important architectural spaces of Greek and Roman cities, a process as inexorable and as successful as had been the earlier efforts of Augustus to colonise the central spaces of Roman cities with imperial symbols (Zanker 1988). The evidence for this is still all around us, in the dominant position at the centres of cities, towns and villages of the church or cathedral, containing within it the memorials or shrines or graves of the saints of the church, and surrounded by the graves of lesser people, the whole oriented to the Christian purpose.

By *The End of Ancient Christianity*, to use R.M. Markus' title, the Christian dead had indeed colonised the central places of the living. Even where extramural cemeteries were maintained, Christians proclaimed their separate and theologically different status. At Poundbury near Dorchester, a huge fourth century CE Christian cemetery with

194

about 4,500 interments is clearly separated from the adjacent pagan burial area. The Christians were buried naked other than for their burial shrouds, the pagans were fully clothed and equipped with grave-goods and food (Painter 1989: 2049). In death, in dress, separation was absolute.

Peter Brown (Brown 1981) emphasises that there was a rather different but parallel process to the 'urbanising of the dead' going on in the eastern parts of the Empire. Here, the shrines of the martyrs were either located in extramural cemeteries, which became in effect 'cities of the dead', or in remote desert places, where they became places of pilgrimage, associated with monastic and ascetic styles of Christianity, somewhat at odds with the this-worldly concerns of the growing number of bishops and other functionaries of the nascent Church.

These are, surely, twin developments, together saying to the pagan world that it was through its dead that the new religion lived – and it was the colonisation of the cities by the dead which was the most startling reversal of ancient practice. This is certainly how Julian the Apostate saw it, when with increasing fury he sought to rid the Empire of the new religion in whose practices he saw the ruin of Rome:

> You keep adding many corpses newly dead to the corpses of long ago. You have filled the whole world with tombs and sepulchres. ... The carrying of the corpses of the dead through a great assembly of people, in the midst of dense crowds, staining the eyes of all with ill-omened sights of the dead. What day so touched with death could be lucky? How, after being present at such ceremonies, could anyone approach the gods and their temples?
>
> (Julian, in Brown 1981: 7)

The 'important' corpses in this process were those of the martyrs and saints, often the same people, and we can turn to Peter Brown for the most succinct summary of the general process:

> The rise of the cult of saints was sensed by contemporaries, in no uncertain manner, to have broken most of the imaginative boundaries which ancient men had placed between heaven and earth, the divine and the human, the living and the dead, the town and its antithesis. ... For the cult of the saints ... designated dead human beings as the recipients of

unalloyed reverence, and it linked these dead and invisible figures in no uncertain manner to precise visible places and, in many areas, to precise living representatives ... part of a greater whole – the lurching forward of an increasing proportion of late antique society toward radically new forms of reverence, shown to new objects in new places, orchestrated by new leaders.

(ibid.: 21–2)

In city, town and village across the Empire, old pagan cultic, civic and cemetery sites were subsumed into the burial architecture and funerary ornament of the religion of Christianity. To quote Brown again, 'late antique Christianity as it impinged on the outside world was shrines and relics' (ibid.: 12) – the shrines and relics of martyrs.

Justin the Apostate, who had clearly inherited the Greco-Roman, and indeed Jewish view of bodies as pollution, was confronted with a religion which, in its foundation stories, has the dead and risen body as the central object of worship and veneration. The story of Jesus' death and bodily resurrection was the centrepiece of Paul's theology. The story of Jesus hugely simplified (at least for a time!) the demographic contours of the space between human life and the heavens, offering in place of the numberless 'gods' and 'demi-gods' and cult-powers, sacrifices and 'heroes' of ancient, Hellenic and late-antique thanatologies, the single expiatory figure of Jesus, the Son of God who had died as a human and who had conquered death through dying. Death, in Christ, becomes holiness, the means to salvation not only for saints and martyrs but also for all Christians. Death was the *dies natalis*, the day of birth into eternity, a time of joy. Christians (or Christian martyrs anyway) died facing with joy the next world, their backs to this one; pagans, as we have seen from Greek and Roman epitaphs, died with their backs to the next world, which they either feared or resented, and facing into this one for the sense and meaning of their existence.

Early Christian writings such as the Didascalia make it very clear that 'it was not to the martyrs alone that He promised the resurrection, but to all men', and provided a description of how this dispensation was to be experienced:

God Almighty raises us up through God our Saviour, as He has promised. However, He raises us up from the dead as we are – in this form in which we are now, nevertheless in the great glory of everlasting life, with nothing wanting to us. Indeed, though we be thrown into the depth of the sea, or scattered by the winds like chaff, we are still within the world, and the whole world itself is enclosed beneath the hand of God. From within His hand therefore He will raise us up, as the Lord our Saviour has said: 'A hair of our head shall not perish, but in your patience shall you possess your souls.'

(The Didascalia Apostolorum 1979: 175–6)

In the early Christian writings of the ante-Nicene Fathers, this message of *resurrection for all* is spelt out, generally in the context of the goodness of the creation, having been spoilt by human folly, now redeemable through Christ, though with concomitant punishment for those who reject him. *God, we are told, loves his creation.* Clement of Alexandria, for example, assures his readers that God loves them: to him they were 'a beautiful breathing instrument of music the Lord made man, after His own image. ... You have, then, God's promise, you have His love' (Clement 1909: 21). In a brilliant polemic, in which Clement demonstrates his familiarity with the basic texts and teachings of Greco-Roman religions and cults, Clement time and time again assures Christians that they are part of a loved creation and that through Jesus they can be saved:

He hath changed sunset into sunrise, and through the Cross brought death to life; and having wrenched man from destruction, He hath raised him to the skies, transplanting mortality into immortality, and translating earth to heaven.

(ibid.: 102)

The corollary, of course, was just as absolute a damnation for those who are hostile to the Christian message, especially heretics, described by Cyprian, Bishop of Carthage (martyred 258 CE) as:

Pests and plagues to the faith, snake-tongued deceivers, skilled corrupters of the truth, spewing deadly venom from their poisonous fangs; whose speech spreads like a canker; whose preaching injects a fatal virus into the hearts and breasts of all ... not sons unto God, but to the devil. Born of a lie, they cannot inherit the truth which was promised; the reward can never come to men who have broken the peace of the Lord by the frenzy of dissent.

(Cyprian 1971: 75)

There is, then, a clear unabashed duality in Christian thought on human nature. *Precisely because* of God's initial love, the punishment of the non-believers and blasphemers will be just as sure in its damnation as the love was in its salvation.

Justin (110–165 CE), a near-contemporary of Clement of Alexandria, assured the Roman Emperor that '[y]ou can kill us but you cannot hurt us' (Justin 1957: 162), thereby expressing the very firm Christian belief that their real existence was in the next world, that they would rise again in the imminently expected Jesus, and that the death of a Christian was, logically, an occasion for rejoicing. Rush quotes Augustine to this effect: 'Let sadness perish where there is so great a consolation; let sorrow be plucked from the heart and let faith drive away sadness' (Rush 1941: 185). Augustine, of course, was well aware that too lavish an expression of this sentiment would make the Christian funeral an object of pagan derision (Augustine 1978: 539–51). Rush's long analysis of early Christian burial practice shows that early Christians did indeed possess an 'optimistic' view of life after death, and that this occasionally saw the Church leaders being forced to insist on restraint, both in behaviour at the actual funeral and in the temptation to seek martyrdom. The actual *process* of the Christian funeral derived essentially from its Jewish origins (see Part II above), adapted where necessary to the particular topographies and customs of that part of the pagan world in which Christians found themselves, but invested with a quite different meaning.

Quintessentially and distinctively, Christians insisted always that the dead were not polluting, and that their deaths and funerals were occasions for displays of hope, not resignation or fear. Rush states that 'from the very beginning the Christian funeral was a religious service ... with a joyful concept of death ... [by pagans] death was regarded as an evil. The Christian concept of death was entirely different' (Rush 1941: 170–4). The Didascalia worked its way through both its Jewish and pagan inheritance and culture, with all their complicated rules and prohibitions about clean and unclean, and instructed the Christians to dissociate themselves from such preoccupations:

> Do not load yourselves again with something which our Lord and Saviour has taken away from you. And do not observe these things, nor think that it is uncleanness; and do not restrain yourselves because of them, and do not seek sprinklings, or baptisms, or purifications for these things.

Indeed, in the second legislation, if one touches a dead man or a tomb, he must be bathed. You, however, according to the Gospel and according to the power of the Holy Spirit, shall be assembled even in the cemeteries, and read the holy Scriptures, and without observance complete your services, and your intercessions to God, and offer an acceptable eucharist, the likeness of the body of the kingdom of Christ, in your congregations and in your cemeteries and on the departures of them that sleep among you, pure bread that is prepared in fire and sanctified through an invocation. Indeed, those who have believed in God, as it is written in the Gospel, even though they should sleep, they are not dead, and our Lord said to the Sadducees: 'About the resurrection of the dead, have you not read that which is written: I am the God of Abraham and the God of Isaac, and the God of Jacob? And he is not the God of the dead but of the living'. ... On this account you are to approach without restraint those who rest and you shall not declare them unclean.

(The Didascalia Apostolorum 1979: 245–6)

Other chapters of the Didascalia provide for the singing of psalms ('the souls of the righteous are in the hands of God') and for prayers for the dead, at both first inhumation and anniversaries. The dead body would have been washed, anointed and sometimes embalmed. In keeping with the belief that the body was not polluting, the gap between death and interment was extended to three or four days, the body was attended by a vigil, and it was carried to the grave on occasion by priest or bishop, with psalms, hymns and prayers, and buried with a eucharist. Face upwards, the body would be oriented feet towards the east, in expression of the hope of new life in the Son (as 'sun', this a clear pagan as well as Christian practice). At fixed periods, again following very ancient practice, friends and relatives would meet for prayer and food (Smith and Cheetham 1875: 251–4). This is, in essence, what we know of 'ordinary' early Christian burial. There were regional variations, and changes over time – the practice of a eucharistic service at the grave site, for example, died out in the fifth century. The actual structure and sequence of events, the funeral 'drama', has some obvious antecedents in the 'Christian origins' in the Ancient Near East.

What was different was the centrality of the resurrection of Christ as the witness, the exemplar, of personal and physical resurrection for each Christian. Resurrection was, as we have seen, *part* of the Jewish inheritance, but it was enunciated now as *the* central indisputable proposition of the new faith. It was enunciated so strongly that (much to the amazement of the Roman authorities) large numbers of Christians came forward to claim their resurrectional rights, as it were, by offering to die, and to do so in the most public and painful of ways. Clearly, many Christian converts, when faced by the demands of the authorities, chose to apostasise, insufficiently sure, perhaps, of the resurrection promise, or simply terrified: the writings of the early Fathers are not infrequently concerned with what to do about those who had, under persecution, 'lapsed' but who later wished to rejoin the community. Equally clearly, large numbers suffered, and smaller numbers died, for their faith, their blood and suffering being the foundation-message of the Church. As Bowersock puts it, 'it was probably through martyrdom that many pagans became aware of Christianity in the first place during the second and third centuries' (Bowersock 1995: 66).

14

THE NATURE OF
MARTYRDOM

> Beliefs and opinions float from place to place and pass over
> from one religion to another wittingly and unwittingly.
> There are conceptions like the Akedah Merit that start out
> at first to act as influence and end up being influenced
> themselves. And it also happens that, in time, owing to
> forgetfulness, traditions get lost, and the loss is recovered
> through contact with an alien culture.
>
> (Spiegel 1979: 118)

In 203 CE, in Roman Carthage, a group of Christians were waiting,
in prison, for the martyrdom they sought. They were Saturninus,
Secundulus, Revocatus and Felicity (two slaves), and Vibia
Perpetua, 'a newly married woman of good family and upbringing'
(Musurillo 1972: 180). They had various concerns. Saturninus, for
example, wanted to be attacked by *all* available beasts so that 'his
crown might be all the more glorious' (ibid.: 127). Secundulus
preferred the leopard to the bear, as leopards killed quickly whereas
bears took their time. Felicity, a pregnant slave, was faced with the
problem that her pregnancy would, under Roman law, stop her
from being martyred along with her mistress Perpetua and other
companions. The group 'in one torrent of common grief' (ibid.:
123) prayed for a 'miracle', which duly came in the form of a
premature birth. The delivery was not easy:

> She suffered a good deal in her labour because of the natural
> difficulty of an eight month's delivery. Hence one of the
> assistants of the prison guards said to her: 'You suffer so
> much now – what will you do when you are tossed to the
> beasts? Little did you think of them when you refused to
> sacrifice.' 'What I am suffering now', she replied, 'I suffer

by myself. But then another will be inside me who will suffer for me, just as I shall be suffering for him.' And she gave birth to a girl, and one of the sisters brought her up as her own daughter.

(ibid.: 123–5)

Two days after the birth, Felicity joined Perpetua in going joyfully into the arena:

The day of their victory dawned and they marched from the prison to the amphitheatre joyfully as though they were going to heaven, with calm faces, trembling, if at all, with joy rather than fear. Perpetua went along with shining countenance and calm step, as the beloved of God, as a wife of Christ, putting down everyone's stare by her own intense gaze. With them also was Felicity, glad that she had safely given birth so that she could now fight the beasts, going from one bloodbath to another, from the midwife to the gladiator, ready to wash after childbirth in a second baptism.

(ibid.: 125–7)

The two women had been stripped naked – but this upset the sensitivities of the crowd: 'even the crowd was horrified when they saw that one was a delicate young girl and the other fresh from childbirth with the milk still dripping from her breasts. And so they were brought back and dressed in unbelted tunics' (ibid.: 129).

Joyce Salisbury (1997: 142) comments that the crowd could have been offended because the lactating breasts might have mimicked the procession of Artemis/Isis in which male priests dripped milk through the multinippled breasts of the goddess. Or they might have been concerned that motherhood and martyrdom did not go together. In the arena, Perpetua was attacked and tossed by a wild heifer. Her first concern after being thrown in the air was to rearrange her tunic, which being ripped was showing too much thigh. Then she asked for a hairpin, 'for it was not right that a martyr should die with her hair in disorder, lest she might seem to be mourning in her hour of triumph' (Musurillo 1972: 129). The two women then had to wait a day before they were taken to the killing-platform, located to maximise the crowd's view of the swords going in – 'that their eyes might be the guilty witnesses of the sword that pierced their flesh' (ibid.: 131). Perpetua, the last to die, had to help her young killer, whose inexperience saw the first thrust hit a bone.

Perpetua had yet, however, to taste more pain. She screamed
as she was struck on the bone; then she took the trembling
hand of the young gladiator and guided it to her throat. It
was as though so great a woman, feared as she was by the
unclean spirit, could not be dispatched unless she herself
were willing.

(ibid.: 131)

As is obvious from that story, religious movements are more than
the recording and formalisation of the exhortatory words or even of
the exemplary deeds of their founder or founders. In order to come
fully into existence, in order to become alive and potent, and to *stay*
alive and potent in the minds of men and women, religions have to
become graphic and to have their noise, taste and smell, their
virility, endlessly reinforced by replays, large and small, of their
story. The deaths of Felicity and Perpetua are a form of noise, a
scream (of pain? of exultation?), deeply ratcheted in the noise, the
moaning death of Jesus, which in turn both amplifies and is amplified by their noise. Even at this distance, we can *hear* the deaths of
Felicity and Perpetua, even if we can in no sense hear ourselves
doing what they did. Rather, we can hear ourselves asking: how,
how could they have *done* what they did? How could they have
wanted to have done what they did? How could people *pay* money to
go and watch this murder?

At times the offered, scholarly, answers seem to be more about
definitions than substance, delimiting the field in a careful, restrictive
way, relying more on the thoughts of contemporary commentators
and philosophisers than on actual deeds or the record of death and
pain. It must be stressed that whatever was 'said', whether 'at the
time' or later, it was the *acts* of the martyrs, not the commentary,
which bloodily made the point. The issue is important beyond the
matter of 'origins' because it lies very close to the nature of contemporary religious identity and therefore to an important aspect of the
socio-political divisions in the world in which we live.

Were the Christian martyrs 'Jewish' in that their deaths are part
of the story of Jewish persecution and suffering, or were they the
heirs of Greco-Roman stoic ideas of heroic and self-denying death?
Or was this something new, a mixing of martyrdom and heroism to
provide a potent and very long-lived 'new' Christian tradition?
Rabbinic Judaism was (and is) far from 'keen' on the idea of
martyrdom, although we have always to bear in mind that 'Judaism'
was at the time of Felicity's death still some way away from being

the 'closed' system of the Rabbis. The imperative, the *mitzvah*, in Rabbinic Judaism is: to live! There is, for example, simply 'no comment' in the Mishnah or the Talmud on the 'heroic' suicides or martyrdoms at Masada, an event heroic certainly to the state of Israel and a story fitting quite well with Euro-Christian notions of soldierly bravery and self-sacrifice (Davies 1995). To Geza Vermes, however, martyrdom is derivable from very ancient Jewish example. The Akedah, the story of the death and 'resurrection' of Isaac was, at least by the first century CE, available independently in Judaism, and was fairly easily taken over into Christianity from that source. The Akedah provided the vocabulary of martyrdom: 'the Eucharistic meal may be understood as the introduction into Christianity of this other element of the Akedah theology: the perpetual remembrance of the one perfect Sacrifice until the Kingdom comes' (Vermes 1961: 227).

Shalom Spiegel is much more hesitant about the function of the Akedah, a story hugely commented on throughout Jewish writings, often enough concerned with the puzzling absence of Isaac on the journey *down* from Mount Moriah. Spiegel's book, *The Last Trial*, is an extended commentary upon a medieval Jewish version of the Akedah in which Abraham actually kills Isaac, who is then resurrected. Spiegel is concerned about the variations *within* Judaism of the story of Abraham and Isaac because of its possible implication of human sacrifice as well as 'martyrdom'. He thinks that there was perhaps a common source 'in the ancient pagan' world for these 'sanguinary' events, and goes on to say:

> What survived from the heritage of idolatry which in Judaism remained peripheral grew to become dominant in the Christian world, which sought to shape and glorify the Golgotha Event into the Akedah image and likeness. And when Christianity placed at the centre of its religion belief in the atoning power of the blood of its messiah, in Israel a need was increasingly felt to blur more and more the remnants of similar, ancient beliefs from pagan times, leaving behind therefore only faint traces in our sources. Withal, however, it is possible to find support for every one of the details of the Haggadah on the slaughter and resurrection of Isaac in the documents of talmudic-midrashic literature itself, independently of ideas or sources from the realm of Christianity.
>
> (Spiegel 1979: 116–18)

Here, Shalom Spiegel is saying that the diffidence in later or Rabbinic Judaism about the story of Isaac is partly because of its annexation, by Christianity, into its central martyrology: in other words, the exigencies of the present re-read the record of the past. Daniel Boyarin presents an even more complex Jewish commentary on martyrdom. In discussing 'The Martyrdom of Rabbi Akiva' (50–135 CE), he traces R. Akiva's midrash back *through the Song of Songs to Genesis and the story of the crossing of the Red Sea*, finding in the Rabbi's thoughts on *that* event 'the idea of martyrdom as a positive religious value *per se*' (Boyarin 1990: 126). Boyarin comments:

> In the past also there was a concept of martyrdom, but it was very different from this one. The former model was that of the Hasmonean period, in which the martyr refuses to violate his or her religious integrity, and is executed for this refusal; now we find martyrdom being actively sought as the only possible fulfilment of a spiritual need. ... In the past martyrs refused to violate a negative commandment (to worship idols); in the present, they are fulfilling through their deaths a positive one (to love God). ... They [R. Akiva and his fellows] *died with joy*, with a mystic conviction; not only was it that their deaths were necessary, but that they were the highest of spiritual experiences.
>
> (Boyarin 1990: 126; my emphasis)

Felicity and Perpetua seem to have died in something of a similar frame of mind: 'with joy'. Elaine Pagels, in her work on Satan, shows that the period between 165 BCE and 100 CE was prolific in producing apocalypses of various types, in which among other things the Jewish sects at Qumran read back into their scriptures to recover a tradition of martyrdom, as well as of militancy. Isaiah, Chronicles and Zechariah are remobilised in writings such as the various books of Enoch, Jubilees and the 'Martyrdom of Isaiah' to produce the 'battle between heaven and hell', the sense of 'separateness' of the true believers from all the rest, and the sense of the true and total salvation of those who risk their all for righteousness (Pagels 1991: 105–28).

Robert Doran, in a discussion of the 'martyrdom' in 2 Maccabees 7 of the mother and her seven sons, traces the varied treatment of this story in Rabbinic writing (which, for example, at some point manages to 'write out' the mother). He concludes that at the most general level we can see here, in Hellenistic Judaism, a definite picture of deaths being incurred because of and for faith, with the resultant exaltation and vindication by the God in whom the martyr trusted (Doran 1980: 200–2). Perhaps we can conclude this discussion of the Jewish tradition or traditions, if that is what they are, with a comment by Alan Segal, in which (again!) we see a tradition being both remade and made:

> Christianity takes themes of (1) death, (2) resurrection, (3) martyrology, (4) vicarious atonement and (5) messiahship from Judaism, but it does not find any one of them ready-made or united in one place in Jewish tradition. Instead it hunts for what it needs and applies it to the events which it is seeking to explain. [The Easter event, an experience] which is predictable if not normal on the part of a Jewish community of the First Century most often in the case of martyrdom, justified the earliest Christian community in thinking that for the first time in Judaism there could be such a thing as a crucified messiah. From this oxymoron everything else derives.
>
> (Segal 1987: 123, 126)

There is, then, this rather complex 'Jewish origin', reflexively and historically constructed and reconstructed, rather than 'scripturally prescribed', a pedigree for what Felicity and Perpetua did in Carthage in 203 CE. (There was, of course, a sizeable Jewish community in Carthage.)

Were there other influences at work? Bowersock feels that 'martyrdoms form a cohesive part of the structure of the Roman Empire, both bureaucratic and social. … *{They} had nothing to do with Judaism or Palestine*. It had everything to do the Greco-Roman world, its tradition, its language, and its cultural tastes' (Bowersock 1995: 28; my emphasis). The 'bureaucratic' refers to the fact, well discussed by Kyle and Coleman (Kyle 1998, Coleman 1990) that the Roman 'penal system' and 'games' provided a standard response to what the authorities saw as criminals. Christians such as Felicity and Perpetua were only two of a much larger number of human beings (prisoners of war, criminals, gladiators) fed through the routine system of public 'games'. Very few of these victims would have considered themselves to be martyrs: they were unfortunates and no doubt on occasion rather nasty people nastily dealt with. For Felicity and Perpetua, however, the Roman penal system provided a stage on which their deaths would be acted as a terrifying public spectacle, a choreographed martyrdom with themselves inevitably in the leading roles.

The 'cultural tastes' to which Bowersock refers include, for example, the 'stoic' views of Seneca, with his emphasis on the endurance of pain for some greater purpose. Seneca, of course, knew through the Roman practice of suicide at the Emperor's command how close life was to death. He was the recipient of such a command, and killed himself. It has to be said that Nero had left him no choice and the evidence from Tacitus is that, given the choice, Seneca would have kept his life. However, Bowersock, in a subtle analysis, is adamant that there is nothing in *Jewish* tradition that gives rise to behaviour such as Felicity's or Perpetua's. Indeed, as already noticed, such self-chosen violent deaths offend the major Jewish injunction 'to live'. I might at this point comment that there is nothing in Seneca's writings which is similar to this very positive affirmation of life and its sense that life is of God. For Rabbi Akiva this, the return to God, is a source of joy. Conversely, Seneca's basic position, in for example 'On Despising Death', was that you lived as long as it suited, then left in as dignified a way as possible, and that was it (Seneca 1917). His was a defeated suicide *from this life, not* a victorious death *into* another, better life with God. The Greco-Roman tradition, as expressed in Seneca, provided for various forms of stoic death for patricians, usually soldiers or officers of state, but not for parturient slaves. In Seneca is to be found the stoic attitude to life, i.e. that it is simply a balance of pain and pleasure, naturally leading to 'very many' perfectly rational acts of self-interested suicide. The 'highway to liberty' from the miseries of life, says Seneca, is 'any vein in your body!' (Seneca 1928: 295). Felicity and Perpetua were not escaping a miserable this-life – they were seeking, through suffering, a higher one: 'They thought', wrote Augustine, 'of how much they should love the things eternal if they were capable of such deep love for things that pass away' (in Brown 1981: 72). One searches fruitlessly in Seneca for such a view. Rome might have provided the stage; it did not provide the script.

Bowersock deals with the 2 and 4 Maccabees issue with the argument that these texts are *Hellenistic*, and that Jewish and Christian traditions have 'a common origin in the imperial Greek of Asia-Minor' (Bowersock 1995: 79): both the Maccabean texts are part of that Hellenistic tradition. This may, or may not, make the origin of notions of 'martyrdom' any the less 'Jewish' unless everything written or thought about 'in Greek' cannot be anything other than only 'Greek'. David Seeley, in *The Noble Death*, essentially agrees with Bowersock in the view that the death of Jesus, *as presented by Paul*, would, could and did derive from the Greco-Roman culture in which Paul himself was so evidently immersed. Seeley, partly by carefully defining 'martyrdom' in such a way as to limit its scope, rejects as source the possibility of 'older' Jewish traditions such as the 'suffering servant' of Isaiah or the Temple cultus (in which *human* sacrifice played no part), as well as the Akedah and indeed of the pagan 'mystery religions'. His conclusion is that the 'noble death' of martyrdom drew for its inspiration on Greco-Roman texts and writers well-known at the time of writing of the New Testament. Paul, in restructuring the 'intellectual atmosphere of the Hellenistic Kingdoms and the early Roman Empire', 'quite naturally' took on the implications of this tradition, which would have included 2 and 4 Maccabees, a Hellenistic (though Jewish) text. Paul gave his own distinctive, apocalyptic twist to the story, thereby creating the particularly powerful imagery of Jesus as the exemplary, atoning, salvific death (Seeley 1990: 147–50).

Is this sufficient to 'explain' Felicity? After all, the Greco-Roman world was quite clear about what it expected from, say, women in their roles as daughters and mothers, yet Felicity and Perpetua were well able to transcend *this* part of their Greco-Roman 'socialisation'. Had Perpetua followed the Greco-Roman rules about obedience to her father, or about her responsibilities as wife and mother, she would have debarred herself from martyrdom. Her father, having tried anger and then pleas, begged her to think of the family reputation: 'Do not abandon me to be the reproach of men. Think of your brothers, think of your mother and your aunt, think of your child, who will not be able to live when you are gone. Give up your pride! You will destroy all of us!' (Musurillo 1972: 113). Felicity, as the mother of a new-born child, would have ordinarily seen in that birth not a miracle freeing her for martyrdom but a demand for her to live in society, in well-prescribed and circumscribed roles. In abandoning parents, husbands and babies, these two young women were adding something quite new (for better or worse) to human participation in the drama of life and death.

As I have tried to argue above, attitudes to death and dying vary – slowly perhaps – with historical change. What determines attitudes to death is the cosmogony of the culture, the sense the culture provides of the nature of the creation and of the place within it of its gods and of humanity. The endless wars of the Romans, the particular wars and killings of the Maccabean era, and later the destruction of the Second Temple clearly produced (for example in 4

Maccabees and in other more expressly apocalyptic Jewish writing, such as the War Scroll of the Essenes) the conditions under which martyrdom became a new reality. As Daniel Boyarin and indeed Shalom Spiegel show, the 'new' reality of late antique Roman Palestine looks back into very ancient scripture, finding in it meanings which are then reformulated, by such as R. Akiva, to 'explain' the present and to reimagine the (in his case) Jewish future. There was no shortage in the history of the Ancient Near East, whether for Jews or other peoples, of direct experience of both natural and man-inflicted disasters.

This was a reality looking for a vocabulary; but the reality, as activity, came first. There are millions of words in the world. They achieve meaning only when ordered by experience. The Maccabean martyrs were Jewish martyrs at a time when Jews were more of an ethno-nation than a formalised religion: it was in their flesh that they knew their history and their martyrs; and the first Christians were ethno-Jews. In the initial historical experience of the early Christians, who were of course Jews as appalled as any other by the destruction of the Temple and what happened afterwards, lay an experience already sensitised to Paul's presentation to them of the figure of Jesus as yet another, greater, martyr in a long tradition. The Roman Empire, whether at war, or at play in its 'games', or in daily life, was a violent place, providing violent death, proclaiming a violent authority in the emperor-state. This violence, whether experienced by Jews in Palestine or by Christians in Carthage, would and did indeed produce, as one potent reaction to it, a dramatically dualistic view of the world and its troubles. In the words of the War Scroll from Qumran:

> The sons of light and the lot of darkness shall battle together for God's might, between the roar of a huge multitude and the shouts of gods and of men, on the day of the calamity. It will be a time of suffering for all the people redeemed by God. Of all their sufferings none will be like this, from its haste until eternal redemption is fulfilled ... God's might will strengthen the hearts of the sons of light ... He will shine out to assist the truth, for the destruction of the sons of darkness.
>
> (Martinez 1994: 122)

That could almost be a description of the experience of the arena. Elaine Pagels is sure that this way of thinking, in which the unity of a God-created universe is, in the face of wars and massacres, fractured into a radical dualism, with salvation totally on one side, was central to the cosmology of the first Christians, as well as of the Essenes of Qumran (Pagels 1991: 124).

It is from this perspective that we can begin, perhaps, to make sense of what Felicity and Perpetua were doing. There is ample evidence that apocalyptic and dualistic views of the world and the fate of humanity were a central and potent part of early Christianity. Such a cosmology has a very long pedigree indeed: we can perhaps summarise this book by reference to this long and persistent theme. The religions of ancient Egypt, of Mesopotamia and of Ugarit, of Persia, and of ancient Canaan and ancient Israel, can be seen as a series of thanatopses, meditations on the fragility of human existence in the face of the power of an essentially unpredictable nature (seen as 'chaos') and of the conditionally unpredictable nature of the cosmocrator, the god(s). The irreducible power of nature, the most adamant proclamation of chaos, is death. Whether as fertility cult, or as calendar and astrological calculation, or as covenant, the impulse in all thanatologies is to secure human life by an alliance with divinities who will control nature by making it predictable. The Egyptians found this predictability in the journey of Re (Ra), regularly arising each day out of the primal waters and descending, only to rise again, into and through the darkness of the underworld. Each human life, in becoming Osiris, parallels this endless or 'immortal' existence, as the Osiris of 'Yesterday' becomes the Re of 'Tomorrow', always repeated (Griffiths 1996: 52). In Ugarit, where the mono-theistic or polytheistic choice seems to have been avoided rather than made, Baal – the fertility or nature-taming god – seems to be but precariously positioned within the pantheon. Indeed, as we have seen, he is swallowed by Mot – death – and is resurrected only to continue the struggle, not to end it: life–fertility remains a problem. In the Atrahasis 'flood' stories of Babylon–Assyria, there is a clear account of the power of nature to destroy human accomplishment and security. The creation story of Babylon is of the great combat of Marduk, first with the other gods of the pantheon and then with the forces of nature. Marduk tells the gods:

> I, not you, will decide the world's nature, the things to come. My decrees will never be altered, never annulled, but my creation endures to the ends of the world.
>
> (Sandars 1971: 82)

Tiamat, the primal and uncreated waters, has other ideas:

> She has loosed the irresistible missile, spawned enormous
> serpents with cutting fangs, chock-full of venom instead of
> blood, snarling dragons wearing their glory like gods.
> Whoever sees this thing receives the shock of death, for
> when they heave those bodies up they never turn them
> back. She has made the Worm, the Dragon, the Female
> Monster, the Great Lion, the Mad Dog, the Man Scorpion,
> the Howling Storm.
>
> (ibid.: 83)

Marduk, in spite of becoming the one god, does not thereby become
all-powerful, since Tiamat and other forces pre-exist him and
continue as a potent threat, the threat of the return of chaos.

Dualism was, of course, very explicit and central in Zoroastrianism.
Within the small universe of the human body, the evil spirit
Ahriman is always dangerous: 'As long as there is', says Zoroastrian
scripture in a rather terrifying dictum, 'in this world a dwelling
even in a single person for a small demon, Ahriman is in the world'
(Williams 1997: 159). The location of evil *within the body* is, in
Zoroastrianism or any other religion, probably the most terrifying
form of dualism, as it is then placed so close to who we are. We carry
it about within ourselves and can get rid of it, as Perpetua saw, only
by the most radical of self-annihilating acts. On the cosmic scale,
Ahriman, like Tiamat, is eternal, arising out of the primal abyss,
creating in nature evils and dangers such as snakes, scorpions,
lizards, poison ivy, weeds and thorns (Nigosian 1993: 85), and
mobilising armies of evil demons and archdemons in a permanent
war with Ahura Mazda, the source of goodness and life. In the 'time
of mixture' (i.e. this world until it is saved) he kills all levels of
creation – the sky, the waters, the soil, fire and all original (i.e.
living) creations: the original plant, original animal, original human
(Cohn 1993: 96).

'Official' Judaism set its face against such dualism. God creates
everything, the creation is *good*, nature and everything else is subor-
dinate to him, he is bound to at least 'his' humans by a fixed
covenant: he *is*. Yet as Jon Levenson (1988) and John Day (1985)
show, there are themes in Hebrew and Jewish writing which
parallel the various Ugarit and Mesopotamian myths and stories
which see evil and the anti-human forces of nature as retaining an
independent, death- and chaos-dealing power. The primal waters

(Tiamat in Mesopotamia) of Genesis and their denizens are contained, not abolished in the Genesis stories. In Job 38: 8–11, God asks Job to consider:

> Who shut up the sea with doors, when it brake forth, as if it
> had issued out of the womb?
> When I made the cloud the garment thereof,
> and thick darkness a swaddling band for it ...
> And said, Hitherto shall thou come, but no further:
> and here shall the proud waves be stayed?

This *seems* to imply the existence of the 'proud waves' *before* creation: at the very least God is clearly threatening that the power of the sea will be unleashed in the event of human misbehaviour. As threat, this can only be effective if the sea is indeed potent and destructive. The chaos-monsters Behemoth, Leviathan and Rahab are 'demonic ... present in subdued form within the earth's seas' (Day 1985: 87). Levenson sees Leviathan in particular as pre-existing creation, whereas (in Job) Behemoth is specifically presented as created by God as his plaything (Levenson 1988: 49). They all, of course, reappear in Isaiah and, much later, in Revelation, as creatures of chaos and destruction, the messengers and forces of the end time.

In Isaiah, and in other prophets, it is the return of chaos, of nature, which is seen as the most potent proof of God's disfavour and of the primal capacity of nature to overwhelm creation and kill. Indeed, in Isaiah it is precisely this terrifying dualism that is brought to an end in the perfection *of the world to come*:

> The abundance of the sea shall be converted unto thee ...
> I will make thee an eternal excellency. ... For brass I will
> bring gold, and for iron I will bring silver, and for wood
> brass, and for stones iron; I will also make thy officers peace,
> and thine exactors righteousness. Violence shall no more be
> heard in thy land, wasting nor destruction within thy
> borders; but thou shalt call thy walls Salvation and thy gates
> Praise. The sun shall be no more thy light by day; neither for
> brightness shall the moon give light unto thee: but the Lord
> shall be unto thee an everlasting light, and thy God thy
> glory. Thy sun shall no more go down, neither shall thy
> moon withdraw itself; for the Lord shall be thine everlasting
> light, and the days of thy mourning shall be ended.
>
> (Isaiah 60: 5–20)

All of this promise of another world is of course conditional upon obedience to the Covenant, which defines the proper behaviour of human beings. The promise, though, is of an end to dualism, the end of nature. In this, as Levenson incisively points out, is a tacit recognition that this world, on its own, is not good enough. It is a terrifying place, a combat zone, a battle to the death between the powers of light and the powers of darkness, the forces of life and the forces of death.

This cosmology, in which the traditions of all of the Ancient Near East seem to me to share, is the larger immanent or permanent apocalypse on which the smaller apocalypses are played. These latter are the particular histories of the participant societies and cultures: as we have seen there was ample cause, in the story of 'Israel', in its two exiles and its eventual destruction by the Romans, for the elaboration of a complementary dualism focused most agonisingly on the fact that chaos (the Pax Romana) had overwhelmed their world more surely than any flood or great Leviathan. The apocalyptic content of Hellenistic Judaism, and hence of Hellenistic Christo-Judaism, is well attested in the Dead Sea Scrolls – and in the Christian Gospel of John:

> The Gospel [of John] presupposes the ancient myth of cosmic combat, transmitted, in the author's own time, especially in apocalyptic texts ... [and] such apocalyptic traditions influenced the Gospel's interpretation ... which presents the death, resurrection and ascent of Jesus as the turning point in the conflict between God and the forces of evil ... the crucifixion was a necessary part of God's plan for the salvation of the world ... the decisive engagement in the cosmic battle between God and Satan.
> (Kovacs 1995: 228, 231–2, 247)

The radical difference between Judaism and, say, Ugarit or cultic Hellenism, lay in Judaism's (and Christianity's) monotheism. When there is only one God of Good, and yet there is an almost equal Evil in the world, then there can only be either saints or sinners, salvation or damnation, transcendence or corruption. The choice is absolute: there are, here, the Sons of Darkness and, there, the Sons of Light.

Perpetua saw this very clearly. In her visions she is not so much leaving this world as going to another. If the one to which she is going is all good, then the one she is leaving must be all bad – hence the joy of suffering. In visions, Perpetua ascends a most terrifying

A home beyond the sky,
Where all who live in Christ with thee
Shall never die.

(*Hymns Ancient and Modern* 1916: Hymn 700)

Epilogue

SACRIFICIAL LIVING AND SACRIFICIAL DYING
Christians in the world

In *The Christian Warrior in the Twentieth Century*, I argued that the martyr-hero basis of Christianity creates, among other things, what I called 'Euro-Christianity', an attitude to war in which the idea of self-sacrifice has the rather ambivalent result of being neither pacifist nor belligerent, but 'dutifully' tolerant of the bearing of arms, of going to war, of laying down one's life in the practice of war. The codes of chivalry and the doctrine of the just war of Christianity, enable Christians to go to war with an approving, though far from easy conscience.

To demonstrate this, I relied mainly on the evidence of the many tens of thousands of European war memorials, most of them constructed after the Great War of 1914–18, a period as full of death as the centuries on either side of the birth of Christ, and a period also as prefaced by 'peace', the Pax Britannica, just as the Roman centuries were prefaced by the Pax Romana. These war memorials are far and away the most widespread of European statuary, and are in many ways the most significant twentieth-century contribution to or redaction of the Christian tradition. They are lapidary texts on an archaeological par with the martyria of early Christianity, or the triumphal arches, battle-site orations and military mausolea of the Ancient Near East. War memorials are, rather unlike martyria or mausolea, direct and genuine demotic records. We have to make assumptions about the older records as to how 'representative' they are, and we will never really know. In twentieth-century war memorials, however, we have a most interesting example of what has been a major theme of this book, that is the way in which thanatologies are constructed 'by experience out of' a religious tradition, however 'dimly' that tradition may be thought to exist.

We have some evidence from art as to how Jesus was 'understood' in late antiquity. In *The Clash of Gods*, Thomas Mathews demonstrates how radically the imperial authority symbolisms of 'Caesar' were negated by the image of the crucified messiah. He notes that an 'imperial' Christ appears once only, as an object of derision to the Roman soldiers attending to the killing who dress him up as 'King of the Jews'. Otherwise, writes Mathews, 'of the thousands of representations of Christ in early Christian art, I know of only two where he dresses in what may be taken for imperial garments ... these being less than one tenth of one per cent of the total' (Mathews 1993: 179). Whether riding (side-saddle like a woman, not a warrior) on an ass (not a war-horse), or touching menstruating (i.e. unclean) women, or as androgynous or even feminine, or as an adolescent-like grave decoration in the catacomb of Domitilla, Christ appears as 'pacific, non-military and non-imperial' (ibid.: 62). There are no paintings of Christ for at least 200 years after his death: when they do appear they deliberately eschew the 'imperial' model, even after the 'triumph' of Christianity within the Empire. The images retain the story of vulnerability, of suffering, of powerlessness – but of a victory, the victory of the martyr over violence, a victory won by *giving* up life. This is the message of war memorials. Whether in France ('pour la France') or in Germany ('für Deutschland') or in the British Empire ('they died for you'), the dead soldiers *give* their lives: greater love hath no man than this, that he lay down his life for his friends. So strongly grounded is this imagery in the longevity of Christianity that it can survive its own evident fictitiousness: soldiers do not give their lives; they are meant to take those of the enemy, an entity which appears hardly at all on these memorials. War memorials are works of fiction, but works of fiction so deeply rooted in martyrology that they remain true.

At times, in particular at times of violent conflict and war, the hard foundation of martyrdom re-emerges, invoked by suffering close to that of Felicity and Perpetua. In 1919 the Church of England produced a report on 'The Army and Religion', in which the Church sought to find out how 'religious' were the millions of troops who had gone through the ranks in the Great War. The general conclusion (after 1,400 years of Christian presence in Great Britain!) was that most of the soldiers had no time for the Church and were estranged from Christ (Army and Religion 1919: xxvii): 'A very small percentage have any relation to the churches nor do they look to them for help ... the churches are the embodiment of cant' (ibid.: 229). And yet:

At the Front the impact of danger awakens the religious consciousness ... most men pray before they go over the parapet ... the idea of salvation by death in battle for one's country has been widely prevalent ... nearly all the serious questions come down in the end to the problem of suffering ... the chaplain who can portray the story of the Cross in terms of the soldiers' own experience will find the soil crying for the seed ... the appeal of the Cross is very strong, but not on its redemptive side. The attraction of the Cross is that, in the main, of a wounded hero, a fellow-sufferer in a good cause ... the thought of Christ's wounds means a lot to a wounded man ... the war seems to have revived something ancestral in these men, something elementally religious ... in wayside Calvaries and in shattered towns the Cross has confronted the marching battalions, they must see something in it, something vital linking up their lives with the Son of Man.

(ibid.: 7, 19, 28, 42, 62, 288)

During the War, as the lists of the dead grew, shrines appeared, quite voluntarily, against Church walls and even in Church grounds: some vicars resisted this 'intrusion'. After the War, all over Christian Europe, hundreds of thousands of war memorials (some great national monuments, but mostly the product of community concern, paid for by collected pennies) remobilised and in some sense reinvented Christianity, turning back over many centuries to the martyr-hero model of Christ, heroic in his self-giving, not in victory, martyred in his millions. Just as the bones of early martyrs were placed in places of worship, and just as the towns and public cemeteries of late antiquity found their spaces occupied by martyria great and small, so, after the War, were the towns and villages of Europe occupied by monuments to war, witnesses to a very long tradition indeed. War memorials occupied the central spaces of European cities, towns and villages just as adamantly as did Christian churches and graveyards in the Roman Empire of late antiquity. These twentieth-century memorials emphasised that the lives they commemorated *had been given*, given so that we who remember may live: they are, that is, proof of vicarious sacrifice, not belligerence. They may well be works of fiction, but a fiction well grounded in fact, new and very ancient.

In Sheffield Cathedral a war memorial is the Akedah, Abraham embracing Isaac, in a Christian cathedral, surrounded by explicitly

Christian memorials.[1] In France, at Thiepval, an empty tomb and soaring arches invoke the empty tomb of Periclean Athens and early Christianity, as well as the sad triumphal ambitions of Rome. Horace's *dulce et decorum est* appears frequently, though very much less so after World War II. In Chartres, a monument – a hand holding a broken sword – commemorates Jean Moulin, 'héros et martyr'. Throughout France, the martyr-heroes are 'children': 'les enfants de Pézou morts pour la France', imagery reaching back to the New Testament and perhaps to 4 Maccabees. At Verdun, the sub-basement windows of a gigantic ossuary contain relics, the bones of tens of thousands of very ordinary French martyr-heroes who 'gave their lives' for France. On the Somme, Castor and Pollux rise on a plinth above the memorial to the South African war dead. Poems and lapidary prose promise eternal life to the dead soldiers. They are presented as having 'saved' the living – as long as the living are properly respectful of them, by which is meant as long as the living are prepared to remember and to do likewise, in imitation of them.

All over Europe, thousands of memorials and hundreds of thousands of ordinary war graves are the benchmark, the template for lives and deaths which are comprehensible only within a tradition which sees in martyrdoms, large and small, ecstatic or mundane, the way in which Christians, especially Christian men, should, dutifully, live – and die.

---

1 The Sheffield Akedah war memorial has been stolen since the completion of this epilogue.

APPENDIX

Les Flavii du Cillium

Poem taken from the mausoleum of the Flavii at Cillium (see Chapter 10 for more details), translated from the French by Ros and Dave Place. The French edition of the poem was produced by the Groupe de Recherches sur l'Afrique Antique as *Les Flavii du Cillium: Etude du Mausolée de Kasserine* (Collection de l'Ecole Française de Rome 169, Rome, Scuola Tipografica S.Pio X, 1993).

Part A

Yes, life is very short and its moments fleeting, our days torn from us pass like a brief hour, our mortal bodies are drawn deep down into the Elysian Fields by malevolent Lachesis bent on cutting the skein of our lives. Suddenly, however, the image was invented, a seductive process. Thanks to it, beings are prolonged into a later age. Memory, made less ephemeral, collects them and keeps many souvenirs: inscriptions are made so that the years endure. Here is a recent gesture of piety of which everyone will approve: it is worthy of glory and endless praise; it is an entirely original example. Flavius Secundus exercising the piety of an ancient tradition has put his mark on it in homage to his father. Who henceforth could stop here without feeling a rush of virtue, who would not admire this masterpiece, who, on seeing this profusion of riches, would not remain thunderstruck before the immense resources that have enabled this monument to be projected into the ether? This is the most honourable way of using one's fortune, it is thus that spending one's money procures imperishable dwelling places. This is the way that money is used for eternity when it is well invested in a durable foundation. What a fine spectacle for those frenzied people who

221

think of nothing but piling up gold and who are carried away by the appeal of money bought at the price of blood. What a fine spectacle also for insolent and prodigal luxury that is spent in vain pleasures, that luxury which has learnt to buy very dearly imported cloths and precious stones whose brightness seduces, or presents from over the Erythrean [?] sea. It is a disease maintained by the competition to which peoples give themselves. Greece offers its boys, Spain offers the products of its fruits of Pallas, Libya offers its hunting, the Orient its 'amome', Egypt the frivolities of Pharos, Gaul the industry of which she is always proud, rich Campania its wines. All that quickly loses its charm, gives only an instant's pleasure, is condemned by its brevity; but if one really wants to take account of all the hazards of life and to take the trouble to measure man by the shortness of his existence, then one will learn to believe that the best way of behaving is to devote all the strength one has in life to prolong oneself in time without failing in the respect one owes the gods. That said, I don't doubt that in the silent darkness of Acheron, if the dead still have feelings, your father must often feel joy, Secundus, and look down on the battalion of the other shades, for he knows that here his tomb continues to exist, eternally new in all its majesty, that these stones, perfectly matched, rise up in all their splendour, that rising from their foundation these tall buildings have seen their beauty grow to such an extent that each of these ridges seems marked out perfectly straight in soft wax. From the movement of the statues the sculptor's art brings into being a new charm; and the crowd of passers-by can without wearying admire these splendours and marvel to see the harmonious balance of the columns shining above their heads. Furthermore you offered to the gods the inscription of the states of service of your father, and your father in person. He has the pleasure of contemplating the gifts that he himself made formerly for the happiness of this place; he introduced there in profusion the gifts of Bacchus, he saw fit to plant the first vine in rows and showed off the groves of trees to best effect by means of streams of running water.

May the Destinies and the King of Styx in his awesome night give me the power to express myself. Now is the time to maintain that your father is immortal, that he has left behind Dis and fled its sinister palace, since he prefers, until the end of time, to follow the fate of this monument and live, thanks to these names inscribed here eternally, to inhabit these familiar woods, to contemplate from here with tenderness the hills of his fatherland and remain, one might say, the master of the household that he has passed on to his children.

Many people perhaps, in making thoughtless remarks about this attitude, will say that one is inviting premature death by erecting during one's lifetime a monument for the future. Personally, I don't have such thoughts on my mind. I believe on the contrary that those who have gone and set up an eternal dwelling place and, displaying an absolute rectitude in their lives, have built walls that will never fall down, are protected. You can't change the route mapped out by the Fates and Atropos doesn't change in the course of her work. Once she has begun to spin the first threads, believe me Secundus, you will go right to the end of your allotted span of years. You will be protected from care, you will fully profit from your wealth without running the risk of creating burdens for other people, without making a will weighed down by obligations, without your heir having to fear the necessity of building a similar monument. No, everything that you leave will go completely to wherever your wishes want it to go.

But the care of the work and its great beauties demand my attention. It is a work of homage that has been built high, that pierces the clouds and measures the course of the sun. You can cast your eye over the line of summits: each one in its turn is dominated by another. You look down to the plain and the earth beneath you disappears. The Colosseum, from what they say, doesn't rise in this way towards the Romulan heights, nor the obelisk of the Circus into the air. The lighthouse at Pharos doesn't indicate from such a height the channels of the sistrum-bearing Nile when its flames, visible from afar, light up the surrounding sea.

What cannot be achieved by filial piety combined with learning? See here the stone pierced by numerous gaps that invite swarms of gentle bees to build their nests of wax, so that this dwelling, forever sweet with the nectar of Thymbrea, distils juices tasting of flowers while the bees produce new honey.

Part B

Come once again Piety, awaken thoughts worthy of respect, and breathe into my verse that charm of which you have the secret. Here before us once again stands Secundus who, with a pure heart, has dedicated to his father not a memorial but the novelty of a temple. Where are you taking me now Calliope, forcing me to depart once again and tread once more roads along which I have already passed? (Come on Calliope, give us all a break.) Have we not expressed the full majesty of the work, spoken also of the smooth, well-jointed stones, the surrounding groves, the appeal of the running waters, the sound of the bees bringing their honey?

Here however is, I believe, the only thing that has escaped our art, at the moment when, intoxicated Muse, you were giving yourself to a thousand fantasies. We have said nothing about this cock with flapping wings that flies high above, much higher, I believe, than the highest cloud. If nature had also given a voice to this body, this cock would force all the gods to get up early in the morning! Now that the façade carries the appointed names and one can see inscribed there the titles with which a life is adorned, I wish you, Secundus, a long and happy life, and hope that you will read the monument that you have brought into being.

BIBLIOGRAPHY

Abercrombie, J. (1984) 'A Short Note on a Siloan Tomb Inscription', *Bulletin of the American School of Oriental Research* 254 (Spring): 61–2.

Aldred, C. (1994) *Egyptian Art in the Days of the Pharoahs, 3100–320 BCE*, London, Thames & Hudson.

Alster, B. (ed.) (1980) *Death in Mesopotamia: Papers Read at the 26th International Assyriological Association*, Copenhagen Studies in Assyriology, vol. 8, Copenhagen, Akademisk Forlag.

Amundsen, D.W. (1996) *Medicine, Society and Faith in the Ancient and Medieval Worlds*, Baltimore, John Hopkins University Press.

Ancient and Modern, Hymns (Standard Edition) (1916), London, Clowes & Sons.

—— (New Standard Edition) (1983), London, William Clowes.

Apuleius, L. (1996) *The Golden Ass*, Ware, Wordsworth Editions.

Aristides, P.A. (1981) *The Complete Works*, ed. C. Behr, Leiden, E.J. Brill.

'(The) Army and Religion: An Enquiry and Its Bearing upon the Religious Life of the Nation' (1919) London, Macmillan.

Augustine (1978) 'On the Care to be had for the Dead', in *Nicene and Post-Nicene Fathers of the Christian Church*, vol. 3, Grand Rapids, Eerdmans Publishing.

Auld, A.G. (1993) *Understanding Poets and Prophets: Essays in Honour of George Wishart Anderson*, Sheffield, Sheffield Academic Press.

Aune, D.E. (1972) *The Cultic Setting of Realized Eschatology in Early Christianity*, Leiden, E.J. Brill.

(The) Babylonian Talmud (1978) ed. I. Epstein, London, Jerusalem and New York, Soncino Press, 18 vols.

Bailey, L.R. (1985) *Biblical Perspectives on Death*, Philadelphia, Fortress Press.

Barclay, J.M.G. (1996) *Jews in the Mediterranean Diaspora: From Alexander to Trajan (323 BCE–117 CE)*, Edinburgh, T. & T. Clark.

Bartlett, J.R. (1982) *Jericho*, Guildford, Surrey, Lutterworth Press.

Bauman, Z. (1992) *Mortality, Immortality and Other Life Strategies*, London, Polity Press.

Bayliss, M. (1973) 'The Cult of the Dead in Assyria and Babylonia', *IRAQ: The Journal of the British School of Archaeology in Iraq* 35: 115–25.

Beard, M. and North, J. (eds) (1990) *Pagan Priests: Religion and Power in the Ancient World*, London, Duckworth.

Bender, A.P. (1894–5) 'Beliefs, Rites and Customs of the Jews, Connected with Death, Burial and Mourning', *Jewish Quarterly Review* 6 (1894): 317–47, 664–71; 7 (1895): 101–18, 259–69.

Berger, P. (1980) *The Heretical Imperative*, London, Collins.

Berger, P. and Luckmann, T. (1966) *The Social Construction of Reality: A Treatise in the Sociology of Knowledge*, New York, Doubleday.

Bernal, M. (1987) *Black Athena: The Afroasiatic Roots of Classical Civilization*, vol. 1, *The Fabrication of Ancient Greece, 1785–1985*, London, Vintage Books.

Bernstein, A.E. (1993) *The Formation of Hell: Death and Retribution in the Ancient Near East and Early Christian Worlds*, London, University College of London Press.

Bialik, H.N. and Ravnitzky, Y.H. (1992) *The Book of Legends: Sefer Ha-Aggadah, Legends from the Talmud and Midrash*, trans. W.G. Braude, New York, Schocken Books.

Bloch-Smith, E. (1992a) 'Judahite Burial Practice and Belief about the Dead', *JSOT Supplement*, Series 123, Sheffield, Sheffield Academic Press.

—— (1992b) 'The Cult of the Dead in Judah: Interpreting the Material Remains', *Journal of Biblical Literature* 111, 2 (Summer): 213–24.

Boardman, J., Griffin, J. and Murray, O. (eds) (1988) *Greece and the Hellenistic World*, Oxford, Oxford University Press.

Bottero, J. (1987) *Mesopotamia: Writing, Reasoning and the Gods*, trans. Z. Bahrani and M. van de Mieroop, Chicago, University of Chicago Press.

Bowersock, G.W. (1995) *Martyrdom and Rome*, Cambridge, Cambridge University Press.

Bowker, J. (1969) *The Targums and Rabbinic Literature: An Introduction to Jewish Interpretations of Scripture*, Cambridge, Cambridge University Press.

Bowman, A.K. (1986) *Egypt After the Pharoahs, 332 BCE–CE 642, from Alexander to the Arab Conquest*, London, British Museum Publications.

Boyarin, D. (1990) *Intertextuality and the Reading of Midrash*, Bloomington and Indianapolis, Indiana University Press.

Boyce, M. (1979) *Zoroastrians: Their Religious Beliefs and Practices*, London, Routledge & Kegan Paul.

Boyd, B. (1995) 'Houses and Hearths, Pits and Burials: Natufian Mortuary Practices at Eynan, Upper Jordan Valley', in S. Campbell and A. Green, *The Archaeology of Death in the Ancient Near East*, Oxford, Oxbow Monograph.

Braund, D.C. (1985) *Augustus to Nero: A Source Book on Roman History*, London, Croom Helm.

Bray, W. and Trump, D. (1982) *Dictionary of Archaeology*, London, Penguin Books.

Bremer, J.M., Van den Hout, Th.P.J. and Peters, R. (eds) (1994) *Hidden Futures: Death and Immortality in Ancient Egypt, Anatolia, the Classical, Biblical and Arab World*, Amsterdam, Amsterdam University Press.

Breslin, J. (undated) *A Greek Prayer: The translation and account of a short burial prayer engraved by an ancient people on a tiny sheet of gold and found among ashes in a cinerary urn*, J. Paul Getty Museum, Malibu, produced by Ambassador College, Pasadena.

Brown, P. (1971) *The World of Late Antiquity*, London, Thames & Hudson.

—— (1972) *Religion and Society in the Age of Saint Augustine*, London, Faber & Faber.

—— (1981) *The Cult of the Saints: Its Rise and Function in Latin Christianity*, Chicago, University of Chicago Press.

—— (1990) *The Body and Society: Men, Women and Sexual Renunciation in Early Christianity*, London, Faber & Faber.

Budge, E.A.W. (1911) *Osiris and the Egyptian Resurrection*, London, Medici Society.

—— (1927) *The Book of the Cave of Treasures: A History of the Patriarchs and the Kings Their Successors from the Creation to the Crucifixion of Christ*, London, Religious Tract Society.

—— (1995) *The Mummy*, London, Studio Editions.

Burkert, W. (1992) *Greek Religion*, Oxford, Blackwell.

Bynum, C.W. (1995) *The Resurrection of the Body in Western Christianity, 200 CE–1336 CE*, New York, Columbia University Press.

Campbell, E. and Freedman, D. (eds) (1983) *The Biblical Archaeologist Reader Four*, Sheffield, The Almond Press, in association with the American Schools of Oriental Research.

Campbell, S. and Green, A. (eds) (1995) *The Archaeology of Death in the Ancient Near East: Proceedings of the Manchester Conference, 1992*, Oxford, Oxbow Books, and Park End Place and Oakville, David Brown Book Company.

Cannon, A. (1989) 'The Historical Dimension in Mortuary Expressions of Status and Sentiment', *Current Anthropology* 30 (4): 437–58.

Charles, R. H. (1908) *The Testaments of the Twelve Patriarchs*, London, Adam & Charles Black.

—— (1968) *Apocrypha and Pseudepigrapha of the Old Testament*, Oxford, Clarendon Press, 2 vols.

Cheyne, T.K. and Black, J.S. (eds) (1899) *Encyclopaedia Biblica*, London, Adam & Charles Black, 4 vols.

Cicero (1971a) *Tusculan Disputations*, London and Cambridge, MA, Heinemann and Harvard University Press.

—— (1971b) *Selected Works*, London, Penguin Classics.

—— (1991) *On Stoic Good and Evil*, ed. and trans. M.R. Wright, Warminster, Aris & Phillips.

Clarke, J.R. (1988) *Looking at Lovemaking: Constructions of Sexuality in Roman Art, 100 BC to AD 250*, Berkeley, University of California Press.

Clement of Alexandria (1909) 'Exhortation to the Heathen', in *The Writings of Clement of Alexandria*, Edinburgh, T. & T. Clark.

Cohn, N. (1995) *Cosmos, Chaos and the World to Come: The Ancient Roots of Apocalyptic Faith*, New Haven, Yale University Press.

Coleman, K.M. (1990) 'Fatal Charades: Roman Executions Staged as Mythological Enactments', *Journal of Roman Studies* 80: 44–73.

Collins, J.J. (1977) *Apocalypticism in the Dead Sea Scrolls*, London, Routledge.

Collins, J.J. and Nickelsburg, G.W.E. (eds) (1980) *Ideal Figures in Ancient Judaism: Profiles and Paradigms*, Missoula, Scholars Press.

Coogan, M.D. (1978) *Stories from Ancient Canaan*, Philadelphia, Westminster Press.

Cornell, T.J. (1995) *The Beginnings of Rome: Italy and Rome from the Bronze Age to the Punic Wars, c.1000–264 BCE* , London, Routledge.

Cullmann, O. (1986) *The Christology of the New Testament*, London, SCM Press.

Curtis, A. (1985) *Ugarit: Ras Shamra*, Cambridge, Lutterworth Press.

Cyprian (1971) 'The Unity of the Catholic Church', in *Cyprian*, text and trans. M. Bevenot, Oxford, Clarendon Press.

Dalley, S. (trans. and annot.) (1991) *Myths from Mesopotamia*, Oxford, Oxford University Press.

Davenport, G.L. (1971) *The Eschatology of the Book of Jubilees*, Leiden, E.J. Brill.

Davies, J. (1994) *Ritual and Remembrance: Responses to Death in Human Societies*, Sheffield, Sheffield Academic Press.

—— (1995) *The Christian Warrior in the Twentieth Century*, Lampeter, Mellen Press.

Davies, W.D. and Finkelstein, L. (eds) (1984) *The Cambridge History of Judaism*, Cambridge, Cambridge University Press.

Davis, S.T., Kendall, D. and O'Collins, G. (eds) (1997) *The Resurrection: An Interdisciplinary Symposium on the Resurrection of Jesus*, Oxford, Oxford University Press.

Day, J. (1985) *God's Conflict with the Dragon and the Sea: Echoes of a Canaanite Myth in the Old Testament*, Cambridge, Cambridge University Press.

De Moor, J.C. (1986) 'The Crisis of Polytheism in Late Bronze Ugarit', *Oud Testamentische Studien* 24: 1–20.

Deroche, V. (1989) 'Delphes: La Christianisation d'un Sanctuaire Paien', in *ACTES of the 11th International Congress of Christian Archaeology, 1986*, Rome, Pontifical Institute of Christian Archaeology, pp. 2713–26.

De Vaux, R. (1974) *Ancient Israel: Its Life and Institutions*, trans. J. McHugh, London, Darton Longman & Todd.

(The) Didascalia Apostolorum (1979) *Corpus Scriptorum Christianorum Orientalium des Universités Catholiques de Louvain et de Washington: Scriptores Syri*, trans. A. Voobus, vol. 408, tomus 180, Louvain, Secretariat du Corpus SCO.

Dilcher, R. (1995) *Studies in Heraclitus*, Spudasmata 56, Hildesheim, Zurich and New York, George Olms.

Dillon, J. (1997) 'Plutarch and the End of History', in J. Mossman (ed.) *Plutarch and His Intellectual World*, Swansea, Duckworth, in association with the Classical Press of Wales, pp. 233–40.

Diodorus Siculus (1933) *An Account of Egypt by Diodorus the Sicilian*, trans. W.G. Waddell, Cairo, University of Egypt.

Donfried, K.P. (1974) *The Setting of Second Clement in Early Christianity*, Leiden, E.J. Brill.

Doran, R. (1980) 'The Martyr: A Synoptic View of the Mother and Her Seven Sons', in Collins and Nickelsburg 1980: 189–205.

Drijvers, H.J.W. (1965) *Bardesan of Edessa*, trans. G.E. Baaren-Pape, Netherlands, Van Gorcum.

Eisenman, R. and Wise, M. (1992) *The Dead Sea Scrolls Uncovered*, Shaftesbury, Element Books.

Elsner, J. (1995) *Art and the Roman Viewer: The Transformation of Art from the Pagan World to Christianity*, Cambridge, Cambridge University Press.

Encyclopaedia Judaica (1972) Jerusalem, Keter Publishing House, 16 vols.

Engels, D. (1990) *Roman Corinth: An Alternative Model for the Classical City*, Chicago, University of Chicago Press.

Erickson, L. (1994) *The Problem of Zoroastrian Influence on Judaism and Christianity*, unpublished paper presented at the Philosophy Department of Cuesta College, University of California, San Luis Obispo County.

Eusebius (1986) *The History of the Church*, London, Penguin Classics.

Evans, C.A. and Hagner, D.A. (eds) (1993) *Anti-Semitism and Early Christianity: Issues of Polemic and Faith*, Minneapolis, Fortress Press.

Faulkner, R.O. (1996) *The Ancient Egyptian Book of the Dead*, London, British Museum Press.

Feldman, L. (1984) 'Abraham the General in Josephus', in F.E. Greenspahn, *Nourished with Peace: Studies in Hellenistic Judaism in Memory of Samuel Sandwell*, Chico, Scholars Press, pp. 43–9.

Ferrua, A. (1991) *The Unknown Catacomb: A Unique Discovery of Early Christian Art*, trans. I. Inglis, New Lanark, Geddes & Grosset.

Fiorenza, E.S .(1983) *In Memory of Her: A Feminist Theological Reconstruction of Christian Origins*, London, SCM Press.

Fishbane, S. and Lightstone, J.N. (1990) *Essays in the Social Scientific Study of Judaism and Jewish Society*, Department of Religion, Concordia University, Montreal.

(Les) Flavii du Cillium: Etude du Mausolée de Kasserine, see Groupe de Recherches sur l'Afrique Antique 1993.

Fontaine, J. (1989) 'Discussion', in *ACTES of the 11th International Congress of Christian Archaeology, 1986*, Rome, Pontifical Institute of Christian Archaeology, pp. 1,152–213.

Fox, R.L. (1988) *Pagans and Christians in the Mediterranean World, from the Second Century CE to the Conversion of Constantine*, London, Penguin Books.

Frankfort, H. (1996) *The Art and Architecture of the Ancient Orient*, Pelican History of Art, New Haven, Yale University Press.

Freedman, D.N. (ed.) (1992) *Anchor Bible Dictionary*, New York, Doubleday, 6 vols.

Frend, W.H.C. (1996) *The Archaeology of Early Christianity*, London, Geoffrey Chapman.

Garlan, Y. (1975) *War in the Ancient World: A Social History*, trans. J. Lloyd, London, Chatto & Windus.

Garland, R. (1985) *The Greek Way of Death*, Ithaca, Cornell University Press.

—— (1992) *Introducing New Gods: The Politics of Athenian Religion*, London, Duckworth.

Garstang, J. (1907) *The Burial Customs of Ancient Egypt as Illustrated by Tombs of the Middle Kingdom, Being a Report of Excavations made at the Necropolis of Beni Hasan during 1902–4*, London, Archibald Constable.

Gaster, T.H. (1961) *Thespis: Ritual, Myth and Drama in the Ancient Near East*, New York, Anchor Books, Doubleday.

Ginzberg, L. (1909–38) *The Legends of the Jews*, trans. H. Szold, Philadelphia: The Jewish Publications Society of America.

Goodenough, E.R. (1953) *Jewish Symbols in the Greco-Roman Period*, Bolingen Series 37, New York, Pantheon Books, 13 vols.

—— (1969) *By Light, Light: The Mystic Gospel of Hellenistic Judaism*, Amsterdam, Philo Press.

Goody, J. (1993) *The Culture of Flowers*, Cambridge, Cambridge University Press.

Gordon, C.H. (1965) *The Common Background of Greek and Hebrew Civilizations*, New York, W.W. Norton.

Grabbe, L.L. (ed.) (1992) *Judaism from Cyrus to Hadrian*, London, SCM Press.

Grant, M. and Kitzinger, R. (eds) (1988) *The Civilization of the Ancient Mediterranean*, vol. 2, *Greece and Rome*, New York, Charles Scribner's Sons.

Greenhut, Z. (1995) 'Early Bronze Age IV Tombs and Burials in Palestine', *Journal of the Institute of Archaeology of Tel Aviv University* 22 (1): 3–46.

Griffiths, J.G. (1996) *Triads and Trinity*, Cardiff, University of Wales Press.

Grimal, P. (1991) *Dictionary of Classical Mythology*, London, Penguin Books.

Groupe de Recherches sur l'Afrique Antique (1993) *Les Flavii du Cillium: Etude du Mausolée de Kasserine*, Collection de l'Ecole Française de Rome 169, Rome, Scuola Tipografica, S.Pio X.

Hachlili, R. and Killebrew, A. (1983) 'Jewish Funerary Customs during the Second Temple Period, in the Light of Excavations at the Jericho Necropolis', *Palestine Exploration Quarterly* 115: 109–39.

Hadidi, A. (1987) 'An Ammonite Tomb at Amman', *Levant* 19: 101–2.

Hastings, J. (ed.) (1912) *Encyclopedia of Religion and Ethics*, Edinburgh, T. & T. Clark.

—— (1914) *Dictionary of the Bible*, Edinburgh, T. & T. Clark.

Healey, J. (1995) 'Death in West Semitic Texts: Ugarit and Nabatea', in Campbell and Green 1995: 186–191.

Heerma van Voss, M. (ed.) (1982) *Studies in Egyptian Religion: Dedicated to Jan Zandee*, Leiden, E.J. Brill.

Heidel, A. (1975) *The Gilgamesh Epic and Old Testament Parallels*, Chicago, University of Chicago Press.

Henrichs, A. (1982) 'Changing Dionysiac Identities', in B.F. Meyer and E.P. Sanders, *Jewish and Christian Self-Definition*, London, CMS Press.

Herford, R.T. (ed. and trans.) (1945) *The Ethics of the Talmud: Sayings of the Fathers, Pirke Aboth*, New York, Schoken Books.

Herodotus (1996) *The Histories*, trans. G. Rawlinson, ed. H. Bowden, London, J.M. Dent: The Everyman Library.

Herzfeld, E.E. (1988) *Iran in the Ancient Near East*, New York, Hacker Art Books.

Hill, C. (1972) *The World Turned Upside Down: Radical Ideas During the English Revolution*, London, Temple Smith.

—— (1988) *A Turbulent, Seditious and Factious People: John Bunyan and his Church 1628–1688*, Oxford, Clarendon Press.

Himmelfarb, M. (1993) *Ascent to Heaven in Jewish and Christian Apocalypses*, Oxford, Oxford University Press.

Hitchener, R.B. (1995) 'The Culture of Death and the Invention of Culture in Roman Africa', *Journal of Roman Archaeology* 8: 493–8.

Homer (1972) *The Odyssey*, trans. E.V. Rieu, London, Penguin Classics.

Hope, M. (1989) *The Elements of the Greek Tradition*, Shaftesbury, Element Books.

Hopkins, K. (1983) *Death and Renewal*, Cambridge, Cambridge University Press.

Horace (1968) *The Odes and Epodes*, trans. C.E. Bennett, London and Cambridge, MA, Heinemann.

—— (1993) *Satires*, trans. P.M. Brown, Warminster, Aris & Phillips.

Hornblower, S. and Spawforth, A. (1996) *The Oxford Classical Dictionary*, Oxford, Oxford University Press.

Hornung, E. (1983) *Conceptions of God in Ancient Egypt: The One and the Many*, London, Routledge & Kegan Paul.

Horsley, G.H.R. (1987) *New Documents Illustrating Early Christianity: A Review of the Greek Inscriptions and Papyri published in 1979*, Ontario, Macquarie University: The Ancient History Documentary Research Centre.

Horsley, R.A. and Hanson, J.S. (1985) *Bandits, Prophets and Messiahs: Popular Movements in the Time of Jesus*, Minneapolis, Winston Press.

Hulin, P. (1959–60) 'A Hemerological Text from Nimrud', *IRAQ: The Journal of the British School of Archaeology in Iraq* 21–2: 42–53.

Humphreys, S.C. (1980) 'Family Tombs and Tomb Cults in Ancient Athens: Tradition or Traditionalism?', *Journal of Hellenic Studies* c.: 96–126.
—— (1981) 'Death and Time', in Humphreys and King 1981: 261–83.
Humphreys, S.C. and King, H. (eds) (1981) *Mortality and Immortality: The Anthropology and Archaeology of Death*, London, Academic Press.
Ions, V. (1968) *Egyptian Mythology*, Middlesex, Paul Hamlyn.
The Jewish Encyclopaedia (1916) ed. R. Dr. I. Singer, New York and London, Funk & Wagnall.
Jones, P. and Sidwell, K. (1997) *The World of Rome*, Cambridge, Cambridge University Press.
Josephus (1841) *Works*, London, George Virtue.
Justin (1957) 'The First Apology', *The Ante-Nicene Fathers: Volume 1 – AD 110–165*, Grand Rapids, Eerdmans Publishing.
Kee, H.C. (1980) *The Origins of Christianity: Sources and Documents*, London, SPCK.
Kennedy, C.A. (1987) 'The Cult of the Dead in Corinth', in Marks and Good 1987: 227–36.
Kingsley, P. (1995) *Ancient Philosophy, Mystery and Magic: Empedocles and the Pythagorean Tradition*, Oxford, Clarendon Press.
Klassen, W. (1996) *Judas: Betrayer or Friend of Jesus?*, London, SCM Press.
Klijn, A.F.J. (1962) *The Acts of Thomas: Introduction, Text, Commentary*, Leiden, E.J. Brill.
Knudsen, E. (1959–60) 'An Incantatory Poem from Nimrud', *IRAQ: The Journal of the British School of Archaeology in Iraq* 21–2: 54–61.
Koortbojian, M. (1995) *Myth, Meaning and Memory on Roman Sarcophagi*, Berkeley, University of California Press.
Kovacs, J. (1995) ' "Now Shall the Ruler of this World be Driven Out": Jesus' Death as Cosmic Battle in John 12: 20–36', *Journal of Biblical Literature* 114 (2): 227–47.
Kraemer, D. (1995) *Responses to Suffering in Classical Rabbinic Literature*, Oxford, Oxford University Press.
Kraemer, R.S. (ed.) (1988) *Maenads, Martyrs, Matrons, Monastics: A Sourcebook on Women's Religions in the Greco-Roman World*, Philadelphia, Fortress Press.
Kyle, D.G. (1998) *Spectacles of Death in Ancient Rome*, London, Routledge.
Laistner, M.L.W. (1978) *Christianity and Pagan Culture in the Later Roman Empire*, Ithaca and London, Cornell University Press.
Lambert, W.G. (1975) *Babylonian Wisdom Literature*, Oxford, Clarendon Press.
—— (1980) 'The Theology of Death', in Alster 1980: 53–66.
Lampe, G.W.H. (ed.) (1969) *The Cambridge History of the Bible*, vol. 2, *The West from the Fathers to the Reformation*, Cambridge, Cambridge University Press.
Lamy, L. (1997) *Egyptian Mysteries*, London, Thames & Hudson.

Lattimore, R. (1942) *Themes in Greek and Latin Epitaphs*, Urbana, University of Illinois Press.

Lefkowitz, M. (1997) *Not Out of Africa*, New York, Basic Books.

Lefkowitz, M. and Rogers, G.M. (eds) (1996) *Black Athena Revisited*, Chapel Hill, University of North Carolina Press.

Levenson, J. (1988) *Creation and the Persistence of Evil: The Jewish Drama of Divine Omnipotence*, San Francisco, Harper & Row.

Levy, T.E. (ed.) (1995) *The Archaeology of Society in the Holy Land*, London and Leicester, Leicester University Press.

Lewis, T.J. (1989) *Cults of the Dead in Ancient Israel and Ugarit*, Harvard Semitic Monographs 39, Atlanta, Scholars Press.

Lincoln, B. (1991) *Death, War and Sacrifice*, Studies in Ideology and Practice, Chicago, University of Chicago Press.

Lindberg, D.C. (1992) *The Beginnings of Western Science: The European Scientific Tradition in Philosophical, Religious and Institutional Context, 600 BCE to CE 1450*, Chicago, University of Chicago Press.

Lindsay, J. (1963) *Daily Life in Roman Egypt*, London, Frederick Muller.

Lloyd, G.E.R. (ed.) (1978) *Hippocratic Writings*, London, Penguin Classics.

Loraux, N. (1986) *The Invention of Athens: The Funeral Oration in the Classical City*, trans. A. Sheridan, Cambridge, MA, Harvard University Press.

Lucan (1992) *Civil War*, trans. S.H. Braund, Oxford: Oxford University Press.

Lucian of Samosata (1905) *Works*, trans. H.W. and F.G. Fowler, Oxford, Clarendon Press, 4 vols.

Lucretius (1994) *On the Nature of the Universe*, London, Penguin Classics.

Ludemann, G. (1996) *Heretics: The Other Side of Early Christianity*, London, SCM Press.

Lyle, E. (1992) *Sacred Architecture in the Traditions of India, China, Judaism and Islam*, Edinburgh, Edinburgh University Press.

Lyons, D. (1997) *Gender and Immortality: Heroines in Ancient Greek Myth and Cult*, Princeton, Princeton University Press.

McCann, A.M. (1978) *Roman Sarcophagi in the Metropolitan Museum of Art*, New York, Metropolitan Museum of Art.

McDermott, W.C. and Orentzel, P. (1979) *Roman Portraits: The Flavian and Trajanic Periods*, Columbia, University of Missouri Press.

Maclagen, D. (1979) *Creation Myths: Man's Introduction to the World*, London, Thames & Hudson.

MacMullen, R. (1981) *Paganism in the Roman Empire*, New Haven, Yale University Press.

Manniche, L. (1987) *Sexual Life in Ancient Egypt*, London, KPI, distributed by Routledge & Kegan Paul, London.

Margalit, B. (1980) 'Death and Dying in the Ugaritic Epics', in B. Alster, *Death in Mesopotamia: Papers Read at the 26th International Assyriological Association*, Copenhagen Studies in Assyriology, vol. 8, Copenhagen, Akademisk Forlag.

Marks, J.H. and Good, R.M. (1987) *Love and Death in the Ancient Near East: Essays in Honour of Marvin H. Pope*, Guildford, CT, Four Quarters Publishing.

Markus, R.A. (1998) *The End of Ancient Christianity*, Cambridge, Cambridge University Press.

Martinez, F.G. (1994) *The Dead Sea Scrolls Translated: The Qumran Texts in English*, trans. W.G.E. Watson, Leiden, E.J. Brill.

Martinez, F.G. and Barrera, J.T. (1995) *The People of the Dead Sea Scrolls: Their Writings, Beliefs and Practices*, trans. W.G.E. Watson, Leiden, E.J. Brill.

Mathews, T.M. (1993) *The Clash of Gods: A Reinterpretation of Early Christian Art*, Princeton, Princeton University Press.

Mathews, V.H. and Benjamin, D.C. (eds) (1991) *Old Testament Parallels: Laws and Stories from the Ancient Near East*, New York, Paulist Press.

Meeks, W. (1983) *The First Urban Christians*, New Haven, Yale University Press.

Merrifield, R. (1987) *The Archaeology of Ritual and Magic*, London, B.T. Batsford.

Meyer, B. and Sanders, E.P. (eds) (1982) *Jewish and Christian Self-Definition: Self-Definition in the Graeco-Roman World*, London, SCM. Press.

Meyer, E.A. (1990) 'Explaining the Epigraphic Habit in the Roman Empire: The Evidence of Epitaphs', in *Journal of Roman Studies* 80: 74–96.

—— (1993) 'Epitaphs and Citizenship in Classical Athens', *Journal of Hellenic Studies* 113: 99–121.

Meyers, E.M. (1971) *Jewish Ossuaries: Reburial and Rebirth*, Rome, Biblical Institute Press.

—— (1983) 'Secondary Burials in Palestine', in Campbell and Freedman 1983: 91–114.

(The) Midrash Rabbah (1977), ed. H. Freedman, London, Jerusalem and New York, Soncino Press, 5 vols.

Mikalson, J. (1983) *Athenian Popular Religion*, Chapel Hill, University of North Carolina Press.

Milde, H. (1994) ' "Going out into the Day": Ancient Egyptian Beliefs and Practices Concerning Death', in J.M. Bremer, T.P.J. van der Hout and R. Peters (eds) *Hidden Futures: Death and Immortality in Ancient Egypt, Anatolia, the Classical, Biblical and Arabic-Islamic World*, Amsterdam, Amsterdam University Press.

Millar, F. (1993) *The Roman Near East, 31 BC to 337 AD*, Cambridge, MA, Harvard University Press.

(The) Mishnah (1967) ed. and trans. H. Danby, Oxford, Oxford University Press.

Morris, I. (1987) *Burial and Ancient Society: The Rise of the Greek City-State*, Cambridge, Cambridge University Press.

Musurillo, H. (1972) *The Acts of the Christian Martyrs*, Oxford, Clarendon Press.

BIBLIOGRAPHY

Negev, A. (1986) *The Archaeological Encyclopedia of the Holy Land*, Nashville, Thomas Nelson.

Neusner, J. and Dupuis, J. (1992) *The Christian Faith: Doctrinal Documents of the Catholic Church*, London, Harper Collins.

Neusner, J. and Frerichs, E.S. (eds) (1985) *'To See Ourselves as Others See Us': Christians, Jews, 'Others' in Late Antiquity*, Chico, Scholars Press.

Nickelsburg, G.W.E. (1979) *Studies on the Testament of Abraham*, Septuagint and Cognate Studies 6, Missoula, Scholars Press.

—— (1981) *Jewish Literature between the Bible and the Mishnah*, London, SCM Press.

Niditch, S. (1993a) *War in the Hebrew Bible: A Study in the Ethics of Violence*, Oxford, Oxford University Press.

—— (1993b) 'War, Women and Defilement in Numbers 13', *SEMEIA* 61: 39–57.

Nigosian, S.A. (1993) *The Zoroastrian Faith: Tradition and Modern Research*, Montreal and Kingston, McGill-Queen's University Press.

Nock, A.D. (1961) *Conversion: The Old and the New in Religion from Alexander the Great to Augustine of Hippo*, Oxford, Oxford University Press.

Noth, M. (1966) *The Old Testament World*, London, Adam & Charles Black.

Nunn, J. (1996) *Ancient Egyptian Medicine*, London, British Museum Press.

Ochs, D.J. (1993) *Consolatory Rhetoric: Grief, Symbol and Ritual in the Greco-Roman Era*, Columbia, University of South Carolina Press.

Ovid (1987) *Metamorphoses*, trans. A.D. Melville, Oxford, Oxford University Press.

Pagels, E. (1991) 'The Social History of Satan: A Preliminary Sketch', *Harvard Theological Review* 84 (2): 105–28.

—— (1994) 'The Social History of Satan', *Journal of the American Academy of Religion* 62 (1, Spring): 17–58.

—— (1996) *The Origin of Satan*, London, Penguin Press.

Painter, K.S. (1989) 'Recent Discoveries in Britain', in *ACTES of the 11th International Congress of Christian Archaeology, 1986*, Rome, Pontifical Institute of Christian Archaeology, pp. 2031–72.

Palumbo, G. (1987) ' "Egalitarian" or "Stratified" Society? Notes on Mortuary Practice and Social Structures at Jericho in Early Bronze IV', *Bulletin of the American Society of Oriental Research* 267 (August): 43–59.

Panofsky, E. (1964) *Tomb Sculpture: Its Changing Aspects from Ancient Egypt to Bernini*, London, Thames & Hudson.

Parker, R. (1996) *Athenian Religion: A History*, Oxford, Clarendon Press.

Pausanias (1917) *Description of Greece*, trans. W.H.S. Jones, London, Heinemann, 6 vols.

Paxton, F.S. (1990) *Christianizing Death: The Creation of a Ritual Process in Early Medieval Europe*, Ithaca and London, Cornell University Press.

Perkins, J. (1995) *The Suffering Self: Pain and Narrative Representation in the Early Christian Era*, London, Routledge.

Petrie, F. (1931) *Egypt and Israel*, London, SPCK.

Pettigrew, T.J. (1834) *History of Egyptian Mummies*, London, Longman Rees.

Philip, G. (1992) 'Warrior Burials in the Ancient Near East Bronze Age: The Evidence from Mesopotamia, Western Iran and Syria-Palestine', in Campbell and Green 1995: 140–54.

Plato (1959) *The Republic*, London, Penguin Books.

Plutarch (1970) *On Isis and Osiris*, trans. J.G. Griffiths, Cambridge, University of Wales Press.

Poliakoff, M.B. (1987) *Combat Sports in the Ancient World: Competition, Violence and Culture*, New Haven, Yale University Press.

Pomeroy, S.B. (1997) *Families in Classical and Hellenistic Greece: Representations and Realities*, Oxford, Clarendon Press.

Pritchard J.B. (ed.) (1971, 1975) *The Ancient Near East: An Anthology of Texts and Pictures*, Princeton, Princeton University Press, 2 vols.

Ramsey, R. (1986) *Beginning to Read the Fathers*, London, Darton, Longman & Todd.

Randsborg, K. (1991) *The First Millennium AD in Europe and the Mediterranean*, Cambridge, Cambridge University Press.

Ray, J. (1997) 'How Black was Socrates? The Roots of European Civilization and the Dangers of Afrocentrism', review of Lefkowitz and Rogers (eds) *Black Athena Revisited* and Lefkowitz *Not Out of Africa*, *The Times Literary Supplement* 1998 (February 14): 3–4.

Ray, J.D. (1978–9) 'The World of North Saqqara', *World Archaeology* 10 (2): 149–57.

Reif, S.C. (1993) *Judaism and Hebrew Prayer: New Perspectives on Jewish Liturgical History*, Cambridge, Cambridge University Press.

Reisner, G.A. (1942) *The Giza Necropolis*, vol. 1, Cambridge, MA, Harvard University Press.

Rice, D.G. and Stambaugh, J.E. (1979) *Sources for the Study of Greek Religion*, Missoula, Scholars Press for the Society of Biblical Literature.

Richmond, I.A. (1950) *Archaeology and the After-Life in Pagan and Christian Imagery*, Oxford, Oxford University Press.

Rogerson, J.W. (1978) *Anthropology and the Old Testament*, Oxford, Blackwell.

Rosenberg, R. (1981) *The Concept of Biblical Sheol Within the Context of Ancient Near Eastern Beliefs*, Ph.D. thesis, Departments of Near Eastern Languages and Civilizations, Harvard University, Cambridge, MA.

Rosenblatt, P.C. *et al.* (1976) *Grief and Mourning in Cross-cultural Perspective*, Minnesota, HRAF Press.

Rowell, G. (1977) *The Liturgy of Christian Burial: An Introductory Study to the Historical Development of Christian Burial Rites*, London, Alcuin Club/SPCK.

Rowland, C. (1985) *Christian Origins: An Account of the Setting and Character of the most Important Messianic Sect of Judaism*, London, SPCK.

Rush, A.C. (1941) *Death and Burial in Christian Antiquity*, Washington, D.C., Catholic University of America Press.

Rutgers, L.V. (1995) *The Jews in Late Ancient Rome: Evidence of Cultural Interaction in the Roman Diaspora*, Leiden, E.J. Brill.

Salisbury, J.E. (1997) *Perpetua's Passion: The Death and Memory of a Young Roman Woman*, New York and London, Routledge.

Saller, R.P. (1994) *Patriarchy, Property and Death in the Roman Family*, Cambridge, Cambridge University Press.

Salles, J.-F. (1995) 'Rituel Mortuaire et Rituel Social a Ras Shamra/Ougarit', in Campbell and Green 1995: 171–84.

Sandars, N.K. (ed. and trans.) (1971) *Poems of Heaven and Hell from Ancient Mesopotamia*, London, Penguin Books.

Sawyer, J. (1973) 'Hebrew Words for the Resurrection of the Dead', *Vitus Testamentum* 23: 218–34.

Scheidel, W. (1996) 'Measuring Sex, Age and Death in the Roman Empire: Explorations in Ancient Demography', *Journal of Roman Archaeology*, Supplementary Series, 21.

Scobie, A. (1986) 'Slums, Sanitation and Mortality in the Roman World', *KLIO* 68: 399–433.

Seeley, D. (1990) *The Noble Death: Graeco-Roman Martyrology and Paul's Concept of Salvation*, Sheffield, Sheffield Academic Press.

Segal, A. (1987) *The Other Judaisms of Late Antiquity*, Brown Judaic Studies, Atlanta, Scholars Press.

—— (1997) 'Life After Death: The Social Sources', in Davis *et al.* 1997: 90–125.

Segal, J.B. (1970) *Edessa 'The Blessed City': 'The City that ... was ruled by Christians and alone served the Lord when, long ago, the whole world in the East was under the sway of pagans'*, Oxford, Clarendon Press.

Seneca (1917) 'On Despising Death', *Letters to Lucilius* 24, New York, Heinemann.

—— (1928) 'On Anger', *Moral Essays*, New York, Heinemann.

—— (1969) *Letters from a Stoic*, London, Penguin Classics.

Shanks, H. (ed.) (1993) *Christianity and Rabbinic Judaism: A Parallel History of their Origins and Early Development*, London, SPCK.

Shaw, B.D. (1984) 'Latin Funerary Epigraphy and Family Life in the Late Roman Empire', in *Historia* 33: 457–97.

—— (1996) 'Seasons of Death: Aspects of Mortality in Imperial Rome', *Journal of Roman Studies* 86: 100–38.

Shelton, J.-A. (1988) *As the Romans Did: A Sourcebook in Roman Social History*, Oxford, Oxford University Press.

Shmueli, E. (1990) *Seven Jewish Cultures: A Reinterpretation of Jewish History and Thought*, trans. G. Shmueli, Cambridge, Cambridge University Press.

Simms, R. (1998) 'Mourning and Community in the Athenian Adonia', *Classical Journal* 93 (2, December–January): 121–41.

Singer, I.B. (1974) *A Crown of Feathers*, London, J. Cape & Sons.

Smith, R.H. (1973) *Pella of the Decapolis*, Wooster, College of Wooster, 2 vols.

Smith, W. and Cheetham, S. (eds) (1875) *A Dictionary of Christian Antiquities, Comprising the History, Institutions and Antiquities of the Christian Church, From the Time of the Apostles to the Age of Charlemagne*, London, John Murray, 2 vols.

Sourvinou-Inwood, C. (1995) *'Reading' Greek Death: To the End of the Classical Period*, Oxford, Clarendon Press.

Speake, G. (1995) *Dictionary of Ancient History*, London, Penguin Books.

Spencer, A.J. (1982) *Death in Ancient Egypt*, London, Penguin Books.

Spiegel, S. (1979) *The Last Trial: On the Legends and Lore of the Command to Abraham to Offer Isaac as a Sacrifice: The Akedah*, Jewish Legacy Book, New York, Behrman House.

Stager, L.E. (1980) 'The Rite of Child Sacrifice at Carthage', in J.G. Pedley (ed.) *New Light on Ancient Carthage*, Ann Arbor, University of Michigan Press, pp. 1–11.

Stambaugh, J. and Balch, D. (1986) *The Social World of the First Christians*, London, SPCK.

Strelan, R. (1996) *Paul, Artemis and the Jews in Ephesus*, Berlin and New York, de Gruyter.

Tal, O. (1995) 'Roman-Byzantine Cemeteries and Tombs around Apollonia', in *Journal of the Institute of Archaeology of Tel Aviv University* 22 (2): 107–20.

(The Babylonian) Talmud, see (The) Babylonian Talmud 1978.

Teixidor, J. (1977) *The Pagan God: Popular Religion in the Graeco-Roman Near East*, Princeton, Princeton University Press.

Testament of Abraham (1972), trans. M. Stone, Missoula, Society of Biblical Literature.

Thucydides (1972) *History of the Peloponnesian War*, London, Penguin Books.

Tigchelaar, E.J.C. (1996) *Prophets of Old and the Day of the End: Zechariah, the Book of Watchers and Apocalyptic*, Leiden, E.J. Brill.

Toynbee, J.M.C. (1971) *Death and Burial in the Roman World*, London, Thames & Hudson.

Tromp, N.J. (1969) *Primitive Conceptions of Death and the Nether World in the Old Testament*, Rome, Pontifical Biblical Institute.

Turcan, R. (1996) *The Cults of the Roman Empire*, trans. A. Nevill, Oxford, Blackwell.

Tyrell, W.B. and Brown, F.S. (1991) *Athenian Myths and Institutions: Words in Action*, Oxford, Oxford University Press.

Urbach, E.E. (1975) *The Sages: Their Concepts and Beliefs*, trans. I. Abrahams, Jerusalem, The Magnes Press, 2 vols.

Vanden Berghe, L. (1968) *A la Decouverte des Civilisations de l'Iran Ancien: Textes et Documents* 239–40, Brussels, Ministère des Affaires Etrangers et du Commerce Exterieur.

Van der Horst, P.W. (1991) *Ancient Jewish Epitaphs: An Introductory Survey of a Millennium of Jewish Funerary Epigraphy (300 BCE–700 CE)*, Kampen, Kok Pharos Publishing.

Van der Meer, F. and Mohrmann, C. (1959) *Atlas of the Early Christian World*, London, Nelson.

Van der Toorn, K. (1994) *From Her Cradle to Her Grave: The Role of Religion in the Life of the Israelite and the Babylonian Woman*, trans. S. Denning-Bolle, Sheffield, Sheffield Academic Press.

Van Henten, J.W. (1997) *The Maccabean Martyrs as Saviours of the Jewish People: A Study of 2 and 4 Maccabees*, Leiden, E.J. Brill.

Vermes, G. (1961) *Scripture and Tradition in Jewish Haggadic Studies*, Leiden, E.J. Brill.

Vernant, J.-P. (1992) *Mortals and Immortals: Collected Essays*, ed. F. Zeitlin, Princeton, Princeton University Press.

Veyne, P.(1988) *Did the Greeks Believe in their Myths? An Essay on the Cognitive Imagination*, trans. P. Wissing, Chicago, University of Chicago Press.

Walker, S. (1985) *Memorials to the Roman Dead*, London, British Museum Publications.

Walters, K.R. (1980) 'Rhetoric as Ritual: The Semiotics of the Attic Funeral Oration', *Florilegeum* 2: 1–27.

Weber, M. (1970) *From Max Weber: Essays in Sociology*, trans. and ed. H. Gerth and C.W. Mills, London, Routledge & Kegan Paul.

Williams, A. (1997) 'Zoroastrianism and the Body', in S. Coakley, *Religion and the Body*, Cambridge, Cambridge University Press.

Witt, R.E. (1997) *Isis in the Modern World*, Baltimore, John Hopkins University Press.

Wolf, S.R. (1993) 'Archaeology in Israel', *American Journal of Archaeology* 97: 135–63.

Zaidman, L.B. and Pantel, D. (1992) *Religion in the Ancient Greek City*, trans. P. Cartledge, Cambridge, Cambridge University Press.

Zandee, J. (1960) *Death as an Enemy in Ancient Egypt*, Leiden, Numen Supplements.

Zanker, P. (1988) *The Power of Images in the Age of Augustus*, trans. A. Shapiro, Ann Arbor, University of Michigan Press.

Zias, J. (1982) 'A Rock-Cut Tomb in Jerusalem', *Bulletin of the American Society of Oriental Research* 245 (Winter): 53–5.

INDEX

responses to 2–3; rituals at 104–5;
sudden/unnatural 68, 92–3;
universal practices of 2
deification: of children 139–40; of
Emperors 142–5, 147
Denkard 46
Deroche, V. 194
Descent of Ishtar to the Underworld
63
Diary of Wen-Amon 51
Didascalia 198–9
Dilcher, R. 183
Diodorus Siculus 28, 35–8
Diogenes of Babylon 25
Domitian, Emperor 139–40, 142
Doran, R. 120, 205–6
Drijvers, H. 25
dualism 116, 210, 215; Greco-
Roman 129–30; influences on
65–6; Zoroastrian 42, 45, 211

Edessa story 24–5
Egypt 24, 50, 210; and creation story
28; history of 28; influence of
27–8, 62; life/death beliefs 28–39
Eleazar, R. 118
Elsner, J. 7
embalming see mummification
practices
Endymion story 159–60
Enkidu 115
Enuma Elish story 53–4
Ephesus 61, 149
Epic of Creation 51–2
Epic of Gilgamesh 15, 41, 50–1, 53,
58, 115
Epicurus 130
epitaphs 108, 110–12, 136–7, 148,
153–4; Christian 176; cost of
172; as family commemoration
172–3, 176; Greek 170–7; on
marriage 175–6; as public
announcement 173–4, 177;
Roman 173; for tradesmen
177–8; women and children 171,
174–5; see also
ornamentation/inscription
Erickson, L. 65–6
Eumeneia 16–17
Euripides 175
Eusebius 14, 187–8
evil 211–12, 213, 215

Eynan 73

family: and funerals 5, 142, 147,
149, 167; and purification
ceremonies 152; and religious
festivals 146
Faulkner, R.O. 39
Feldman, L. 117–18
Felicity 201–2, 206–7, 208, 218
Feralia festival 146
Ferrua, A. 193
Fiorenza, E.S. 123–4
Fontaine, J. 191–2, 194
Fox, R.L. 1, 13, 15, 194
Frankfort, H. 56
Freedman, D.N. 6, 42, 108, 112
Frend, W.H.C. 17
funerals: ceremonies 15, 18; Christian
199; description of 168–9;
Egyptian concept 34–5; as
family/collegial events 142, 147;
Greco-Roman 134–5, 140; Greek
167–70; imperial 141–5, 147–8;
orations at 178, 180–1; public
142–4, 167, 168–9
funerary architecture: African-Roman
150–1; function of 151–2; Greco-
Roman 128–9; Greek 150;
Roman 149–50

games 183–4, 206
Garlan, Y. 10
Garland, R. 161, 169, 171, 179
Garstang, J. 27
Gezer Almanac 51
ghosts 55, 56
Gilgamesh see Epic of Gilgamesh
Ginzberg, L. 85
Giza 32–3
Gnostics 25
God 85, 165; and Abraham 86–8;
attitude to death 91–4; cosmic
capabilities of 88–9; inscrutability
of 91, 112, 114; as just,
beneficent, powerful 116
gods 26, 196; absorption of 163–4;
attitude to men 182–3;
Babylonian 48–9, 51–4; belief in
135; Egyptian 68; Greco-Roman
127, 128, 132–4, 158–62;
invention of 163; Mesopotamian